More Alive and Less Lonely

MORE ALIVE *and* LESS LONELY

On Books and Writers

JONATHAN LETHEM

Edited and with an Introduction by Christopher Boucher

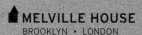

MELVILLE HOUSE
BROOKLYN • LONDON

Also by Jonathan Lethem

MORE ALIVE *and* LESS LONELY

First Melville House Printing: March 2017

Permissions located in the back of the book

Melville House Publishing   8 Blackstock Mews
    46 John Street   and   Islington
    Brooklyn, NY 11201   London N4 2BT

mhpbooks.com   facebook.com/mhpbooks   @melvillehouse

ISBN: 978-1-61219-603-9

Design by Fritz Metsch

The Library of Congress has catalogued the hardcover edition as follows:

Lethem, Jonathan, author. | Boucher, Christopher, editor.
  More alive and less lonely : on books and writers / Jonathan Lethem ;
  edited and with an introduction by Christopher Boucher.
LCSH: Literature--History and criticism--Theory, etc. | Authors and
  readers. | Books and reading. | Authorship. | BISAC: LITERARY CRITICISM /
  Books & Reading. | LITERARY COLLECTIONS / Essays.
LCC PS3562.E8544 M67 2017 (print) | LCC PS3562.E8544 (ebook)
  | DDC 814/.54--dc23

Printed in the United States of America
1   3   5   7   9   10   8   6   4   2

Contents

III

Objects in Furious Motion

IV

Lost Worlds

V

Ecstatic Depictions of Consciousness

VIII

FAN MAIL

Introduction

by Christopher Boucher

The barber, the cheese man, and the book were all named Carmine—oh yeah, wheels within wheels, *big time.*

—Motherless Brooklyn

I first heard about the project that would become *More Alive and Less Lonely* at Fenway Park in the summer of 2015. I'd gone to the Red Sox game with my good friend Jaime Clarke, a Boston-based writer, editor, and bookseller, to see them play the Phillies. Sometime around the fifth or sixth inning, Jaime mentioned that his friend Jonathan Lethem was interested in working with my publisher, Melville House, on a nonfiction book. Jaime thought I should consider editing the project—was I interested?

With that question, the game stopped mid-pitch and everyone at Fenway froze—the players, the crowd, the vendors, perhaps all of Boston. Not only is Lethem one of the most important writers of my generation, but he's also one of the brightest stars in my literary solar system—a star I've steered by for my entire writing career. The game resumed, but I can't tell you a single thing about it—my attention was elsewhere.

• • •

Jaime put Lethem and me in touch, and Lethem sent me the work he'd collected—roughly seventy-five pieces, some never before published—all written over the past two decades or so. I was charged with identifying a framework and a focus. I didn't have to look too hard. The theme of books and book culture jumped out at me immediately. What's more, I was struck by how well these pieces cohered. Collectively, they formed a sustained meditation on the endeavors of reading and writing; a celebration of a life spent in books; a readerly call-to-action. Without knowing it, I'd been waiting to read a book like this for years. Grateful as I was to glean lessons on craft from Lethem's fiction, I did so only by inference and assumption. But this is a hotline—rare, direct access to Lethem's X-ray-like critical insight; his mental library; his infectious hunger for books of all kinds.

Because these selections are culled from a twenty year span and a variety of publications, *More Alive and Less Lonely* invites you to travel in time a little. You might turn a page and find yourself in 1985, sitting next to Lethem at a reading by Anthony Burgess ("Anthony Burgess Answers Two Questions"). From there you can hop forward to 2009, where readers are eagerly awaiting Lorrie Moore's first book in eleven years. Flip from there, perhaps, back to 1983, where a teenage Lethem confronts the beat hero Herbert Huncke at a Brooklyn bookstore. There are delightful surprises at every turn: anthems for books you might not be familiar with (Walter Tevis's *Mockingbird*, for example, or Tanguy Viel's *Beyond Suspicion*), radically creative anthology contributions (an essay on footnotes, for example, which itself takes the form of self-referencing footnotes), and tributes that correlate directly to Lethem's novels (most notably, "The Original Piece of Wood I Left in Your Head," a fictional interview between the film director Spike Jonze and *Chronic City*'s Perkus Tooth).

By and large, the chapter headings divide the selections according to their mission: The work in "Lost Worlds" shines light on obscure or out-of-print titles, for example, while "Engulf and Devour" collects writing about books in the canon. "OK You Mugs" amasses Lethem's writings on media, while the selections in "It Can Still Take Me There" reflect—either directly or indirectly—on the entity of the book itself.

I see these chapters as temporary containers, though, suggested routes that I'm sure you'll abandon to cut your own paths. Some readers may gravitate towards Lethem's writing on one particular writer or topic—Thomas Berger, say, or the notion of amnesia as a narrative device—while others will surely look to *More Alive* as a partial portrait of contemporary literature in the late twentieth and early twenty-first century. Lethem completists, meanwhile, might comb these writings for biographical details—I'd direct them to Lethem's anecdotes about his surprise visit to Chester Brown in Toronto ("A Furtive Exchange"), or the time he made Philip Roth laugh at a party ("The Counter-Roth").

Some of the lines of motion here are more subtle. As a student of Lethem's fiction, I found myself tracking his analysis of other writers' styles, for example. I love his description of Moore's "innate thingliness of words . . . their plastic capacity," the way he rejects abstraction in the work of Thomas Pynchon (". . . figuring out what it is like to read Pynchon is what it is like to read Pynchon. You're never done with it.") and his reverence for *Moby-Dick*—which, Lethem writes, "installs itself in your brain as a kind of second brain, bigger than that which contains it, much like swallowing an ocean of language and implication."

Look, too, for those tendrils that run between this book and others by Lethem. In one of my favorite moments in 2012's *The Ecstasy of Influence*, for example, Lethem writes that "Language, as a vehicle, is a lemon, a hot rod painted with thrilling flames but crazily erratic to drive, riddled with bugs like innate self-consciousness, embedded metaphors and symbols, helpless intertextuality, and so forth." Pair that with what Lethem says about Franz Kafka here—that "[he] grasped that language itself—even the very plainest and most direct—is innately metaphorical, fabulated, and grotesque. What's worse, consciousness, being constructed from language, has that same unholy drift . . ." ("The Figure in the Castle").

Finally, take note of the new, unpublished writing that appears here for the first time—the footnotes on Berger and Sylvie Selig, for example—and the spirit of restless inquiry therein. Like a detective on a case, Lethem circles back, re-examines the evidence, corrects himself and reframes anecdotes from new perspectives. It's not the answers that drive him, after all, but the questions' persistence—and, to borrow from his words on Philip K. Dick, the "beauty of their asking."

In the end, I confess I was driven by my own selfish interests here; I curated a book that I myself wanted to own—one I could carry with me into bookstores, sip on the fly or gulp from in longer sittings, look to for both short bursts of insight and sustained inquiries. This book, after all, is a node, its objective to lead you to other nodes—those mentioned here, and then to other books by those authors, then to books that influenced those authors, through an infinitely expanding web of texts.

Driving these connections, though, is Lethem's remarkable generosity of spirit and gratitude. Ultimately, in fact, I regard

More Alive and Less Lonely as a love letter—one addressed to books, writers and readers alike. Lethem says as much in the pages that follow. He writes:

"I followed the higher principle of pleasure, tried to end up where I'd started: with writing I loved and wanted to recommend to someone else. That is to say, you."

I

Engulf and Devour

The Loneliest Book I've Read

I'm writing today about the loneliest book I've read—lonely in the wonderful sense that I've still never met anyone else who's ever read it. This has increasingly seemed a wonderful thing to me. I've learned to value, actually to crave, that old privacy which used to be my constant familiar when I read, whether I was still selecting children's books or making my earliest explorations of the grown-up's shelves. Books weren't surrounded, for me then, by reviews, awards, consensus, zeitgeist or buzz. I never felt guilty for being the last to discover something, never felt smug or self-improving for reading something difficult. Instead, it was forever only me and a book on a lonely exploration. Me in a secret garden. And my loneliest book really *was* a secret garden—a children's book called *The Happy Valley*, it concerned an isolated land where people were permanently happy and strange. No one but me has ever broken in there, to *The Happy Valley*, so far as I know (I realize I'll change that by writing this essay). The irony, though, is that my lonely book was written by one of the most famous authors in the world, at least at the time he wrote it.

His name was Eric Berne and if you were around in 1963 you probably read his famous book *Games People Play*, which held a spot on *New York Times* bestsellers lists for more than two years. Berne was among the fathers of something called

"Transactional Analysis," and in *Games* he became its popular explicator as well, and some kind of cultural star. This was that same moment when the Beatles dawned, and with them the "real" sixties; our parents were ready for a fully credentialed, fully bespectacled psychiatrist to explain hostilities and neuroses as "bad games" that could be identified and banished. The book is lucid and clever, with an air of existential empowerment, an anti-authoritarian tinge: institutions played bad games, whether they were governments, colleges, or families, relationships, or one's own hidebound mind. Autonomy was the higher sport. If you'd found yourself backsliding into a round of "Frigid Woman" or "Courtroom" or "Now I've Got You, you Son of a Bitch," well, it was only a game: start over. Berne's genius title found its meme-like way into the culture, giving title and lyric to both a country song by Joe South and a soul number by The Spinners—and that's how it's likeliest to be remembered now.

Then, as now, a pop guru with a two-year bestseller could rely on having his ephemeral jottings published, even if only as a courtesy—if Deepak Chopra has a children's book in him, you can bet his publisher will put it in hardcovers. Eric *Games People Play* Berne did have a children's book in him, *The Happy Valley*. Grove Press published it in 1968. Grove published it, some adult purchased it, removed the jacket (and thereby any evidence of its connection to *Games*) and gave it to me.

I've never had confirmation of the book's existence besides the copy now here in my hands. Unlike Bosco, The Bugaloos, Quisp and Quake, *Free to Be You and Me*, and other touchstones of my child-cultural experience which have not only been confirmed, but burnished into kitsch talismans, no one I've mentioned it to has ever heard of, let alone read, *The Happy Valley*. The book might as well have been scooped from an alternate world. Like any book in the mind of a child, it had the authority of its existence, which was all it needed then. My friends had *Alice In Wonderland, The Phantom Tollbooth, The Lion, the Witch and the Wardrobe* and *A Wrinkle in Time*: I had all of these and *The Happy Valley*, too. For me it was just as deep as those books, equally as singular and self-contained a fantasy. And unlike the others, it has never been decanted into adult context—no erotic photography or disguised Benjamin Disraeli, no Christian allegory, no disappointing movie adaptations. In my early twenties I worked in a bookstore which specialized in Oz books and Oziana. There my glimpses of the nerdish frenzy of the collectors, and the showoffy one-upmanship of the scholarly types, who sonorously graded the deficiencies of the commissioned sequels by Ruth Plumly Thomson, forever ruptured the magic bubble of the first book. This can never happen to *The Happy Valley*. *The Happy Valley* is mine, and it is safe.

The book isn't nearly as innocuous—okay, insipid—as its title. It's thrillingly weird. The protagonist is a blue python named Shardlu, who is introduced as "not very handsome to look at, and not very clever . . . the only way he could earn a living was by being kind to people on Tuesday night and Friday morning. He was listed on the payroll as 'Friend & Companion.'" Shardlu has a bad dream that causes him to curl into a ball and roll downhill, where he bumps into a sign, which sets the unpretentious, unforced surrealist tone for the book:

You are now entering the valley of Lamador. Everybody will see something different here. You will see one thing and your father and mother and dog will see something else. A father will see big trees, big birds, and big animals. A mother will see little flowers, little birds, and butterflies. A dog will see little animals, big and little trees, and bones, but he will smell more than he will see. But the main thing that *you* will see is to see what happens next.

What does happen next has the deliriously digressive quality of a sunlit dream, or possibly four or five dreams drifting together like clouds. It involves Shardlu's engagement with the citizens of Lamador—a caravan of dressed, talking animals that include a rabbit named Dulcy and a sheep named Flossie. The animals are led by a strange idiot-sage elder with a long white beard, named Abe, who never answers questions, but often volunteers wisdom impromptu, such as his speculation that Shardlu has come to them from Australia: "I knew that the Australians were going to fall off sometime, and now it has happened . . . any fool can see that the Australians are hanging head downward." Also drifting through are an elegant Prince and a Princess with the air of spoiled, distracted lovers, not quite concerned with the main plot, and an explorer named "The Restless Nogo," who confesses he discovered Lamador the first time he ever left his house. A temperate crisis is caused by Shardlu's hunger, which he directs at Dulcy the rabbit—Shardlu recalls that his mother advised him to "always keep a little bunny for a rainy day." In this he falls into alliance with the Princess, who's been eyeing Dulcy's pelt for a rabbit-skin umbrella to protect the fragile jelly-bean house she's built to honor the Prince. Further mild conflict is provided by the arrival—by parachute—of three Robbers, fleeing their native land of Rodamal:

"How is business?" said the Princess.

"Very good," said the leader. "Except we had to run away. A man got very angry and chased us. So here we are. This is Shamrock, this is Mustache, and my name is Tobedwego." They explain further: "You see, we jumped on this man and beat him up."

"We gave him a bloody nose," said Shamrock.

"And a black eye," said Mustache.

"And a sprained wrist," said Tobedwego.

"We punched him in the chest," said Shamrock.

"And kicked him in the shins," said Mustache.

"And took all his money," said Tobedwego.

"We took his watch," said Shamrock.

"And his ring," said Mustache.

"And then we forgave him," said Tobedwego.

"What did you forgive him for?" said Flossie.

"For getting angry," said Tobedwego.

"After we forgave him," said Shamrock, "we decided to admire ourselves for doing it."

"We decided that we had been generous," said Mustache.

This vein of amoral generosity runs deep in Lamador—the creatures work diligently on a guilt trip good enough to persuade Dulcy to sacrifice herself to the python's hunger and the rabbit-skin umbrella, which, as the Princess points out to the Prince, "I promised you, and what's more important, I promised my conscience too." This wouldn't be 1968, though, if all apparently societal problems weren't in fact solvable in the realm of personal transformation. Handily, Shardlu has begun to itch, warning him that he may be ready for a major shedding. Everyone helpfully tugs at Shardlu's outer skin together, while he clamps his teeth around a tree—but the unforeseen effect is that the python flips inside out. He turns a bright pink color, and loses his reason and eyesight as well, so gives blind, ravenous chase to Tobedwego, mistaking the lead Robber for a meal. When Tobedwego escapes, Shardlu blissfully swallows himself, and vanishes.

Any time I've shown *The Happy Valley* to someone familiar with children's books, they have the same quick response: that there's way too much text on the pages for a colorfully-illustrated picture book, which is what it resembles in every other way. This may have dictated the book's failure in its day (I don't know this for a fact), but it isn't fair. I try not to get defensive—after all, anyone who resists is only confirming more deeply my private relationship to the book, the sense in which it is a dream recounted that only I'll ever completely understand. And the people I've handed the book to aren't children, so they can never approach it with the same receptiveness I did. And not everyone resists.

If you sit and read the book on its own terms the proportion of incident to illustration is, I think, quite reasonable. And what fills the pages are the lovely paradoxical dialogues:

"Do you know why you have to face front in an elevator?"
"No," said Dulcy.
"Neither do I," said Abe. "So I always face the rear. It makes everyone nervous as a cat."
"Cats *are* nervous," said Flossie. "He's right, as usual."

These invariably enchant anyone of any age who I've managed to induce to dip into them.

A mention of the illustrations, which are by Sylvie Selig. The bright-hued pages are certainly characteristic of their era, for a certain paisley-decorative splendor, and for the bell-bottoms and Nehru collars on the animals' two-piece suits. The style, though, is mysterious and wonderful and slightly naïve, less Peter Max-slick than a sort of cross between Henri Rousseau's paintings and Klaus Voorman's jacket art for the Beatles' *Revolver*. And the drawings play a nice trick I've never much seen elsewhere, one which made the book particularly spellbinding and rereadable for me as a child: they contradict and amplify and even sometimes seem to mock the text itself. For instance, where Shardlu's work as "Friend & Companion" is described, the story also mentions his schedule of "breakfast on Monday morning, lunch on Wednesday at noon, and dinner on Friday evening." Nothing more, but Selig has depicted Shardlu grinning over a plate of live—shrew? vole? Hard to tell—which pleads for its life. This nicely sends up "Friend & Companion" as well as prefiguring the rabbit-eating plot. Extra animals, unmentioned in the tale, clutter the peripheries—pigs, monkeys, alligators, even lobsters and giant beetles are shown joining in the communal hubbub. And as wordy as the book is, it stops several times for silent pages, where Selig's lush, mysterious art bleeds to every margin. This has the effect of stopping time, much in the manner of a Japanese film where scenes are lingered over, the camera considering all corners of a room before resuming the plot. When I pick up *The Happy Valley*, which is often, I'm frequently going back to gaze deeper into the odd depths of the drawings, rather than rereading the tale from beginning to end.

But what about the plot? It needs finishing. Though he never quite "tuned in," Shardlu has, of course, dropped out and turned on quite heroically. His transformation doubly spares Dulcy's life, since the blue skin he shed before swallowing himself makes the Princess a fine umbrella. The Robbers are likewise reconciled by a suggestion from Abe: that their intrinsic necessity of robbing be satisfied by robbing one another. The Restless Nogo might have to wander on to find things to discover, until he is offered, by Abe, this insight: why not discover himself?

Finally a happy banquet is laid out for all the creatures, including the suddenly returning Shardlu, who explains:

"I changed my mind. So I unswallowed myself backward so I would be right side out again, and here I am."

"Oh, my!" said Dulcy.

"Don't worry," said Shardlu. "I discovered that if you once swallow yourself, you can never be the same afterward. I don't want to eat Dulcy anymore. Now all I want are flowers and toys and hardware and jelly beans, and there are plenty of those things around."

"How did you change your mind?" asked the Princess.

Shardlu doesn't know how to answer, but Abe does, and it is here Berne tips his hat just slightly to his great model, Lewis Carroll: "You either swallow yourself or get to the other side of a mirror. I was there myself when I was younger."

So, there's the gift *The Happy Valley* brought me—it took me as far on the other side of the mirror as the Carroll books, its Hippie aura no less poignant and affecting than the Victorianisms of Alice. Here's the odd gift it brings me now: since *The Happy Valley* is entirely mine, it can still take me there, a little. I can still visit Lamador and have my bad vibes smoothed out by the happy inhabitants, the ever-so-slightly sexy sheep and rabbits, the droll Zen Koan-ish wisdom of Abe, which in truth stands for the naïve Utopian yearning of our parents' sweetest, most hopeful selves. Unlike The Restless Nogo, they may not have convinced me (or the world) to stay back there in the late sixties. But like Shardlu, I can roll in for a visit.

—from *Remarkable Reads: 34 Writers and Their Adventures in Reading*, 2004

Footnote on Sylvie Selig

I'm not a writer who hides. The result is that I'm destined be reached out to by the real people mentioned, or who feel their lives indirectly evoked, in the work. Everywhere on book tour I meet kids who went to public schools in Brooklyn in the 1970s; some of them are my actual schoolmates, like Rusty Cole, who appeared at a bookshop in San Diego a year or two after *The Fortress of Solitude* was published, and who I hadn't seen since fourth grade.

People stick around. When they don't they leave DNA crumb trails. I got to exchange letters with Russell Greenan, and to know Daniel Fuch's son, and Italo Calvino's daughter. Out of my solitary memoryscape, I've stocked my life with unexpected acquaintances, as if my lonely teenage bookshelves were animating into faces. Surely the most magical among these was when I received an e-mail from Sylvie Selig, the illustrator of *The Happy Valley*. The obscurity of the book, and the fact that I'd barely focused on the illustrations (though I love them), and the fact that she'd spent the rest of her career as a painter, not a book illustrator, and the fact that she was a (then) sixty-four year-old Frenchwoman— all made it feel that time and space and probability had collapsed.

At this point, the story is best taken up by a short piece I wrote for a French catalogue of Sylvie's paintings, which has never been published in English until now:

Five or six years ago I described a lost and esoteric children's book called *The Happy Valley*, written by Eric Berne and published in 1968 and then forgotten, the dreamlike power of which swayed me deeply as a child. In my attempt to account for this power, I wrote: *A mention of the illustrations, which are by Sylvie Selig. The bright-hued pages are certainly characteristic of their era, for a certain paisley-decorative splendor, and for the bell-bottoms and Nehru collars on the animals' two-piece suits. The style, though, is mysterious and wonderful and slightly naïve, less Peter Max-slick than a sort of cross between Henri Rousseau's paintings and Klaus Voorman's jacket art for the Beatles'* Revolver. In using her name with such passing familiarity, it may seem to the reader that I was versed in—or had any idea at all—of Sylvie Selig's wider existence. This impression would be completely wrong. For me, her name might as well have been the name of one of the characters in *The Happy Valley*, for I knew it not at all outside the boundaries of my single copy of that book—a book which seemed to me to have dropped from the sky—and had never seen another of Selig's illustrations, let alone known of the existence of her extraordinary body of paintings.

Then one day a year or two after writing those words, and seeing them published, a letter magically appeared in the mailbox of my computer, as if summoned up by my unconscious, bearing the name Sylvie Selig. The painter, from her home in France, had come across my essay mentioning her illustrations, also due to internet magic. In her letter, Selig expressed her astonishment that anyone recalled *The Happy Valley*, let alone that a child influenced by the book and its illustrator would become a writer who'd happen to publicly resurrect the book in my tiny remembrance. Well, she hardly could have been more astonished than me. Selig explained that she'd long since left illustration behind, and resumed her career as a painter. And within a few moments I browsed an on-line gallery of her artworks.

At that instant, Sylvie Selig's imagery re-colonized my imagination at the level of a childhood dream, consoling and disturbing me like an intervention, a *preemption*, at a level before language or category (painting, film, surrealism, metaphor, symbol, etcetera) could intrude. Past and future became fused in my total responsiveness to her vision. I couldn't possibly exaggerate how natural this seemed to me.

Of course Sylvie Selig adored both Lewis Carroll and David Lynch—in my own imaginings she'd connected the two already, her ominous and helpless rabbits, first in *The Happy Valley*, and now in these parallel paintings, ushering my sensibility from Carroll's March Hare to the situation-comedy bunnies in David Lynch's *Inland Empire*, never mind that those didn't exist yet. Though it would be decades before I could finish the journey from Carroll to Lynch, Selig was secretly with me, and inside me, all the way. And anyway, it wasn't a journey in the sense of moving from one thing to the other: Sylvie Selig knows that we never leave Lewis Carroll behind (and for my part I still write stories with talking animals in them). And of course her brush collects film directors, detecting the tender closet surrealism of Hitchcock and Lubitsch, as well as the more obvious European examples, even while it also still gathers up the menagerie of fellow animals that cover our earth—and treats both, directors and creatures, as exotic and familiar, as dream companions.

I'm disinclined to trouble with art-historical language, or any attempt to place Sylvie Selig in a continuum of painting *per se*, if only because it would nudge her from her privileged place in my dreaming gallery, where she preceded them all, but also because her gathering up of literary quotations and film actor's faces and so many other gifts from the cultural sphere so beautifully expresses the ecstasy of influence (as opposed to Bloom's anxiety of influence), making the work a timeless celebration of her life as a reader, filmgoer, and human being. So, Sylvie Selig, my mysterious imaginary unmet French parent, would it be an affront if I confessed that I wonder if I dreamed you into existence? We've still never met. Yet in her "film fictions" Selig has seemingly read my mind again, using the universal language of externalized dream: the cinema, making the visual vocabularies of so many quintessential directors briefly and brilliantly her own, encompassing so many of my favorite film icons and symbols that I am forced to consider the opposite explanation: Sylvie Selig dreamed me.

Shortly after writing this, I traveled to Paris with my family. One afternoon my wife and I and our two boys enjoyed Sylvie's hospitality at her extraordinary studio in Paris. And a tiny Selig canvas depicting a flying man-rabbit now hangs in the boys' bedroom in California.

Engulf and Devour

You know *Moby-Dick* before you know it. You feel it coming before you read it, like Ishmael in the book, enduring the global duration of the voyage and suffering the thrill and agony of delay of the title character's actual appearance. The title alone is a cultural "meme"—Elvis Presley, in his "Comeback Special," in 1968, raises his microphone stand like a harpoon and sneer-shouts it—"Moby Dick." He raises a laugh of recognition from a crowd of fans in a TV studio. You might be a John Huston completist, or an Orson Welles partisan, or a Ray Bradbury fan, and come into contact with the 1956 film. You might read the Classic Comic, or come across one of any number of the paraphrases or references that trickle through popular culture.

Or you might be me, who walked into a stranger's downtown renovated loft one night—I was there not on any literary or bookish errand, but because I'd been promised a good dance party—to find a wall of four or five long bookshelves. I always step up to bookshelves when I visit a home for the first time. It's probably rude, but I can't stop myself. These shelves, astonishingly, consisted of nothing but different editions of *Moby-Dick*. Hundreds of them. It was a kind of parlor trick or art installation; anyway, one of the most breathtaking surprises I've ever seen in my book-loving life. What did these shelves mean to the person—the book-collector as obsessed Ahab—who'd assembled them? Was he or she satisfied yet? Probably not.

My stepmother, when I was fifteen, was keen on whales, on saving them, of course, but also on taking whale-watching boat tours in the Atlantic, listening to whale songs on scratchy LPs, and on re-reading *Moby Dick* once a year. She claimed it was best read "just for the story," and that this could easily be accomplished by simply skipping every other chapter. Now, this isn't strictly true, not even close; the philosophy and epistemology and ontology and also the freaky poetical crypto-zoological musings interpenetrate the "story," just as the story interpenetrates many of the (seemingly) digressive "fugue" chapters. But her suggestion strongly shaped my first reading, which came five or six years later—the point being, you too, dear reader, arrive at page one with expectations, anticipations, your breath held, your narrative-seeking brain boiling helplessly with "spoilers."

Well, then, if you are lucky enough to be reading *Moby-Dick* for the first time, you'll find the book can encompass every one of these—engulf and devour them, one and all—and satisfy and discharge every impulse that brought you, and that you brought, to its opening page. It takes up such a ridiculous amount of space in the cultural imagination for the very simplest of reasons: for the amount of space it occupies in the private imagination of each individual reader. *Moby Dick* installs itself in your brain as a kind of second brain, bigger than that which contains it, much like swallowing an ocean of language and implication. And that, in turn, connects your engorged mental container to all the others, through time, that have made the same encounter. As the whale is too big for Ahab or Ishmael to fully digest in their apprehension and awe, so is the book to our literary imagination. The unknown reader who filled those shelves (as I've begun, slowly, to do in emulation—I have twelve or fifteen different editions now) was trying to explain what had happened to him—those fathomless shelves were an externalized model of a book which *is itself a hologram of consciousness*, in its variousness and paradox, endlessly altered each time it touches the world and at each point where it mysteriously contacts itself.

—*Moby-Dick, The Norton Critical Edition,* 2016

The Figure in the Castle

The first time I read Kafka I thought I'd been duped. This was in high school, of course, when I had a tendency to suspect I'd been duped by most anything, particularly anything that, like adulthood itself, drew me nearer to it by some irresistible force and yet which baffled me. Specifically, I couldn't accept that Kafka's novel *The Castle* had no ending. Nobody warned me—I wasn't reading Kafka for a class, but had taken him from the school library, driven by the same erratic booklust that had driven me that same year through volumes of Priestley, Dreiser and Camus, as well as Alan Drury's *Advise and Consent*—and when I got to the last page, which ends mid-sentence, I felt betrayed. This was meant to be one of the century's greatest writers' greatest novels, and he couldn't even *finish* it? I was a stubbornly literal reader then, filleting books for their raw plots, absorbed (I thought) not by the music of the prose or by the evocations of theme or symbol, but by the behavior of characters as they moved toward their fates. In this way I was as stubborn and literal as Kafka's main character in *The Castle*, the not-quite-named K., who goes on trying to enter the castle, or at least to get the full attention of its operatives, long after savvy readers will have concluded his efforts are not only un-likely to be rewarded, but intrinsically hopeless—hopeless, indeed, in a way that seems to define the essence of Kafka's art. Consummately un-savvy, at that instant when I turned the last page and met with my disenchantment—K.'s not gonna make it!—I may have been both Kafka's worst reader, and his best. Or anyway, his most committed.

Three years later, in a freshman Lit class, a professor had us read Kafka's story of a father and son's mortal struggle, "The Judgment," in tandem with the writer's undelivered epistle, "A Letter to His Father." This was 1982, early in what has become a literary age of relentless psychobiographical curiosity about authors, yet it was hardly unusual to examine Kafka this way; really, it was deeply traditional. Has there ever been an author more embedded in his own personal context of letters and diaries—as well as in the image created by his neurasthenic gaze in the famous photographs, and by the biographical details of his pensiveness, suffering and early death? This may be the inevitable legacy of a literary genius who left such an epic disproportion of letters and diaries to intentional literary works. (And, if we recall Kafka's instructions to his friend Max Brod to destroy the unfinished novels and a majority of the other writings, aren't we violating Kafka's privacy anytime we read beyond *In the Penal Colony*, that modest volume that assembles every piece of prose whose publication he approved?) Yet Kafka is luminescent in every mode and medium. His capacity for anticipating any response we find in ourselves as we read him, can tend to make us feel he has overmastered any commentator the moment they issue a single interpretation. As long as we keep our own mouths shut, and all theories at bay, we can assure ourselves that we alone have mingled with the "true" Franz Kafka.

The history of Kafka studies is one of proprietary sniping among claimants for Existentialism, Judaism, antifascism and anti-Communism between Freudians and anti-Freudians and deconstructionists and anti-deconstructionists. The battles take place on ground struck by Brod and by Kafka's early translators into English, the Scots Willa and Edwin Muir, against whom every subsequent commentator has been obliged to react. Brod and the Muirs preferred to see the writer's teasing nightmares of futility and paradox as a vast allegory of Man's attempted negotiation with an absconded and yet somehow menacing spiritual authority—call it *God*, if you like, though taking my college professor's hint, it often enough resembles *Dad*. These debates, while in character seeming old as the Talmud, are, like terrorist cellphone chatter, boiling away any time we care to tune in: if you don't believe me, visit the letters pages of *The New York Review of Books*. The irony is that Kafka may seem to resemble the invisible authorities lurking inside *The Castle*, or behind the operations of *The Trial*: impossible to approach without transgression, and without sinking into a mire of petty bureaucratic obstacles.

Kafka's presence in extra- or para-literary culture is also feverish, and contested. At this point, denouncing the adjective "Kafkaesque" as a travesty of Kafka has itself become a cliché. But then Kafka's evocative persona and his most famous signifiers—particularly the insect of "The Metamorphosis"—seem to beg for travesty, for appropriation into icon and cartoon, into Philip Roth's novel *The Breast*, Steven Soderberg's movie *Kafka*, and dozens if not hundreds of others. (Mea culpa: in *Kafka Americana*, with co-conspirator Carter Scholz, I morphed Kafka with Frank Capra, Batman, and Orson Welles). The cartoonist R. Crumb, with writer David Zane Mairowitz, in *Introducing Kafka*, denounced Soderberg's movie and the Kafka T-shirts sold in Prague as "kitsch," even while offering up unsqeamishly detailed renderings of the insect Kafka fought to keep off the front jacket of the book edition of "The

Metamorphosis." In travesty, as in interpretation, only one's own effort is likely to seem wholly excusable.

Now, striding across this field comes the Italian essayist Robert Calasso, who proposes, by a single gesture of minimizing interpretive context or precedent, to restore the fragmentary Kafka to an immaculate wholeness. He also proposes Kafka as a visionary of ontology—an ontology which hints everywhere at theological traditions, though Calasso might be horrified to have his project described this way. Calasso's brash method, established in the justly celebrated *Marriage of Cadmus and Harmony* and continued in *Ka*, is to reinscribe, persistently, the essential power of the myths and stories he considers, largely by the act of retelling them in his philosophically muscular prose. In *Cadmus and Harmony* he did this for the Greek myths, in *Ka* for the gods of the East, the Vedic and Brahmanic pantheons; in each case his encompassing awareness created for the reader a breathtaking immersion in the force and implication of these ancient stories, offering a series of epiphanies as to their relevance to contemporary literature and life. Rather than surrounding his subject with information, Calasso seems to cause it to glow from within, like fingers cupped around the bulb of a flashlight, so that that which has been taken for granted becomes translucent and revelatory.

In Calasso's Kafka, infinity is not a state of mind, let alone a version of obsessive-compulsive or manic-depressive oscillation, but a peek at the cosmos, the eternal order before which mankind inevitably shudders:

> Certainly it's not the case, as some continue to maintain, that the religious or the sacred or the divine has been shattered, dissolved, obviated, by some outside agent, by the light of the Enlightenment . . . What happened instead is that such things as the religious or the sacred

or the divine, by an obscure process of osmosis, were absorbed and hidden in something alien, which no longer has need of such names because it is self-sufficient and is content to be described as society . . . With Kafka a phenomenon bursts onto the scene: the commixture. There is no sordid corner that can't be described as a vast abstraction, and no vast abstraction that can't be treated as a sordid corner.

It's a measure of Calasso's accomplishment that his readings feel familiar, as though his erudition were inside us, a pre-existing condition only waiting for diagnosis. His tone, while epic, is also welcoming. It's a measure of Kafka's genius, though, that Calasso's book still feels like an interpretation, and therefore partial at best.

What if, as in Henry James's "The Figure in the Carpet"—that perfect parable of critics coming to grief in the attempt at interpreting fiction—the secret of Kafka is that there's no secret? What if behind the machinations of *The Castle* lies not so much the ineffable mythos of Calasso's reverent speculation, but the Great and Powerful Oz? In fact, anytime K. glimpses the Castle's operatives they look a lot like a bunch of old guys smoking cigars and cavorting with trollops. It's easy to complain that Calasso, like every critic before him, has missed Kafka's humor (to read Kafka is to feel that everyone before you has missed his humor—hence the almost wearisome popularity of the anecdote that Kafka and his friends were convulsed with laughter when he read *The Trial* aloud). But Calasso, for all his transubstantiation with these texts, may have, in his bias for excavating Gods, missed Kafka's grubby, self-effacing foolishness, his insistent embarrassment at grandiosity, his peculiar and magical refusal to keep his eye on the ball—in a word, Kafka's shrug.

All of this is only to say that the difficulty with Calasso's *K.* is precisely that this great distiller of distant myths has taken as his subject not some vast and elusive array of ancient texts, but the readily available and eminently readable works of a modern author. It is useless to read *K.* before one has read Kafka. Indeed, to sample Calasso's communion with Kafka is to feel the immediate need to reread the novels and stories, if only out of envy for the galvanic charge the activity has plainly put into Calasso. And to read Kafka is to locate one's own intensely personal relationship to the writer's glorious and terrifying conundrums. Your Kafka, however less brilliantly articulated, is unlikely to be exactly Calasso's.

My own Kafka does keep company with ancient archetypes, sure, but he's also a fiction writer from the not-yet-irretrievable twentieth century (You caught me: I'm claiming him for my own tribe now). Manipulator of characters, scenes, dialogue and plot; painstaking emulator of Dickens and Flaubert; and self-taunting blocked writer, Kafka is as accessible to readers as he is esoteric to interpreters. In his communing with the unnamable, Kafka may be drawn into the company of gnostic seers, yes. But he's also (Warning: I offer you now a bouquet of comparisons-as-travesties) as strange and cool as the best M.C. Escher drawing you ever got cross-eyed over; as disconcertingly ribald as not only Philip Roth and Samuel Beckett but also the aforementioned R. Crumb; as toxic and shuddery as Poe and David Lynch. His prose, among the most exacting and incisive ever put on the page (hence the inevitability of his translators' doubts, and our doubts of his translators), may be taken as a reproach to all us lesser writers. But it also takes the top of your head off, like a line of cocaine.

If for most readers Kafka demolishes the quarantine between waking and dream, for working writers like Anita Brookner, who has reconciled Kafka with Jane Austen, or

Thomas Berger, who appropriated Kafka for genres like the policier and the screwball farce, Kafka represents a writerly pressure on individual moments of lived experience, of lived consciousness, to a degree previously unknown in fiction. For anyone who has dared attempt picking up where Kafka left off it is the quarantine between realist and anti-realist methods in fiction that his writing has made seem permanent nonsense. Kafka grasped that language itself—even the very plainest and most direct—is innately metaphorical, fabulated, and grotesque. What's worse, consciousness, being constructed from language, has that same unholy drift, like the staggering gait of a golem, or the puttering and sifting activities of the mole-like creature in "The Burrow." To follow where language and consciousness lead, to chart a mind's self-devouring narcissism and anxiety as it encounters and defends itself from an indifferent universe, is the higher realism. Language itself dreams, and all thinking is wishful, or else morbid. Usually both. One of the most poignant moments in all of Kafka's writing is when this compulsive epistolary filibusterer, whose volumes of brilliantly self-justifying and self-abnegating letters to his sweethearts rival his fiction in both volume and hypnotic power, remarks: "These letters do nothing but cause anguish, and if they don't cause any anguish it's even worse."

Kafka's characters are both defiled and enraptured by the world. They defile and enrapture it in turn: Calasso isolates a perverse moment in *The Trial*, when Joseph K. recognizes the sexual allure that attaches to him because of his predicament: "Defendants are the loveliest of all . . . it can't be guilt that renders them beautiful . . . It must result from the proceedings being brought against them, which somehow adhere to them." Similarly, each of Kafka's readers will be defiled and enraptured in the maze of the writer's texts; no interpretation can protect one from the world's grasp, or from the grasp of stories. One of Kafka's parables concerns leopards breaking into a temple and drinking from the sacred vessels; after a period of years the leopards are relied upon as an aspect of the holy ceremonies. As with the leopards, so with this ritual of interpretation (and defense from interpretation) of Kafka's writing. Kafka's readers must become leopards and transgress in order to visit the temple in the first place.

Three essential books: *The Castle*, *The Trial*, and *The Collected Stories*. Throw in *Amerika* for dessert. Kafka's the greatest writer, by a long shot, who you can polish off in two or three weeks' reading. And yet, a warning: As Kafka found it impossible to finish his own novels—some days, his diaries reveal, he believed he had not even begun his work—so you may find it impossible to be finished with Kafka. The Castle's up there on the hill. Set out anytime you like. The horizon, you'll find, recedes as you approach it; you may approach wearing a Kafka t-shirt, or not.

—*The New York Times*, 2005

The Greatest Animal Novelist of All Time

I have a suggestion: Forget London. Forget, for now, the nineteenth century, forget the whole assertion that the value of the "late," or "mature," Dickens—a construction whose first evidence is usually located by commentators here, in *Dombey and Son*—rests on his staging his sentimental melodramas and grotesques within an increasingly deliberate and nuanced social panorama, of his city. Forget *institutions*, forget *reform*. Please indulge me, and forget for the moment any questions of confession or self-portraiture, despite *Dombey*'s being the book which preceded that great dam-bursting of the autobiographical impulse, *David Copperfield* (in fact, *Dombey* contains a tiny leak in that dam in the form of Mrs. Pipchin, the first character Dickens said was drawn from a figure from his life). Forget it all, and then forgive what will surely seem a diminishing suggestion from me, which is that you abandon all context, ye who enter here, and read *Dombey and Son* as though it were a book about animals.

Read it as though the characters are all covered in fur, beginning with Dombey and his little newborn heir on the glorious first page: read this book as if it were *The Wind in the Willows*, or *Watership Down*), one of those droll stories about anthropomorphized creatures, clever eccentric badgers and rabbits and crows, as well as feral predators, foxes and cats, tucked into Victorian suits and dresses—read it as if Dickens were the *greatest animal novelist of all times*. If this seems impossible, note the head start Dickens has given you in naming *Dombey*'s characters: Cuttle, Chick, Nipper, Gills, MacStinger and, of course, The Game Chicken. Note the descriptions: "Mrs. Pipchin hovered behind the victim, with her sable plumage and her hooked beak, like a bird of ill-omen." There's Mrs. Skewton, "whose vigilance . . . no lynx could have surpassed." Doctor Blimber "looked at Paul as if he were a little mouse"—then, a page later, "seemed to survey Paul with the sort of interest that might attach to some choice little animal he was going to stuff." Mrs. Brown is shown "hovering about" Florence Dombey "like some new kind of butterfly." Or consider the description of Mr. Toodle feeding his brood of children, which omits any overt animal reference yet still sounds like narration from the Nature Channel:

> In satisfying himself, however, Mr. Toodle was not regardless of the younger branches about him, who, although they had made their own evening repast, were on the look-out for irregular morsels . . . These he distributed now and then to the expectant circle, by holding out great wedges of bread and butter, to be bitten at by the family in lawful succession, and by serving out small doses of tea in a like manner with a spoon; which snacks had such relish in the mouths of these young Toodles, that, after partaking of the same, they performed private dances of ecstasy among themselves, and stood on one leg apiece, and hopped . . . they gradually closed around Mr. Toodle again, and eyed him hard as he got through more bread and butter and tea . . .

Then there is of course our skulking white-collar criminal, Carker:

. . . feline from sole to crown was Mr. Carker the Manager, as he basked in the strip of summer-light and warmth that shone upon his table and the ground . . . With hair and whiskers deficient in colour at all times, but feebler than common in the rich sunshine, and more like the coat of a sandy tortoise-shell cat; with long nails, nicely pared and sharpened . . . Mr. Carker the Manager, sly of manner, sharp of tooth, soft of foot, watchful of eye, oily of tongue, cruel of heart, nice of habit, sat with a dainty steadfastness and patience at his work, as if he were waiting at a mouse's hole.

Mary Gaitskill, in her introduction to *Bleak House*, describes the force such protean imagery stirs up from underneath the surface of Dickens's ostensibly lucid stories:

With all the roaring energy he summons . . . and all the ranting little heads popping out of his fantastic landscape, Dickens is excessive by modern standards. But modern standards have become excessive, and Dickens is excessive like Nature; like living things his creatures must twist and turn, expand out or tunnel in until they have utterly fulfilled what they are.

Susan Horton, in *The Reader in the Dickens World*, takes the observation further:

Although these images are called up in metaphors which presumably are meant to carry forward the plot action, they often seem to accumulate in such a way that they create an entirely separate and separable world . . . This beastlike world is a world of real mystery rather than contrived plot mystery . . . and it is in this figurative rendering of the experience of living . . . that Dickens's power and his vision lie.

Mark Spilka, in *Dickens and Kafka*, offers a comparison of *Dombey and Son's* comic-grotesque leading-man, Captain Cuttle, with the obsessive digging creature who narrates Kafka's long tale "The Burrow." Cuttle, through the middle of the novel, has taken flight from Mrs. MacStinger, and from his fears of marriage and children, to barricade himself inside Sol Gills's anachronistic sea-instrument shop. As Spilka points out, "the enemy in each case is the prospect of adult involvement, and the defensive preparations are equally elaborate":

> What the Captain suffered . . . whenever a bonnet passed, or how often he darted out of the shop to elude imaginary MacStingers, and sought safety in the attic, cannot be told. But to avoid the fatigues attendant on this means of self-preservation, the Captain curtained the glass door of communication between the shop and parlour . . . and cut a small hole of espial in the wall.

Cuttle then lives "a very close and retired life; seldom stirring abroad until after dark; venturing even then only into the obscurest streets . . . and both within and without the walls of his retreat, avoiding bonnets, as if they were worn by raging lions."

So, see the proud and alienated Dombey as some sort of arctic falcon. I know there's no such thing as an arctic falcon, yet Dombey's relentlessly characterized as *frozen, frigid, and remote*, and yet he's too high-strung and vulnerable to be a polar bear, and far too preening and fierce to be a penguin. The great ice-creature's chill and hauteur are the fundamental problem to be solved in this book, while around him, seeking or awaiting a solution, a host of other beasts gibber and beseech and pine and scheme, every one of them in their way more accepting of his or her animal nature, and animal destiny, than Dombey himself. Dombey's error is that, seeing the world in mercantile terms, he denies familial truth; he sees his offspring principally as methods of extending his Dealings and his Firm. He's wearing the wrong spectacles: they filter out the natural truths all around him. They filter out his daughter. Dickens wants us to feel this as a blindness, one as poignant as it is infuriating. When Dombey orders a tombstone prepared for his deceased son and heir, he asks that it read: "beloved and only child." It takes the stonecarver to point out the mistake:

"It should be 'son', I think, Sir?"
"You are right. Of course. Make the correction."

But every approach to Dickens, apart from "Read him, damn it!," seems patronizing and reductive, doesn't it? Fur-covering his characters is only an absurd example. How can it be that this most generous and diverse and intricate and inventive of novelists, in whose pages nearly every subsequent narrative mode seems—whether as a result of conscious experiment or exuberant, instinctive doodling—to have been anticipated, is nearly always introduced by critics or followers (and *any* writer of fiction is a follower of Dickens, I insist on this, whether like Gissing and Kafka and Dostoevsky and Christina Stead and Peter Carey a conscious follower, or like me, until my shameful awakening five years ago, a blind and unconscious one) who say, one after the other, in so many words: "Dickens only half-knew what he was doing" or "Dickens was often great despite himself"?

The trick of Dickens is that it is only easy to say what he wasn't. Basically, he wasn't George Eliot. He wasn't the inventor of the interior, psychological mode in English fiction, the mode which can be legibly traced from Richardson and Austen through Modernism to the preponderance of contemporary fictional styles. Having excluded this, and having muttered a few apologies for his *broad* or *theatrical* or *popular* or *sentimental* tendencies, commentators are often at a loss to say what Dickens was. This is because he was everything, and to be everything is to be paradoxical and overwhelming, and leave your reader grappling for a handhold. It's not that Dickens *isn't* what he's said to be, and what a thousand paraphrases into movies and Classic Comics and all sorts of other mediums have suggested: theatrical and sentimental, absolutely. The man's the all-time beguiler, flatterer, and manipulator of readers, to great comic and bathetic effect in virtually every chapter. The trick is that he deals in proto-Modernist ambiguity and disjunction too. For everything Dickens is plainly wishing you to understand and feel, he also provides a fistful of arrows pointing elsewhere, to uneasy, vagrant thoughts and feelings, "signifiers" which a reader tends to feel Dickens is ignorant of, or resistant to, himself, but which he endlessly shares anyway.

His genius, then, is at one with the genius of the form of the novel itself: Dickens willed into existence the most capacious and elastic and versatile kind of novel that could be, one big enough for his vast sentimental yearnings and for every hunger and fear and hesitation in him that cut against those yearnings too. Never parsimonious and frequently contradictory, he always gives us everything he can, everything he's planned to give, and then more. This from one of the most energetic souls to ever walk the planet, or specifically the streets of London, which he famously did, in daily marathons of ten miles or more, where one presumes he generated material in the collision of his fevered imagination with the varieties of life he encountered in the streets, and with the life of the streets themselves, the buildings and railroads of an increasingly industrial century.

Take for instance the famous "theatricality," which might seem one of the least arguable assertions about Dickens. He adored the theater, yes. And his characters do present themselves to the reader and to one another in declamatory, presentational modes which seem specifically derived from Victorian melodrama. Yet it's worth pointing out that Dickens shows an aggressive impatience with the most basic and inherent limitation of theatrical presentation: the stage. He's forever sliding from the main action to focus on peculiar side-issues, on reaction shots of minor characters, or simply to vent the camera-eye of his prose to the rooftops, to the sky. He's constantly panning the crowd, in what can begin to seem a kind of claustrophobic avoidance of whatever main stage he's set. Take for instance Dombey's wedding. It begins with a wide shot: "Dawn with its passionless blank face, steals shivering to the church . . ." We're given pages of steeple-clock, spire, a super-anthropomorphized "dawn," the church's mice, the beadle, and Mrs. Miff, the pew-opener, none of them previously introduced, nor relevant to the book's design. The chapter ranges over the reactions of the pastry-cook and others on the serving-staff, winding up with nameless partygoing throngs and with those mice again. Or, consider Little Paul's death, which is presented as a recurring shot of waves ceaselessly pounding the shore, as if to reinforce the fateful universality of the event, and distract us from its meaning in terms of the central theatrical unit—the Dombey family.

Dickens works to keep us aware of the variety he's met in the street, and of the possibility that, if his eye happened to settle elsewhere, in place of the story underway we'd find another story going on. These methods anticipate film: the distended ensembles of Robert Altman's *Nashville* or *A Wedding*, the rhythmic cityscapes Yasujiro Ozu employs to widen the context of his family dramas in *Late Autumn* or *Tokyo Story*. This isn't to say Dickens would have hightailed it to Hollywood if he'd lived in our century. One only has to measure his torrential, visceral engagement with language to know this is as silly as speculating that Beethoven could have been tempted from music, or De Kooning from paint. Still, the most famous page in *Dombey* is a fantastic wish for the ultimate wide shot. It echoes the utopian intent of a filmmaker like Godard, who used a cutaway set to anatomize social reality in *Tout Va Bien*:

> Oh, for a good spirit who would take the house tops off, with a more potent and benignant hand than the lame demons in the tale, and show a Christian people what dark shapes issue from amidst their homes . . . For only one night's view of the pale phantoms rising from the scenes of our too-long neglect; and from the thick and sullen air where Vice and Fever propagate together . . . Not the less bright and blest would that day be for rousing some who never have looked out upon the world of human life around them, to a knowledge of their own relation to it . . .

In *Dombey*, Dickens brings in the outside world in his portraits of the (then-new) London suburbs, and of the railway as it crushes its way through the heart of London. These are usually taken as proof that Dickens was beginning to anchor his drama in the larger socio-economic world. *Dombey and Son* (its full title: *Dealings with the Firm of Dombey and Son Wholesale, Retail and for Exportation*) is the first book in which he places an institution at the center of his story, a move he'd expand and deepen in *Bleak House* and *Hard Times*.

That's just one of the ways in which *Dombey* is a watershed for Dickens. If four or five of his novels are more cherished by contemporary readers, all roads somehow lead to *Dombey*: welcome, here, to the heart of the heart of Dickens. As I said at the top, this book contains his first conscious use of autobiographical sources. It's also the first in which Dickens drew a clear blueprint beforehand, rather than relying on improvisation to get him through his plot—and because he was impressed by his own new capacity to make plans, he documented them carefully in his letters to his friend (and eventual biographer) John Forster. So we know, for instance, of Dickens's enthusiastic effort to shift sympathy quickly from Paul to Florence, after the boy's death, and of his vetoed scheme to have Carker and Edith Dombey consummate their self-loathing tryst.

What's more, it was after the occasion of a reading of the second installment of *Dombey* to a group of close friends that Dickens wrote to Forster:

"I was thinking the other day that . . . a great deal of money might possibly be made . . . by one's having Readings of one's own books. It would be an *odd* thing. I think it would take immensely. What do you say?"

This is not just to blame *Dombey* for the whole modern-day rigmarole of book touring, or to say that it was here Dickens learned the trick that, taken to grueling extremes on American and British stages, likely killed him. It changed his writing, too. Mark Lambert, in *Dickens and the Suspended Quotation*, suggests that the public readings siphoned off a significant portion of Dickens's craving for the flattering approval of a human audience. By venting the grossly comedic and sentimental aspects of his temperament live on stage, Dickens may have freed himself to be the more remote, obscure and generally less people-pleasing author of subsequent books. Perhaps this confluence—autobiography, social criticism, increased planning, and the readings, all attributable to *Dombey*—is what created the "late" style.

"*Dombey and Son* makes the impression of a leafless tree illuminated fitfully by twinkling lights . . . (which) reveal to us the whole person and house of Dombey in all their aridity and arrogance." That description comes from Una Pope-Hennessy's (largely supplanted) 1945 biography. Another way of putting it is that the character at the center of this book is a cold fish, whom Dickens exposes by the warmth of the menagerie around him, and by the steady loving gaze of his daughter, Florence. Critics have often taken Dickens to task for his "perfect girls," of which Florence is a classic example. Gaitskill defends the function of Esther in *Bleak House*, another of those angels, this way: "When Dickens looks at certain wicked or complex characters through her ingenuous eyes, he can perceive their gross faults with naïve clarity while pretending . . . not to know what's wrong with them." Florence, similarly, serves as a simple but powerful lens roaming through these pages, amplifying, by her proximity, any tender emotion. Her patience, at her father's chilly threshold, stands for Dickens's ultimate faith that in a world of rigid grotesques we are nevertheless required, in the sphere of our intimate experience, to embrace the possibility of growth and change. Dickens's innocent girls aren't more persuasive as characters because he doesn't *need* them to be. What he needs them for is to cut against the grain of his "beastly" world. Rather than their being relics of the earlier, more sentimental style, it is with *Dombey* that he begins to require those girls more urgently, in order to contradict the monolithic, even punishing design of the later books.

Dombey's house, and his novel, becomes a kind of deprivation chamber: how much warmth and charm can Dickens banish from this space and still have a tale to tell? One after another, Toodles, Walter, Paul, Edith, Florence, Susan Nipper, all the abiding hearts, are pushed away to heighten the eeriness of Dombey's stand in his room, alone. This is a book partly about solitude, and Dombey is mirrored not only by Cuttle in his shop-burrow but by Carker smugly plotting in his living room, and by Toots spacing out in his attic—all, perhaps, oblique self-portraits of a writer alone in his workshop, images that range from the self-lampooning to the self-outraged.

Dickens declared this book an indictment of the excesses of capital-p Pride. I'd say it's also his Anatomy of Sycophancy. The book catalogues a host of divergent postures in respect to Dombey's power. Dickens, fresh from a buffeting by extremes of adulation and rejection by American crowds, had a lot to tell us on this subject. Major Bagstock is, of course, the most delirious flatterer, always ready to cover himself in any butter he's spreading:

"Dombey," said the Major, "I'm glad to see you. I'm proud to see you. There are not many men in Europe to whom J. Bagstock would say that—for Josh is blunt. Sir: it's his nature—but Joey B. is proud to see you, Dombey."

"Major," returned Mr. Dombey, "you are very obliging."

"No, sir," said the Major, "Devil a bit! That's not my character. If that had been Joe's character, Joe might have been, by this time, Lieutenant-General Sir Joseph Bagstock, K.C.B., and might have received you in very different quarters. You don't know old Joe yet, I find. But this occasion, being special, is a source of pride to me. By the Lord, Sir," said the Major resolutely, "it's an honour to me!"

Bagstock's sycophancy, and Mrs. Skewton's, provide the book an engine of misunderstanding, whisking Dombey into his disastrous marriage. Dickens shows how other misguided postures of homage have their own grievous results: it is Captain Cuttle's cultivation of Dombey that dooms Walter Gay to his exile on the high seas. Rob the Grinder's wheedling at the feet of Carker and Mrs. Brown is portrayed with outright disgust.

Seeing sycophancy overthrown provides one of the novel's chief satisfactions. Take Susan Nipper's confrontation with Dombey: it's silly but quite wonderful that we can still have our breath taken away to see a maidservant shuck off her deference. And one of the book's great comic set-pieces is Cuttle's buddy and confidant Bunsby unexpectedly switching allegiance to the husband-hunting MacStinger. Bunsby-Cuttle-MacStinger, though, are only a comic echo of the book's key triangle: Carker-Dombey-Edith. In each case the ultimate insult in an affair of the heart is in learning that someone else, someone unexpectedly nearby, may want what one has cast off.

The relationship between Carker the Manager and Edith Dombey is Dickens's darkest and shrewdest presentation of the evils of sycophancy. In an analysis of "slave mentality" worthy of Nietzsche, Dickens details the baroque self-loathing of proud souls brought to heel by Dombey's wealth, and by his oblivious arrogance. Carker and Edith, in their hypocrisy and nihilism, are unmistakable to one another, though Carker fatally mistakes the compulsion between them for a sexual To Do list. That Dickens censored his original plan to give the pair a night or two to exorcise their lust, and to make Dombey an official cuckold, is hardly important—Edith's hatred would surely have outstripped her carnality before long. Dickens is a pretty sexaverse writer—note how he has to banish Florence and Walter to a remote offstage land to consummate even the happiest union. But this revision is a good one, underlining the morbid psychology instead, in one the most modern sequences in all of Dickens. In the words of David Gates, "the man knew a thing or two about sadism and shame."

For all this, Dombey's pride *is* the novel's ultimate subject—and because Dickens felt a paradoxical identification with Dombey, it remains the novel's ultimate mystery. Old Dombey's humbling last-minute capitulation at the novel's end only comes, after all, due to his infirmity and bankruptcy. Dickens himself couldn't afford to wait that long to confront his own severity, and snobbery, or his resistance to the images of home and hearth he'd become a celebrity for endorsing. The novel's most tormenting moment, for me, comes after Little Paul's death, as Dombey boards the train on his way to the resort where he will meet Edith. On the platform he runs into the stoker, Toodle, whose wife had been Paul's wet-nurse. Dombey, characteristically, offers charity—munificence being one of the simplest ways to inscribe the distance between classes. But Toodle doesn't want money. He wants to discuss their two sons, Rob the Grinder and Little Paul. Dombey can't handle this. Turning away, he notices a bit of crape on the stoker's cap: Toodle is publicly *mourning* Paul. At this, Dombey becomes enraged:

> To think of this presumptuous raker among coals and ashes going on before there, with his sign of mourning! To think that he dared to enter, even by a common show like that, into the trial and disappointment of a proud gentleman's secret heart! To think that this lost child, who was to have divided with him his riches, and his projects, and his power, and allied with whom he was to have shut out all the world as with a double door of gold, should have let in such a herd to insult him with their knowledge of his defeated hopes, and their boasts of claiming community of feeling with himself, so far removed: if not of having crept into the place wherein he would have lorded it, alone!

This reminds me of Alfred Lambert, the St. Louis paterfamilias in Jonathan Franzen's *The Corrections*. Franzen's is a definitive contemporary portrayal of this typically middle-class rage for quarantines—quarantines not only between classes, but between realms of life. Dombey is the nineteenth century antecedent. Each man believes the beastly, shitty, unworthy, overwhelming world can be held at bay, be banished from his house. Each writers sympathizes with, and puzzles over, this adamant, hopeless belief. In *Dombey*, Dickens was in part asking himself: How, if I am the great hero of domesticity, can I want to spend so much time alone in my room, or racing through the London streets? Why do I act as if my children have disappointed me? What was their crime? And: I'm the great lover and champion of the poor, sure, but do I hold them at arm's length with my charity? It is Dickens's genius that even while he impersonates Dombey, he is also with us in the form of Florence, waiting at Dombey's door, wondering how to get inside, and framing for us in her despair the unanswerable question: What would actually happen if he came out?

—Introduction to Charles Dickens's *Dombey and Son*, 2003.
Reprinted that same year in *The Believer*

The Counter-Roth

1.

I'd taken the train out to East Hampton, Long Island, bringing with me to read only the first volume of John Cowper Powys's *Wolf Solent*. This was an ambiguous mission I was on—I'd been invited to a very nice rich girl's family's summer house, and I'm justified in calling her a girl because this was the summer after my first year of college and I was 19, a boy of 19. We'd been only friends at college but might be more, away from college: that was the ambiguous mission. I didn't know what I wanted.

On the train I stared out the window, not making it past more than a chapter of the Powys. The girl and her mother picked me up at the station, a five-minute drive there and back, just long enough that by the time we entered the house, through the kitchen, the girl's younger brother was caught in the act of pulling from the broiler two overdone, smoldering lobsters, their red partly blacked. The mother chided him, but affectionately, and insisted the lobsters be dumped immediately in the trash. I thought *I'll eat those*, but no. This was a period in my life where I was persistently being startled, to the point of violation, by the behavior of the wealthy. No reading—not Powys, nor F. Scott Fitzgerald, nor Karl Marx—could have prepared me to witness such a thing in real life. We ate something other than lobsters. Then I was shown to the guest room. It was beautifully quiet, with a scattering of books on the shelves.

An evening seemed to yawn before me—the girl and I would have time to be confused about one another tomorrow and the next day. Everything was done very graciously in this house, no hurry. Left alone there with ponderous Powys, I reached instead for a book I hadn't known existed: Philip Roth's novella *The Breast*.

I'd at that point in my reading life kept a useless partition against Roth, who, thanks to the intimidating aura generated by a paperback copy of *Letting Go* on my mother's shelves, I'd decided was a bestselling writer of grown-up realist novels of a sort that couldn't possibly interest me. Oh judgmental and defended youth! But wait, now I had to consider the claims of the book's dust jacket, that Roth worked in the realm of morbid fantasy, too. The realm of Kafka. This wasn't fair, I thought. Kafka should belong to me.

Alone in the East Hampton guest room, I gobbled *The Breast* in one gulp. That's how it came about, that's how I began taking Roth aboard, the first tiny dose a kind of inoculation to make me ready for the long readerly sickness I still endure. For it is a sickness, most especially for a reader who wants to be a writer, to open oneself to a voice as torrential and encompassing, as demanding and rewarding, as that of Roth.

2.

My situation in the East Hampton summer house was the stuff of Jewish comedy, if I'd had my Jewish antennae up. Had the brother been played by Christopher Walken, I was in a scene from *Annie Hall*. But I not only didn't have my Jewish antennae up, I didn't know I possessed any. By chance, and unlike a majority of Jews, I'd been raised so as not to take being Jewish, or in my case half-Jewish, in any way personally. I'd have to acquire those antennae elsewhere, by my reading.

It took overtly Jewish-American writing—by Bernard Malamud, who'd retired but was still lingering, thrillingly, around at the college the girl and I attended, and Saul Bellow, and yes, sometimes Roth, who is sometimes, when it serves the cause of the writing, overtly Jewish—to illuminate the connection between what I knew semi-consciously from the writing of the less-overt, such as Nathanael West or Barry Malzberg or Norman Mailer, as well as from sources like Groucho Marx and Abbie Hoffman and my Uncle Fred. What was it that was illuminated? That something aggravated and torrential in my voice, or perhaps I should call it my attempt at having a voice, was cultural in origin, even if aggravated and torrential frequently in the cause of disputing or even denying that point of origin.

As Roth points out, the books aren't Jewish because they have Jews in them. The books are Jewish in how they won't shut up or cease contradicting themselves, they're Jewish in the way they're sprung both from harangue and from defense against harangue, they're Jewishly ruminative and provocative. Roth once said of Bellow that he closed the distance between Damon Runyon and Thomas Mann—well, given the generation of reader I'm from, Roth in turn closed the difference between Saul Bellow and *Mad* magazine. That's to say, once I'd gained access to what he had to offer, Roth catalyzed my yearnings to high seriousness with the sense that the contemporary texture of reality demanded not only remorseless interrogation, but also remorseless caricature and ribbing. Contemporary reality, including perhaps especially the yearning to high seriousness, needed to be serially goosed.

3.

Speaking of caricature, I'm aware I may appear to have lapsed into schtick—a conflation of potted Rothian syntax and shameless confession. My only defense is that I'm employing tools Roth helped instill in me, tools that may in fact be all I've got: a reliance on the ear, for devising a voice and then following where the voices insist on going, and a helpless inclination to abide with the self—with one's own inclinations and appetites—as a lens for seeing what's willing to be seen, and as a medium for saying what wants to be said.

Call me instead a Counter-Roth. For it is the fate of a Roth, being the rare sort of writer whose major phases sprawl across decades, whose work encompasses and transcends modes of historical fiction, metafiction, memoir, the maximalist (or putters-in), the minimalist (or takers-out), the picaresque and counterfactual, etcetera and so forth—being the sort of writer who in his generosity half blots out the sky of possibility for those who come along after—to generate in his ambitious followers a sort of army of Counter-Roths. I'll say it simply: the one certainty in my generation of writers, not otherwise unified, is that we all have some feeling about Roth. We can't not. Mostly it involves some kind of strongly opinionated, half-aggrieved love.

4.

So, another confession: more than ten years after that encounter in East Hampton, I'd become a published novelist invited, for the first time, to a residence at the artist's colony called Yaddo. By this time I'd pursued my Roth obsession to both ends of his bookshelf, as it existed at the time, as I was to continue following it, right up to the present. On my arrival at Yaddo, a fellow writer who helped me to my room at West House mentioned famous personages who'd written masterpieces behind the various windows—Sylvia Plath here, John Cheever there—and then, opening the door to what was to be my residence and studio both, unveiled a circular turret featuring a smooth domed ceiling: "The Breast Room," he announced. I laughed, thinking he referred only to the shape. Then he explained that Roth, inspired by dwelling within the room's contour, wrote *The Breast* there. As with many circumstances in a young writer's life, I was exalted and humbled simultaneously—having been delivered by the Yaddo invitation into what I thought was my maturity, it turned out I was again to suckle at the fount of apprenticeship. Incidentally, if this story isn't true, I don't ever want to find out.

5.

Of course, I'm beyond my apprenticeship now and no longer even remotely young. In fact, as a college professor, it's sometimes my duty to counsel other young aspirants navigating an overwhelming encounter with Roth. I'm chagrined to admit that a quite brilliant English major under my care recently quit work on a thesis on Roth's 1974 novel *My Life As a Man*, in despair. With his permission, I quote from the e-mail he sent when, like Nixon, he resigned.

What can I say about Philip Roth that Philip Roth hasn't already said (and denied) (and said again) himself? It's farcical how much *My Life As a Man* exemplifies this tendency. I was being pretty arrogant: if established literary critics cannot produce the kind of scholarship I feel is worthy of Roth's fiction, how could I possibly think myself capable of rising to that challenge, without even reading the work *my* work would supposedly surpass? I feel like a guy taking on the Marines with a single pocketknife. Going forward, here are the options, as I see them: 1) Write as much of a shitty first draft of this chapter as I can and send it to you, then come back to school next semester and write chapters three and four while taking a fuller course load than I did this semester and applying to jobs so that I have somewhere to live and something to do when I graduate. Or, 2) Tolerate the "Incomplete" on my transcript and take Prof. Dettmar's "Irony in the Public Sphere" instead. My gut is strongly telling me to choose the latter. I know I fucked up. If I had done the substantial work I should have done earlier this semester, I would either have made this decision at a better time or not made it at all. But here I am. This is okay with me. I'm not going to grad school and I won't be any less fascinated by Philip Roth in letting go of my academic obligation to his books.

I quote at length here simply for the pleasure of hearing how the disease has taken hold of the e-mail itself, which bubbles with Rothian vitality, even arriving at the key phrase, "Letting Go."

5.

I only ever made Philip Roth laugh twice, to my knowledge. That's weak recompense for the thousand hilarities Roth's bestowed on me—bitter snorts of recognition, giggles of astonishment at narrative derring-do, sheer earthy guffaws. Of course, I've only ever met him a couple of times. The first time I made Roth laugh was in recounting a conversation I overheard while on line for a hot dog between innings at Shea Stadium, between two boorish men confessing to one another their preference for a glimpse of tight Spandex even over that of bare skin; I mention this if only for the pleasure of bragging that Roth and I suffer the same fannish encumbrance, for anyone who knows the inside of Shea Stadium has earned whatever joy can be salvaged on the hot dog line. The second time I made Roth laugh is more important to me: we stood together in the late stages of an Upper West Side brunch party, where I dandled my infant son while Roth looked quite reasonably impatient to be elsewhere. In a quiet panic, bobbing up and down to sooth the six-month-old, I found myself monologuing to Roth's increasingly arched eyebrows. Finally, straining for a reference that would interest my hero, I turned the boy's head slightly to the side, displaying the fat curve of his cheek, and said, "It resembles one of those disembodied unshaven cigar-smoking heads in a Philip Guston painting, don't you think?" The juxtaposition of my pink son and the grotesques of Guston, like the earlier juxtaposition of Shea and Spandex, did the trick. And this was another lesson from Roth: In putting across what wants putting across, in seeking a rise from the listener, *do whatever it takes*, grab any advantage, employ even the baby in your arms. I would have *juggled* the baby if it would have helped.

6.

To finish, then, with a final confession, according to the Rothian principle of crypto-confessional storytelling: that though you may hold your cards quite close to your vest, it is best to create the thrilling illusion of having laid oneself generously bare, of having told all. That's simply to say, I don't want to leave you hanging in that East Hampton guest room. Did I get anywhere with the very nice rich girl? The answer is no. I saw as little action in East Hampton as I'd seen of those lobsters on their voyage from the broiler to the kitchen garbage pail. Less, even, than I'd seen of the lobsters. The only breast I fondled in East Hampton was Roth's.

—*The New Statesman*, 2013

II

It Can Still Take Me There

The Only Human Superhero

My two-year-old has a favorite superhero: Batman. He's firm on this, though he's never read a Batman comic, nor seen a Batman movie. How does he know? He was given a Batman lunchbox, despite that, being two, he has no need of a lunchbox. He was given this Batman lunchbox to offset his older brother's being given a lunchbox featuring some other icon. Why did I select the Batman lunchbox? Impulsively. Perhaps it was some unconscious gesture. The first superhero I loved was Batman. The first drawing I recall attempting was a drawing of Batman. I remember painstakingly working to reproduce the bat-emblem on his chest, the capsules lining his belt. I never renounced Batman; instead, it is as if his outline contains every other curiosity that would later overtake me; it is as if his outline contains me.

Perhaps Batman endures and remains interesting simply because he has a good name and a good mask, a non-clown costume, and no superpowers. The least infected by the absurdity of his category, he gives that hopeless category some small possibilities. Superman wears choo-choo train pajamas; Batman wears an athletic version of a conservative suit and overcoat. He's our first and most essential *human* superhero.

His original venue was *Detective Comics*. The overcoat that transforms into a cape and a cloak is a hard-boiled detective's trench coat. He cuts the figure of an ass-kicking Philip Marlowe, another self-appointed, solitary figure—"down these mean streets a man must walk," etc.—with the code of an urban knight. And he bears the stigma of his trauma, an injury in the past, much like the hard-boiled detective, whose own trauma is encoded in the meaning of a trench coat: trench warfare. The detective in a trench coat is a returning World War veteran. Batman is veteran of a secret war of the self, injured in a way no civilian could ever adequately comprehend.

Another simple factor to his lasting appeal: Batman has the deepest rogues gallery of any hero. If the enemy makes the man, he's made. Batman's greatest enemy is, of course, the Joker. Yet so many of his other nemeses, those coin-flippers, those flightless birds, reproduce the Joker's unnerving *unseriousness*. In a deeper sense Batman's real enemy is joking itself—mirth, mockery. He stands in opposition to the *comical* even as he arises in the habitat of the *comic* book. Batman in his cowl and monotone conveys some grain of severity, of grim resolution, that is persistently betrayed by the glib, slick, and foolish. He emits an urgent call to our serious selves, but Batman, who fights both crime and the existential abyss with the inadequate weapons of fists and gritted teeth, teeters on the brink of the ludicrous. It is our belief in his great purpose that sustains him—as we clap for Tinkerbell, we despise irony on Batman's behalf.

Batman's famous and stirring refusal to wield a gun, the weapon that killed his parents, links him to the classic problem of the western frontier, embodied by John Wayne and Jimmy Stewart in films like *The Searchers*, *Destry Rides Again*, and *The Man Who Shot Liberty Valance*. That question being: Is the man violent enough to clear the path for civilization himself unfit to participate in civilized society? Batman resolves this paradox simply by removing his mask. In fact, his code is ludicrous on its face. The very first criminal he confronts, in *Detective Comics*

#27, plummets into a vat of acid; Batman declares this "A fitting ending for his kind." And his various gun-surrogates—boomerangs, planes, money—are as lethal as they need to be. Batman *is* death. He's death denied, or mediated through the crude morality of Fate.

Batman is also Goth. His unbearable whiteness, his revenger's isolation, his animal-cultist's affiliations, his occupation of *Goth*am City. He stands as the hinge between the image of the superhero and that of the undead: vampires, werewolves, ghosts. In the shadow of Batman's legitimacy lurks a righteously Americanized Dracula—nocturnal, subterranean, a ladykiller. More than a trace of the decadent European image of the aristocratic monster still resides in Batman's secret identity. Yet the more seriously we take Bruce Wayne the more likely we'll reject this rageful one-percenter, perpetuating his cycle of abuse. Wayne shares in none of Batman's deep existential necessity. Better to believe Batman is the true self, Bruce Wayne a mere shred, a residue. Batman only pretends still to be Bruce Wayne.

Adam West's Batman was axiomatic. He's impossible to erase, not because he exposed the Batman image as ludicrous but because the campiness made it all the more disturbing that a grain of intensity was nonetheless conveyed. And the cowl, never better. We would literally dream about the texture of the cowl; was it rubber, plastic, something else? Who drew those weird eyebrows? Why were the bat-ears so small, yet perfect? This alchemy eluded later masters of Hollywood costume design. If Batman is a barometer on collective feelings about authority and state power, then Adam West was a Yippie's image of Batman, the equivalent of nominating a piglet for president. In any era, we get the Batman we deserve. The Christopher Nolan version takes Frank Miller's brilliantly reactionary nihilist Batman of the '80s and leaches out all the tragedy—leaving a state-sponsored psychopath Batman for our era of triumphalist remote-control revenge. He's the manned drone of twenty-first century urban warfare.

Yet the character won't sit still. All the contradictory Batmen resound through each successive version, pointing up the baseline incoherence of the original. Go back again to *Detective #27*. There you discover that the point-of-view character in the story isn't Wayne or Batman, but Commissioner Gordon, who seems to conjure Batman as a furtive extension of his own denied impulses. The true Batman comes into focus at this crossroads, where a creature worthy of Kafka—emerging from his burrow wearing his traumatic identity humiliatingly on the outside of his body, like a bug's shell—meets the sadistic daydreams of a tired, sedentary policeman.

To make sense of it all, to resolve this cloud of contradictions into something magnificent again, you'd need to go back to that other beginning: you'd need to be two years old. You'd need to remember what it first felt like to glimpse a cowled avenger crossing a patch of night sky, his cape flared expressively as he pounced on wrongdoers from above. You'd need a lunchbox.

—*Rolling Stone*, 2012

Forget This Introduction

A writer sat in a featureless white room trying to remember a genre which had never existed.

Real, diagnosable amnesia—people getting knocked on the head and forgetting their names—is mostly just a rumor in the world. It's a rare condition, and usually a brief one. In books and movies, though, versions of amnesia lurk everywhere, from episodes of *Mission Impossible* to metafictional and absurdist masterpieces, with dozens of stops in between. Amnesiacs may not much exist, but amnesiac characters stumble everywhere through comic books, movies, and our dreams. We've all met them and been them.

This book of literary amnesia began as an observation of certain resemblances in two or three novels I admired—a passing notion, a reader's list. I had no intention of editing a book, let alone identifying a genre. But amnesia turned up more the harder I looked, and meant more the harder I thought about it. At first it was the obvious, gaudy cases, amnesia breaking out into an overt premise or plot symptom—there were more of these than I'd ever imagined (in fact I'd written more than one myself). Elsewhere amnesia appeared pulsing just beneath the surface, an existential syndrome that seemed to nag at fictional characters with increasing frequency, a floating metaphor very much in the air. Amnesia, it turned out when I began to pay attention, is a modern mood, and a very American one.

Not that there's any question that literary amnesia has European grandfathers: Franz Kafka and Samuel Beckett. If it's usually felt that every compelling novel is in some sense a *mystery*, the examples of Kafka and Beckett suggest that *amnesia* can be seen as a basic condition for characters enmeshed in fiction's web. Conjured out of the void by a thin thread of sentences, every fictional assertion exists as a speck on a background of consummate blankness. There's a joke among writing teachers that apprentice writers, at a loss for an idea, will usually commit some version of the story that begins: "A man woke alone in a room with bare white walls . . ." unconsciously replicating their plight before the blank page and hoping that compositional momentum will garb the naked story in identity, meaning, and plot. Our hero might have blood on his hands, or answer a ringing phone, or find himself wiggling an antennae—we'll improvise as we go along. Kafka and Beckett dance beautifully at the edge of that void which has always loomed for fiction, has always been waiting to be noticed and flirted with. They're the very soul of amnesia.

The body that soul would come to inhabit, however, was provided by pop culture's appropriation of Freud. The explosion of psychotheraputic metaphors into the narrative arts in the twentieth century is so complete and pervasive it would be hard to overstate; a profound sense of before-and-after is traceable in nervous jokes about how well Gissing or Poe might have responded to a course of Prozac. Or, say, try imagining Emily Brontë if she'd scrutinized her characters with the neurological vocabulary available to writers like Philip K. Dick, Lawrence Shainberg, and Dennis Potter. The ease with which these writers—and their audiences—grasp those new vocabularies for human perceptual life creates fresh textures in fiction, both particular and universal. Anyone's been Heathcliff on a bad day, but, unlike Heathcliff we've had our brooding shaped by diagnosis (either accepted or refused); had romance and faith decanted into symptom, codependence, and past-life trauma; seen childhood sexual abuse converted into alien abduction and back again.

But what about that sharp blow to the head? And who fired this smoking gun in my hand if it wasn't me? Amnesia is film noir, too, a vehicle made of pure plot, one that gobbles psychoanalysis passingly, for cheap fuel. Cornell Woolrich and John Franklin Bardin are collected here to stand for many others: David Goodis and Richard Neely and Orson Welles (in *Lady From Shanghai* and *Mr. Arkadin*), plus another thousand haunted, desperate protagonists wandering the black-and-white streets of the Noir Metropolis wondering if they really did something terrible during their boozy binge, and trying to persuade the cops to give them a chance, like O.J. Simpson, to hunt for the real killers and redeem the memory of that tragic, unworkable love affair. Amnesia plots are, however inadvertently, often stories about guilt—a trail which leads right back to Kafka, of course. (Maybe Kafka's the real killer!)

Beckett's Amnesia, to give another strain its diagnostic name, is characterized by meditation on the absent, circular, and amnesiac nature of human existence, as well as on the vast indifference of the universe to matters of identity. His novella *The Lost Ones* is an eerily dispassionate meditation on the plight of a group of bereft human bodies stuck in a cramped metal cylinder. It prefigures the disembodied-brains-dreaming subgenre of amnesia, which often arises in science fiction. In stories like A. A. Attanasio's *Solis* and Joseph McElroy's *Plus*, brains implanted into machines are plagued into malfunction by sticky emotional residue from their forsaken human lives. Ambrose Bierce's "Occurrence at Owl Creek Bridge" is the most famous version of a closely related amnesia archetype, where a character discovers that the bewildering events of his story were only the strobelike hallucinations of a dying brain. A couple of the novels excerpted here or listed in the bibliography adopt this *darn, I was dead the whole time* template, but to name them would be to give away the endings to several wonderful ontological mystery stories—even if those endings are all essentially the same.

Perhaps an even more disheartening realization for an amnesiac is that he's *only a fictional character*. Call it Pirandello's Syndrome. Those elusive memories never existed, because the author never bothered to imagine them, having abandoned the mimetic pretense—which is hard on those of us who prefer to believe we live in a three-dimensional world. Thomas Disch, Paul Auster and Vladimir Nabokov are among the writers prone to tipping their hands metafictionally—confessing authorial whim as readily as a Warner Brother's animator depriving Daffy Duck of the ground he stands on, instead warping the edge of his celluloid prison inward to reveal the sprocket holes.

Another form of amnesia is the collective political type, identified by Orwell, Huxley and Yevgeny Zamyatin and extended, refined and watered down by an army of science fiction writers ever since ("Soylent Green is—people!"). Taken in its direst and dryest sense, this version of amnesia points to theories of social or institutional knowing and forgetting, to theorists and critics like Michel Foucault, Marshall McLuhan, Fredric Jameson, Allan Bloom, and G.W.S. Trow. Obviously, I risk spilling my precious and only-recently-distilled vial of amnesia fiction into the broad streams of dystopian writing and cultural critique, but, well, that's what genres *do* under study: merge and disappear into others. (Noir, dystopia, theory, metafiction: watch amnesia swirl and be lost in them, like James Stewart in *Vertigo*'s dream sequence.) Anyway, any good dystopian tyrant knows the use and value of controlled collective amnesia, or he loses his job.

As I reread and weighed the fiction on my list, it was possible at times to enter into a state of forgetting what I'd meant by distinguishing *amnesia* from *fiction*—by declaring one the modifier of the other—in the first place. Genres are also like false oases, only visible in the middle distance. Get too close and they atomize into unrelated particles. Eventually, though, I achieved editorial déjà vu, remembering what I couldn't have already known: I had in mind fiction that, more than just presenting a character who'd suffered memory loss, *entered into an amnesiac state at some level of the narrative itself*—and invited the reader to do the same. Fiction that made something of the white spaces which are fiction's native habitat or somehow induced a dreamy state of loss of identity's grip. I knew I'd identified a genre—even if I was its whole audience as well as its only scholar—when I came across an excellent book containing a scene of literal amnesia, yet which didn't actually fit my parameters; in the same week I came across another novel that struck me as precious and airless yet provided a thrill of discovery: it perfectly *exemplified* the *principles* of amnesia fiction. Now I was an amnesia nerd!

In gathering these stories, essays and excerpts I willfully ignored the boundaries of my new genre. There's some real science in here, as well as cryptoscience, and reverse amnesia, and one straight-up alcoholic blackout. I followed the higher principle of pleasure, tried to end where I'd started: with writing I loved and wanted to recommend to someone else. That is to say, you. Let this introduction be a ghostly scrim in front of the stories, then, a vanishing scroll of words like the preamble of backstory before the start of an engrossing movie, or like the rantings of the captive amnesiac in Thomas Disch's "The Squirrel Cage," which vanish into air as they are typed. What good is a genre? Genres should vanish and be forgotten, this one especially—it was made for it. Forget this introduction. Here are some stories. Here's a book.

—Introduction to *The Vintage Book of Amnesia*, 2000

What's Old Is New (NYRB)

Funny how things call up their opposites. We're in the age of radical damage to the attention-span-o-sphere, everyone knows that except the denialists. And web culture is distributed, collaborative, appropriative—fan fiction rules. So, right, naturally we crave long-quest immersion in vast narratives generated by a single brain—*2666, 1Q84, Infinite Jest, My Struggle,* etc. The long novel has never been better exalted. (We even dig pretending our television serials are generated by a similarly consummate and mysterious Authority, the showrunner.)

Consideration of books and writing has never before been so oppressed by the tyranny of "The Long Now"—or "present shock," to steal a phrase from Douglas Rushkoff. Or at least it seems that way to me, permanent retrograde citizen of the out of print and out of fashion; I developed my passion for novels while working in used bookstores. I've spent my life since that time being baffled at how difficult it is to get a conversation started about noncanonical writing that's more than a few years old. Even the early novels of a towering figure still among us, DeLillo, say, can seem too dwindled in the rear-view mirror. Wasn't this supposed to be the news that stayed news? This isn't only crankiness about late-capitalist "Tweet or Perish" publishing, or about the killing-the-father imperative that collaborates with the former to make first novels more valued, per se, than fifth novels (which are so often better). It's crankiness about both, and if you want to tell me that I'm yelling at kids to get off my lawn, my only defense is that I've been wanting them off my lawn since I was a kid. In other words, I know it wasn't better before. But it's certainly worse now.

My vote, therefore, for the best development in the world of books and writing during the twenty-year span of *Bookforum's* existence is the miraculous appearance and persistence of the New York Review of Books "Classics" imprint. If you love this sort of thing, you know how unlikely it is, and that the shelves of used bookstores are littered with the false starts and short reigns of similar "reissue" or "reintroduction" campaign. Yes, Faulkner and Henry James are both canonical due to being reintroduced (by Malcolm Cowley and James Laughlin's New Directions, respectively), and we owe our awareness of Henry Roth and Paula Fox and Dawn Powell to similar efforts. But that was pretty much the whole head count, right there, until Edwin Frank of NYRB, and his brilliant helpers, began, in 1999, reinjecting dozens of lost books back into a literary bloodstream starved by "presentism." Their list numbers into the hundreds now, many, like Olivia Manning's *Fortunes of War: The Balkan Trilogy* or Oakley Hall's *Warlock* or Elaine Dundy's *The Old Man and Me*, just hidden from view in the fatal middle distance of minor reputation and noncontroversy. The NYRB editions of John Williams's *Stoner* and Renata Adler's *Speedboat* were as much the "It Books" of their respective years of republication as anything actually new, which is pretty crazy, in a good way. For dessert on top of dinner, the books are gorgeous and well bound in good paper, and offer the most gently authoritative standard paperback-series design since the original Penguins. (Their nice physical form could be seen as another reaction against our current state of ether-reality.) In all, it's practically as good as a world littered, as it once was, with used bookstores. The crank in me is chagrined to admit that for many purposes it might in fact be better.

—*Bookforum*'s twentieth-anniversary issue, 2015

To Catch a Beat

Brooklyn in the early eighties, like all of New York City, could still sustain innumerable hole-in-the-wall used bookstores. These weren't moneymaking enterprises, but, rather, outposts in a minor cultural ecosystem on the verge of disappearing. They were fronted by weary men who lived in bubbles of time-gone-by that hadn't yet burst. These men had a haunted look. As a teenage book collector with a crush on a dying guild, I did my best to apprentice myself to every one of them. I'd buy books, then hang around the counter and strike up conversations designed to flaunt my expertise, trying to insinuate my voice into the house tone of these grumpy fiefdoms. A handful of the shops gave me work, though my pay was usually taken home entirely in books.

Under gentrification, the storefronts that had housed the bookstores I'd worked in seemed to share the same fate: they all gave way first to dry-cleaning joints, then to real-estate agents' offices. The storefront of Clinton Street Books, in Brooklyn Heights, went through precisely those iterations after the shop closed, sometime in the late eighties. I've forgotten the proprietor's name, but for a while in high school I was his afternoon sidekick. He'd leave me to man the small counter while he skulked off for coffee on Montague Street. I'd sit and make sales and look up prices in *Books In Print*—mostly the latter, as the shop was awfully quiet.

Like any such store, Clinton Street tolerated a few eccentric regulars. One of these was the Beat Generation icon Herbert Huncke, who, though he was known in the forties and fifties as "the mayor of Forty-Second Street," and ended his life living in the Chelsea Hotel, was at that time a resident of the Heights. Huncke, a major and legendary junkie, hustler, vagrant, and muse, and a minor, though vivid, writer, may or may not have been the source of the term "Beat"; he appears in lightly fictionalized form in William S. Burroughs's *Junky*, Jack Kerouac's *On the Road*, and John Clellon Holmes's *Go*. He was also one of the local guides on Alfred Kinsey's safari into the sexual underground, ushering any number of his fellow Forty-Second Street denizens to Kinsey's Manhattan hotel room for interviews.

Huncke was still very much the squirrely ex-con and drug fiend, but he was also marvelously unthreatening, despite a certain doomy charisma. As for books, he wasn't buying but selling, or trying to. At some point, demonstrating characteristic munificence, Allen Ginsberg had taken a carton of copies of his poetry collection *Planet News*, in the distinctive square, black-and-white City Lights format that *Howl* made famous, and autographed every copy "To Herbert, from Allen, with love." He then gave them to Huncke to sell periodically, in order to alleviate a day's or a week's worth of his lifelong dire financial straits. In the bookseller's or collector's jargon, a copy inscribed thus, from one major Beat figure to another, was a singular and irreplaceable "association copy": in principle, a valuable book. The fact that dozens existed was ticklish, though: that wasn't the level of scarcity the signature implied.

Sometime before I began working at Clinton Street, the proprietor had taken one off Huncke's hands, to offer for sale on the shop's "autographed and first editions" shelf. It hadn't sold. I remember the proprietor having to lecture Huncke, more than once, on why we couldn't purchase a second: two were less valuable than one. He'd have to wait until the first sold before we'd relieve him of another. For months, Huncke's rounds included dropping in to see whether the copy had been snapped up yet, because he so wanted to sell us a second. Giving him the bad news that it still hadn't been, so that he couldn't unload another, became one of my own regular duties. Huncke would be crestfallen. I think it drove him nuts, feeling he had this carton of riches to liquidate, and being denied. I'd shrug and wait for him to slouch back onto the sidewalk. I'd also been warned that when I was alone in the shop I should watch Huncke like a hawk, for fear that he'd shoplift—not fear, really, but the certainty he'd try. This wasn't unusual in a bookshop in Brooklyn in 1983. You watched every customer like a hawk.

Sure enough, one day I had the honor of joining the long procession of those who, over the decades, had laid a bust on the sweet scoundrel Huncke. He'd been browsing while I paged through *Books In Print*. The rare-books shelf was to my back, but I sensed activity, and turned in time to see him hurrying an item into his coat. I held out my hand, and Huncke, with saintly intensity, surrendered the article and left the store. He could have filched any number of books priced more expensively, but no: it was Ginsberg's *Planet News*. He just couldn't wait a day longer for the moment when he'd be able to come in and exclaim that it had sold.

—*The New Yorker*, 2011

Footnote[1]

1. Best always to keep in mind you'd be lucky even to be one.[2]
2. A footnote, that is.[3]
3. I teach at Pomona College, where I occupy the Roy E. Disney '51 Chair in Creative Writing. I'm the second occupant of the Disney Chair; the first was David Foster Wallace.[4] In this sense, I'm Wallace's footnote. Roy E. Disney was Walt Disney's brother and business partner, generally credited with building up the financial side of the business, rather than concerning himself with creative matters; Roy is his brother's footnote. Arguably, therefore, I may be a more fitting occupant of Roy's Chair than Wallace, though he'll forever "own" it in the public imagination.[5]
4. David Foster Wallace is generally understood to be contemporary writing's master of the footnote as a literary device—to such an extent that he's often taken in some sense to be the technique's "originator," which is, almost needless to say, absurd on its face.[6] He's instead the footnote's triumphant popularizer. As it happens, though, his monolithic use of footnotes in the manuscript of his canonical book, the super-long novel *Infinite Jest*, was converted by his editor, against Wallace's initial preference, into endnotes—almost a hundred pages of them.
5. I never met Wallace.

6. Most of those inclined to recall the immediate pre-Wallace context for the literary footnote point to Nicholson Baker's[7] *The Mezzanine*.[8] Indeed, Baker's prominent and dazzling use of footnotes is probably even more integral, formally, to his book's intent and purposes than those in Wallace's fiction.[9] But it's silly to pit these two writers against one another; they're comrades-in-arms, I think, in employing the footnote ultimately as a signifier of cognition's bursting the linear framework of temporality—an urgent correction to the hidebound moment-to-moment progress of stuff across a printed page. What Wallace calls "brain voice" and Baker calls "the shape of thoughts" are both, ultimately, names for each writer's request that we acknowledge the polymorphous and disobedient nature of our attentive and ruminative selves, which refuse the prison-house of experience and behavior, at least as these are traditionally represented.[10]

7. When I was twenty-seven, and living in Berkeley, California, and had only published a handful of short stories in obscure literary journals and science fiction magazines, and Nicholson Baker's *The Mezzanine* had just made a tremendous impression on me and my friend Angus MacDonald, and I was hanging out with a lot of graduate students in UC Berkeley's graduate program in rhetoric, a program which featured a number of "star" theorists, the most intimidating and mysterious of whom was a woman known as Avital Ronell, I sometimes used to visit a café called Roma, on College Avenue and Ashby. There, more than once, I found myself seated at a table within shouting distance, on one side, of Nicholson Baker and, on the other, Avital Ronell. Baker would be correcting page proofs from *The New Yorker*, and Ronell would be writing on a laptop.[11] Berkeley's not a small town, exactly, but it's not the big city either, and I'd get a little jolt of celebrity electricity from

sitting between them and thinking *I'm the only person in this café—including them—who knows who they both are.*[12]

8. I'd also point readers to Gilbert Sorrentino's superbly disorienting use of footnotes in *Imaginative Qualities of Actual Things*.[13] An example: "This sentence is an example of automatic writing." Another: "No attempt will be made to describe this famous bar, thank God."

9. In the mid-eighties, at the start of my years in Berkeley, before I'd read any Wallace or Baker or Sorrentino's *Imaginative Qualities of Actual Things*, I conceived of a short story that would take the form of a sequence of footnotes, one blooming from the next, so that the original text would be completely dwarfed and forgotten. In my conception this story would be very firmly in the manner of Jorge Luis Borges, who's a touchstone for any writer incorporating scholarly apparatus into literary forms (I believe Wallace has written and spoken of his admiration for Borges; I have no idea whether Baker has expressed any; I'd expect Sorrentino to have been very familiar, at the least). I never worked out the technical necessities for such a story, nor landed on any subject matter that seemed to demand this treatment, so it went unwritten. J. G. Ballard, around that same time, wrote and published "Notes Towards A Mental Breakdown," a short story consisting of a single sentence with each of its eighteen component words lengthily footnoted, but I was unaware of Ballard's story until it was collected in *War Fever* in 1990.

10. Even more simply, both writers seem to want to make time *slow the fuck down*.[14]

11. Ronell's signature work of that period, *The Telephone Book*, consists of a critical text disrupted and enhanced by a torrent of typographical and design elements, among them excessive footnotes.[15]

12. Because life is infinitely strange, Nicholson Baker now lives in Maine, a few miles from my father, and he and my father sometimes attend the same Quaker Meeting.

13. I once spoke with Gilbert Sorrentino on the telephone, but we never met. I've been friends since high school, however, with Gilbert's son Christopher, himself a novelist of note. In high school I never knew that Chris's dad was a writer, and when I first discovered Gilbert's writing, I failed to put the two Sorrentinos together.[16] I wouldn't until I was almost thirty.

14. Wallace also frequently employs the footnote as a pre-tense-puncturing device, one providing tonal admonition to the reader and himself not to take all his theoretical posturing too seriously—and, in this cause, typically resorts to sudden idiomatic speech, or profanity. This is usually good for a brief, sharp guffaw. I'm afraid it also becomes very rapidly formulaic, and is surely the most irritating tic common to writers taking Wallace's example.

15. Avital Ronell and I were later on the faculty at NYU at the same time, but we never met.

16. When I say that I "discovered" Gilbert Sorrentino's writing, what I actually mean is that I found a copy of *Imaginative Qualities of Actual Things* at a used bookstore in Vermont, while I was briefly enrolled at a college there, and purchased it, and kept it on my shelf unread for, literally, decades. I have the copy in front of me here as I write, and I can completely recall how and why I fell in love with the book's distinctive design: it is a hardcover tricked up to look like a publisher's rough galley, with the words "Jacket front panel" typed in twelve-point courier font on the front jacket, and below it, named in equally modest font, all the various specifications that a designer would be expected to add to the jacket: author's name, copy, publisher's imprint,

etc. It is like a book titled "book," or, more exactly, a book design consisting of the words "book design."[17] On the first flyleaf[18] my name is written—"J. Lethem"—in a block handwriting distinctive to that time in my life (and, indeed, the practice of writing my name on the flyleaf of books was limited to my two-odd years in Vermont, though that was hardly the only period in my life when I was certain my shelves were subject to the predation of book-thief acquaintances). Tucked inside the same flyleaf, much more recently, is Gilbert Sorrentino's *Los Angeles Times* obituary, painstakingly clipped from the newspaper. (The *New York Times* did him barely any justice at all.)

17. The band XTC's second album, called *Go 2*, has a jacket design employing a very similar trick. I like it, too.

18. The building housing the English department at Pomona College includes an office containing a scattering of half-filled bookshelves, into which has been thrown a measure of cursory organization—a few categories clumped together, and a central run of literature which has been alphabetized. The office belongs to no member of the permanent faculty, but is sporadically put in use by visiting professors. Salvador Plascencia occupied it one semester, and Maggie Nelson all last year. Some portion of these books are, unmistakably, the ass-end leavings of David Foster Wallace's office library, the better portion of which were surely collected by his family or shipped to the Harry Ransom Center in Austin Texas, which holds Wallace's papers. Certainly, any books featuring Wallace's marginal annotations, which have become justly famous for their eccentricity and wit,[19] have been shipped off to the Ransom Center. The books left behind, unremarkable titles in themselves, featuring nothing personal to Wallace, could therefore be considered a footnote to the Ransom Center's important collection of

his books. The first time I browsed through those shelves, however, I found that a number of novels—titles by Ann Beattie, John Updike, Dostoevsky, and others—featured lively marginal remarks on many of their pages. The hand-writing even looked to me like Wallace's, at least at first. What a discovery! That the books had been left behind seemed a terrible oversight, until I further discovered that the witty, eccentric remarks scattered through their pages weren't Wallace's, but rather those of some other person, who'd helpfully written his name on the flyleaf of every book belonging to him, if only I'd looked: J. W. Heist. At first, in the heat of my selfish wish to be the rescuer of unique Wallace annotations,[20] the name seemed obviously fictitious—"J.W. Heist indeed!"—yet I was finally forced to acknowledge that the handwriting wasn't really the same as Wallace's, nor were some of the annotations character-istic, exactly, of his. There were anachronisms, too, in the cultural references within the remarks. Though no amount of asking around the English Department or googling J.W. Heist's name seemed to produce any confirmation of his existence, I did eventually find tucked into one of these books a deeply-yellowed Chicago newspaper clipping that included Heist's name among the listed winners of a college literary scholarship award.[21] The spare office's bookshelves conflated a bunch of different items—some mostly un-impressive Wallace books, many more Heist books, a few other things as well—which some anonymous volunteer had later organized.

19. Unique marginal annotations, especially those by a person of distinction (as opposed to the majority of hand-written markings in books, which are only distracting or annoying, and spoil the reading) could be seen as "artisanal footnotes."

20. Speaking of selfish, in my investigations in that office I did

put claim on one volume, which now lives in my office: a first edition of John Berryman's *Recovery*. *Recovery* is an unfinished novel, on the subject of alcoholism and treatment, published posthumously after the great poet's suicide in 1972. There are no markings to prove it was Wallace's (nor any that prove it was Heist's); if it was Wallace's, there's no way to prove he read it. But I believe it was, and that he did. If the Ransom Center comes calling now, I suppose I might surrender it. But I might not.

21. I'm not making any of this fucking shit up.

—from *The Thing The Book: A Monument to the Book as Object*, 2014

III

Objects in Furious Motion

Fierce Attachments

Preparing to introduce a book you've loved for years, you might find yourself leafing through the previous edition, turning it in your hands as well as plunging in to reencounter certain sentences to marvel again at their slant and freshness, their capacity for permanent surprise. You might also flip to the beginning, hoping to discover that your introduction's already there, already written—which is the feeling that this artifact has given you time and time again: that it knows your thoughts. The book is an object in furious motion, humming with its own energy, and all you might wish to do is touch it, alter its trajectory barely, so as to nudge it into universal view.

Couldn't I just say that you must read Vivian Gornick's *Fierce Attachments*? That I am here to insist this book become a banner in the wide world, as it is a banner already in my mind, one I march behind? And yet, cradling this earlier edition, I notice eight endorsements, all quite eloquent, all by women; could it somehow be that I am the first man to testify for this book? (I check an earlier edition, also on my shelf, and of course this isn't actually the case.) Vivian's Gornick's memoir has that mad, brilliant, absolute quality that tends to loft a book out of context, then to be admired, rightly, as "timeless" and "classic." Yet it is a memoir centered, at least apparently, on the intricacies of a mother-daughter relationship, a memoir written in the eighties (before the boom) by a writer associated, proudly if unsimply, with the Feminist movement. Is it mine to love, then, let alone to brandish as a piece of my own heart? Yes. The reader's path into the entrancement of *Fierce Attachments* is neither by way of gawking curiosity about the specifics of Gornick's or her mother's life, nor by the easy identification that depends on resemblance—on overlapping circumstances—not even the resemblance of femaleness.

Identification, in *Fierce Attachments*, works another way. Immersing ourselves in the book's searing yet seemingly offhand honesty, we find that we simply become Vivian Gornick (or the speaker bearing her name), just as we become her mother, and then Nettie Levine, the passionate and nihilistic young neighbor who emerges as the book's third major character, forming with mother and daughter what Richard Howard has called "that affective, erotic plot by which, just so, we triangulate our lives." Yet our sense of transubstantiation isn't limited to these three. Gornick draws us into brief, scalding alliances with three men, lovers and husbands along the path of her self-uncovering: Stefan, Davey, and Joe. And too, passingly, with a half-dozen other neighbors in the Bronx, and a psychiatrist, and of course the elusive father. By giving every actor in turn eyes with which to see the narrator who has seen them, and voices to rival the narrator's in acuity, however briefly, Gornick has burned these figures onto the page. Not only does no one escape her gaze, but she escapes no one else's. I'm not speaking of fairness, an overrated virtue in literature, and perhaps in life as well. Gornick might be said to demolish her cast of players, but by that standard she also demolishes herself. I prefer to say that like a magician pulling the tablecloth from under a table full of settings, she miraculously leaves herself and her cast intact, and shining with what I suppose can only be described as love. Tough love; that's what they call it.

This would probably be a fine place to quit, only I'm driven to give just a bit more of a writerly tribute, and a personal one, to the memoirist and essayist who along with Phillip Lopate and Geoff Dyer taught me whatever I know about flaying the bullshit from sentences about myself. I hate to saddle her with the epithet "writer's writer," but *Fierce Attachments* demands honor as the work of a breathtaking technician, one whose control of a distilled form of scene and dialogue, of withheld punch lines, and of the use of the white spaces on the page, makes me still wonder why she has never tackled fiction, the love of which she so eloquently professes in her critical essays. Like much of the writing I love most, *Fierce Attachments* draws strength from the method of paradox. These pages contain my favorite description of a would-be writer's realization that she simply *is* a writer, for better or worse and no matter how unclear the path before her:

> In the second year of my marriage the rectangular space made its first appearance inside me. I was writing an essay, a piece of graduate-student criticism that had flowered without warning into thought, radiant shapely thought. The sentences began pushing up in me, struggling to get out, each one moving swiftly to add itself to the one that preceded it. I realized suddenly that an image had taken control of me: I saw its shape and its outline clearly. The sentences were trying to fill in the shape. The image was the wholeness of my thought. In that instant I felt myself open wide. My insides cleared out into a rectangle, all clean air and uncluttered space, that began in my forehead and ended in my groin. In the middle of the rectangle only my image, waiting patiently to clarify itself. I experienced a joy then I knew nothing else would ever equal.

Later in the book, Gornick seems to mourn the inability of this rectangle to thrive, expand, encompass more of her life. The paradox is double: by the evidence of the book in your hands, the very book that describes this resistance and frustration, Gornick's rectangle has done precisely that, grown to encompass not only her life, but, for the duration of the book, her reader's. And yet for all it encompasses, it remains exactly as intimate and local as her first description of its appearance: exactly the size of her body.

—Introduction to *Fierce Attachments*, 1987

Attention Drifting Beautifully
(Donald Barthelme)

Welcome to the wacky world of.

Donald Barthelme is the consummate jester of the American short story, but to say that is perhaps to risk a slight. For it is Barthelme's great achievement that during his heyday (and perhaps no American writer has ever had so hey a day as Barthelme, if you wish to go back and study the record of his prolificity and consistency in the decades of the 1960s and '70s) his "jesting" made as essential a contribution to the literary life of his times as any story writer ever has—Hemingway, Beattie, Carver.

The three stories here ("Robert Kennedy Saved From Drowning," "A City Of Churches" and "The School") show wonderful evidence of the things Barthelme did well—though it is odd to speak of "doing well" at things that, especially at the time they were done, nobody else had ever dreamed of or dared to do. Barthelme is a demon of compression, and surprise. He never bothers with dull transitions, rote explanations, or any kind of apology for what interests or amuses him. Instead, the man made an art of letting his writerly attention drift into silliness, gloom, parody, restlessness, and self-mocking, all within the space of stories that were each relentlessly well-conceived, each a kind of formal proposal for a new kind of story.

Barthelme's in love with voice, as any story writer ought to be, but the voices he loves are unexpected ones: the tedious complainer, the pompous aesthete or windy literary professor, the writers of bureaucratic press releases or technical manuals. He finds the hidden beauty and hilarity and sadness in the sound of the human voice pretending and failing to know what the hell it is talking about, or to admit what's really on its mind. The result is that if the word postmodern didn't need to exist before Barthelme, it sure did after—though by the time you're done struggling over a definition for that problematic word you'll wish you'd just pointed to Barthelme instead: he singlehandedly authenticates and exhausts "the postmodern short story"; he corners the market.

"Robert Kennedy Saved From Drowning" (which, as it is collected in Barthelme's *Sixty Stories*, is touchingly dated "April 1968" so that the reader will understand that it anticipates Kennedy's assassination rather than being a commentary after the fact) is the story among these three which most shows evidence of Barthelme's "laboratory" techniques (the word is Barthelme's—he spoke often in interviews of the laboratory of his fiction). The partitioned structure frees the ventriloquizing voice to wander in and out of the language of recounted dreams, of bureaucratic hagiography, and of corny anecdotes. Nevertheless, the story is unified by an underlying voice—would it be foolish to call it Barthelme's?—which ultimately confesses a tender feeling, a perhaps grandiosely tender feeling, toward the depressive Kennedy.

"A City Of Churches" and "The School" play more at the conventions of the traditional story. Still, the restless absurdities and ghoulish irreverence of "The School," and the unembarrassed fascination with lists and the metafictional aside about a CBS news story with the title "A City of Churches" in "A City of Churches"—as well as the frank sexual fantasizing in both stories—all reveal Barthelme's impatience with the consistency and earnestness of slice-of-life fiction, even when he briefly arouses more conventional expectations in the reader. Both stories read partly like fables, or allegories, except that they resist any easy diagrammatical interpretation. Barthelme loves to tease at moralizing, but his universe is often one of cheery horror.

Barthelme's had many imitators, and not only in his own medium. His work connects literature to performance art, and to comic routines, and *Saturday Night Live* skits. What makes it literature, however, and irreplaceable no matter how complete its subsequent assimilation into the culture, is the immaculate and luminous quality of his sentences, of his paragraphs. His attention drifts *beautifully*. Donald Barthelme may seem to throw the baby out with the bathwater, and from a very high window. But when you rush downstairs to look, both baby and bathwater have come to a gentle and happy landing in the garden.

—Introduction to "Donald Barthelme" in *3 x 33: Short Fiction by 33 Writers*, edited by Mark Winegardner

Rock of Ages

In *Midnight's Children*, Salman Rushdie's hero was born at the inception of India's modern history. Ormus Cama, the expatriate protagonist of Rushdie's sprawling, omnivorous and millennial *The Ground Beneath Her Feet*, is exactly the same age as another great and indefinable bastard nation: rock and roll. Like some overwhelming Rhino Records box set, the novel tries to encompass four decades of pop culture as well as the clash of East and West through Ormus Cama's imagined life and career. But this overloaded ark of a novel does more than span goatherders in Bombay and the New York of Lou Reed and Andy Warhol: Rushdie bumps his ship into the realm of alternate history—usually the province of genre experts like Philip K. Dick and Robert Harris—and in one big, sloppy leap, colonizes it.

Cama, born to a convoluted and fabulous Bombay family, is, like Elvis Presley (and Philip K. Dick), the surviving sibling of a dead baby twin. He's also a paradigmatic child of rock and roll, born fingering an air guitar and mouthing nonsense lyrics that foretell the hit songs about to transform the culture of the far-off United States. Ormus is a godlike amalgam of Gatsby and Dylan and Orpheus, and by the end of the book he's a little bit of David Bowie's character in *The Man Who Fell to Earth* as well. His significant other is Vina Apsara, an orphan emigrant-in-reverse who ascends to Madonna-esque stardom singing lead vocals in Cama's music and dies in an earthquake, then becomes the center of a Princess Diana-sized posthumous cult.

They're larger than life. The third leg of the triangle at the book's center is the narrator, another Bombayan, and a Wee-gee-like photographer who conquers the worlds of front-line wartime photojournalism, fashion, and high art in turn. He serves as footman, documentarian, and confessor for the rock-star couple, all while carrying a torch for—and carrying on an affair with—Apsara. He's also Rushdie's mouthpiece for a series of ruminative discourses on exile and loss, pages in which humble reality threaten to inadvertently expose the relative hot air of the rock star genius-is-pain, fame-is-hell stuff.

Because he's part Pynchon, Rushdie's language cascades and spirals, a cornucopia of referents, puns, and rhymes; because he's part John Irving, his narratives are clotted with backstory, genealogy and momentum-slaughtering foreshadowing. Because he's both Pynchon and Irving at once he's never met a coincidence or doubling he didn't like. The notion of laying his royal flushes on the table one tantalizing card at a time never seems to cross his mind.

Rushdie cues his alternate history by trotting out a warhorse: in his reality, Kennedy survives the assassination attempt (Oswald's rifle jams, while Zapruder conks the grassy-knoll gunman on the head with his movie camera). But Rushdie's concerns are less political than cultural, and subsequent embellishments are less *JFK* than *The Doors* or *Natural Born Killers*: Dionysian rituals of communion and hallucinatory ruptures in the fabric of reality. Ormus Cama is the reluctant witness to this gap between the worlds, and though his music is inspired by these visionary glimpses he—in one of the nicer touches—takes to wearing an eyepatch to cut down on the double vision.

The novel's sense of which histories are worth tweaking, and which rock and roll matters, reveals Rushdie as a real '60s guy.

Punk (renamed "Runt") is dismissed in a brazenly silly one-page aside, and though Ormus's band has some glam overtones, Rushdie's notion of the '70s centers on '60s lions in maturity or decline: Andy Warhol, the Rolling Stones, and Lennon. The 1980s and '90s are a summary blur. Rushdie only pauses to extol U2 (flimsily disguised as "Vox Pop")—who are, in the bizarre alternate reality we all inhabit, reportedly about to record one of Rushdie's fictional smash hit lyrics.

Ah, the lyrics. Rushdie can't avoid the trap that snared Don DeLillo, Scott Spencer, Norman Spinrad and others: his genius's song lyrics die on the page. He shouldn't feel bad—so do many of Dylan's. The music's inaudible, for nearly 600 pages. This leaves Rushdie stranded in a protests-too-much valley of hyperbole:

> . . . it was the voice that did it, it's always the voice; the beat catches your attention and the melody makes you remember but it's the voice against which you're defenceless . . . *Never mind what kind of voice. When you hear it, the real thing, you're done for, trust me on this.*

Ground resumes Rushdie's interrupted fall towards the culture of the West, after the retreat into allegory and the East of *Haroun and the Sea of Stories* and *The Moor's Last Sigh*. The notorious earthward tumble that opens *The Satanic Verses* is recapitulated here, not once but many times: between earthquakes (which plague Rushdie's alternate present), helicopters, jets, and the upsweep of global fame, Rushdie's characters have ground beneath their feet less often than not. It's probably telling that several of the most closely observed and finely written passages take place on airplanes. Plenty of recent writers have turned out novels that show evidence of being written during grueling book tours; Rushdie has, by direst necessity, gone them all one better. If he now identifies with martyrs and exiles, who can blame him?

Yet. Martyrs and exiles are one thing, but these characters are practically pantheistic deities. Again and again Rushdie makes it clear that for Cama and Apsara the only real obstacles lie within; for these titans mortal dilemmas are shrugged off as easily as their thousands of discarded lovers. Maybe the photographer-narrator was meant as tonic, a paparazzo to play off against Princess Di. If so, Rushdie blew it by making him nearly as famous and as much a genius as his subjects.

The novel form, baggy and panoramic as it may be, also thrives on privacies, on moments of humble particularity that play against the banners of history and legend. In Rushdie's breathless vision of worlds in collision his players touch gritty earth too infrequently, and his wide-screen spectacular finally has not quite enough in focus in the foreground. Earthquakes and the history of rock and roll: their scale ultimately defies fiction, unless tempered by the worm's eye view—or the ignominious fan's. In *The Ground Beneath Her Feet*, as in the real world, the hits (of various kinds) just keep on coming, but we're left yearning for the story behind the top 40.

—*The Village Voice*, 1999

My Hero: Karl Ove Knausgaard

Though it was not long ago, I can't remember when I first heard the whisper in the literary sounding-room: that a Norwegian writer, more or less my age, had belched out a brooding six-volume autobiographical sequence of novels under the provocative title *My Struggle*; that it had taken his national literature by storm and that in his homeland he was being read and gossiped about as avidly as J. K. Rowling at Pottermania's apex. I must have read two or three reviews or mentions by other writers before I happened across the first volume, *A Death in the Family*, in a bookshop. Of course it seemed preposterous: the vast claims, comparisons to Proust, the peculiar specificity of Norway—when had I last read a living Norwegian? Had I ever? First rumors of a previously unknown great writer invariably feel like a hoax—I remember when word of Roberto Bolaño slipped out, fifteen years earlier. I remember when, at eighteen, someone revealed to me the existence of Gaddis's *The Recognitions*, a book, I was told, to rival *Moby-Dick*. Resistance is aroused, for a writer, in the form of rivalrous skepticism. As a reader, one suffers the dread of disappointment, the reluctance to glimpse a naked emperor. Yet for me, from the very first page, all rumors, doubts, or preemptive weariness evaporated, replaced by the oxygen-blast of this vast novel's utterly absorbing tone of remorseless, questing curiosity toward the problem of existence. The book investigates the bottomless accumulation of mysteries everyday life imposes, from the vantage of a helplessly undisguised narrator: a stroller-dad, navigating a mundane world of diapers and tantrums on train platforms, who suspects he is the possessor of literary genius, and finds these selves bitterly incommensurate. He's also enmeshed in the earlier selves that delivered him to this present one: a pensive son of a depressed drunkard, a friend, a citizen, a subject of global modernity. Knausgaard's approach is plain and scrupulous, sometimes casual, yet he never writes down. His subject is nothing less than the beauty and terror of the fact that all of life coexists with itself. Knausgaard's a hero, who landed on greatness, seemingly in a flash, by abandoning every typical literary feint, an emperor whose nakedness surpasses royal finery. I can't wait for the translator to finish the last three volumes.

—*The Guardian*, 2014

A *New Life* (Malamud)

In conversation with a friend, I once tried to account for my particular fascination with Philip Roth's early novel *Letting Go*. In attempting to characterize the book and how it stood apart from Roth's oeuvre, I blurted out: "*Letting Go* is Roth's Richard Yates book." What I meant, I guess, was that for one book Roth had tried to write a normatively autobiographical novel of postwar American life, outside any conjuration of the mythic or absurd. Tried to paint within the lines. In order to confront the suffocating fullness of American life in the fifties, Roth had run his character up against the possibilities of marriage and children and a conventional career, and by doing so tried to isolate the theme of freedom-versus-responsibility that was so deeply implicit in the life of those times. Richard Yates wrote that book over and over again, Roth and Bernard Malamud only once.

I don't mean to suggest any possibility of direct influence. In fact, *Letting Go*, *Revolutionary Road*, and Malamud's *A New Life* were all published within a year of one another. Rather, I wonder if it might be some kind of principle—that many writers had felt they had to try writing such a novel, that the moment determined the necessity of such books. So, call *A New Life* Malamud's Yates novel.

Certainly it is his most traditional, and least mythic. Though

I don't mean to point to biography (I honestly don't know the facts of a life story about which Malamud was famously reticent, and don't think it important to know them), the book is *tonally* autobiographical. The story is archetypal, but for a change Malamud doesn't emphasize archetype. Samuel Levin, formerly a drunkard, as the first sentence beautifully informs us, takes a teaching job in a rainy Western state, not understanding why he's been chosen from among hundreds of candidates, too grateful to care or look closely enough to discern he's coming to teach at an agricultural college, not a liberal arts school. Levin's a definitive Eastern outsider, flinching from past failure and eager to make the new life that migration Westward has always promised.

The genre is the Western, but the nearest Malamud can bring himself to the genre is in its refusal. For Levin, tenderfoot with a tender heart, is also a schlemiel, prone to absurd crises, so ill-suited to his adopted landscape that he's not yet a driver of cars. Decorous in his own mind, in outward behavior he nearly always commits too much, blurts his thoughts, stays too long, makes Hail Mary passes into an end-zone full of players from the opposing team. This pattern proliferates in comic miniatures in the picaresque first half of the book. Then farce mires, and Levin lurches into tragic inextricability in his affair with an English Department colleague's wife. Tragic or comic, Levin's a reverse Zeno. While he pictures himself a slow beginner advancing on his future by half steps, in truth each time he lifts his foot he takes a step and a half, at least.

A New Life, seemingly the least Jewish of Malamud's books, plays at being secular. The word *Jew* is only mentioned once, practically on the last page. When it comes it's nearly as a sigh of acceptance: yes, of course there's also this, I am one of the Chosen People, if things weren't already bad enough. There's an Irish red-herring, too: Joyce is quoted in an epigraph, and the book fools with Joycean streams and puns (Life, Lev, Love) a few times. The elderly grammarian who dies in Levin's arms mumbling about the mysteries not of the infinite but of the *infinitive* is a jape worthy of Flann O'Brien.

More intimately, Levin is haunted throughout his year of teaching by a precursor-ghost at the college, the dissident Irishman Leo Duffy. Inheriting Duffy's office, and his role as faculty agitator, Levin becomes fascinated and intimidated by the strong impression left by Duffy's flameout (though he'll far outdo Duffy by the end). And Duffy's suicide note, with its own abrupt, Beckettian pun, seems to move Levin to an ultimate commitment to his fate. How many characters who fail to appear in the novel in which they are named have such vivid life?

Then there's Gilley, Levin's grating, grinding pedant of a rival, with his pathetic compulsion to photograph what he doesn't understand. And Fabrikant, the dour mysterious scholar on horseback, who with his odd Germanic name may perhaps be another image of the Jew, one assimilated to the dark side of the moon. But Levin refuses all these images of a possible alternate self, or of a defining antagonist, in favor of the affections of his Olive-Oylish girlfriend.

Here is finally why the book refuses to be any kind of Western: because unlike a Western hero, whose primary engagement is with other men, Levin is in his lonely heart a lover of women. Not an incompetent one, either. In the end, *A New Life* commits itself, with beautiful discomfort, to being a love story, full of private feeling made into the most passionate sort of art. When the schlemiel drives his family out of the frame of Gilley's camera, and into the future, the book's title is revealed as absolutely sincere. Malamud's Yates novel is also his funniest and most embracing, an underrated masterpiece.

—Introduction to *A New Life*, 2004

A Mug's Game

I recently eavesdropped—literally, lurking behind a half-open NYU conference-room door—as John Ashbery gave a "craft talk" to a packed-to-the-rafters room full of aspirants to the condition of poetry. Ashbery, in the form of a patient, barely-ever-annoyed question-and-answer session, quite diligently composed a long first draft of a John Ashbery poem in front of the students, though I'm not certain any of them, Ashbery included, knew that that was what he was doing. Each time a questioner attempted to grab up a little bit of the Ashbery essence with the eyedropper of his or her inquiry to him, that same essence spilled and slithered away, like a blob of mercury, to immerse itself deeper and deeper through a three-dimensional maze of Ashbery's own sensibility. Several students asked him in sequence to weigh in on the difficulty of "content" in poetry such as his. After ignoring the word the first instance or two, Ashbery suddenly wheeled on it, and delivered this apparent certainty: "Content is only the sides and bottom of a box." He drew a box in the air with his hands. "Nothing more." The students contented themselves with this, or discontented themselves, and Ashbery went on with his solemnly merry improvisations on the subject of a writing life, more or less reminiscing in interior monologue, leaving out only names, dates, and other identifying furniture of his life. Half an hour passed before another courageous student pressed at this lingering image, the "box" Ashbery had helpfully sketched. "Sir, if content is a box, may I ask what is inside?"

"I'm sorry?" said the disconcerted poet.

"What does the box hold?"

"Oh! Nothing at all," Ashbery said. "It's entirely empty."

We're all, no matter how lucid, stuck within the unworkable conundrum of our selves, and frequently most confounding precisely when we feel we're speaking most plainly. Gilbert Sorrentino spent fifty years telling us directly who he suspected he was and what he suspected he knew, about Brooklyn, poetry, social class, ambition, jazz, influence, form-versus-content, capitalism, and "realism," a word I'd need to place in scare quotes as a testament to Sorrentino's long passionate skepticism as to its value if I didn't suspect it myself. In Sorrentino's writing, we again and again encounter a mind whose only way of handling a first introduction is to blurt out "Don't we know one another already?" and this sensation utterly permeates *Something Said*, a 1984 collection of Sorrentino's essays (a book I possess in its luscious North Point Press edition, a tall, jacketed, mint-green-now-fading-to-dun paperback, which still bears the pencil price of "7.75"—half-off the publisher's list of 15.50!—scrawled in it by one of my colleagues at Pegasus Books, in Berkeley, where I took it home from the literature section two or three years after it was published). *Something Said* would certainly seem to be a Jupiter's-moon in the great solar system of the poet-novelist's works, and there's little about the book (or its non-history of reception) to evidence any vast claims for Sorrentino's significance as a critical voice. The pieces themselves, bearing dates and watermarks as various and sporadic as *"New York Times Book Review*, 1977"; *"Kulchur*, 1963"; *"The Nation*, 1962"; *"Sixpack*, 1974"; and *"Unpublished*, 1959" are mostly short. Not "brief" though. These little two- and three-pagers are compressed, barked-out like James Cagney monologues, by a writer evidently only quitting work on the present poem or chapter long enough to *get it exactly right*, and then forget he had to do it at all. Sorrentino, as a critic, is superbly impatient. Often he couldn't be bothered even to paragraph.

He was also superbly right, a fact I've butted my head against in my own attempts to write about Edward Dahlberg and Nathanael West, each of whose chimerical essence finds itself encircled in a wizardly fashion in the pages of *Something Said* (in the piece on West, written in 1967, Sorrentino even manages to predict the presidency of Ronald Reagan!). "The critic is either subsumed in his criticism, the latter becoming, relentlessly and imperceptibly, a kind of natural effusion of the collective intelligence; or he is forever identified as 'the one who said that . . .' and reviled for such rank stupidity": that's from Sorrentino's introduction, in which he apologizes for participating in what he calls "a mug's game." Well, I don't know if the "collective" has yet reached Sorrentino's stratum of intelligence, but (from my angle of view as a now middle-aged reader, writer, and teacher of fiction), as per his evaluations, we're certainly still contending with the magnitudes of Gaddis and Calvino, not troubling too much with Larry Woiwode and John Gardner. The book is, of course, helplessly personal, not-so-quietly-outraged, and blackly funny. Sorrentino's long point, if you're willing to listen, was always that a true embrace of life's absurdity led not to a sterile or abstracted ivory-tower Modernism, but to a riotously humane embrace of culture per se, and *Something Said* ends, probably not accidentally, with two traditional jokes, one Italian and one Irish. For Sorrentino, a writer is merely a man decorated with evidence of his persistence in the face of it all. The decorations are more than enough.

—*The Review of Contemporary Fiction*, 2011

Steven Millhauser's Ghost Stories

Among the impostures of book reviewing, the suggestion that a book is encountered in a vacuum of preconceptions is one that's best debunked in the case of a "New and Selected Stories." Here's a career capstone for a writer good (and industrious) enough to rate the honor, a writer not only still walking the earth but also still adding goodies to the pile. It's no time to play dumb. If you weren't already reading the fellow, what business would you have weighing in now?

I'm a Steven Millhauser fan. Three of the four books from which the "selected" stories in *We Others* were selected are sitting on my shelves; additional stories I'd already met in magazines. If this kind of a book is a story-writer's crown, it's also a Frankenstein's monster, assembled from the bodies of others. This review, then, is its pale twin: My own New and Selected Feelings About Steven Millhauser, stitched together to resemble a book review.

That Millhauser is a quiet, enigmatic master of the medium-long-to-long story (he's also written three volumes of novellas, not represented here); that his characteristic method mingles dreamlike and often morbid or perverse fantasies with meticulous realist observation; that his prose temperature is coolly feverish, drawing equally on Nabokovian rapture, Borgesian enigma and the plain-spoken white-picket-fence wistfulness of

Sherwood Anderson; that he writes about magicians and inventors in stories that are themselves presto-chango contraptions; that he peppers his largely well-mannered dream worlds with little salacious uprisings, luscious peeps into the sexy-mermaid part of his imagination's carnival: these things I'd have said going in. But Millhauser's also protean. Although his stories have much in common only with themselves, he seems to demand fresh terms of himself for each project he begins. Generalizations will take you just so far.

The new stories come first. Three of these have an amplitude that makes them real advances in Millhauser's art, but they're also terrific lenses for gazing at the retrospective selection that follows.

The title novella, "We Others," is a painstakingly gradual grown-up ghost story that makes explicit Millhauser's allegiance to the tradition of Henry James (as opposed to that of, say, Hemingway). Many of Millhauser's stories suggest they are allegories of the artist's existential condition, but rarely so forcefully as in this story's opening lines: "We others are not like you. We are more prickly, more jittery, more restless, more reckless, more secretive, more desperate, more cowardly, more bold. We live at the edges of ourselves, not in the middle places. We leave that to you. Did I say: more watchful? That above all. We watch you, we follow you, we spy on you, we obsess over you."

The speaker's a ghost, a dead person who's stuck around to haunt the living. Millhauser is the master of what might be called the Homeopathic School of Fantastic Writing: just the barest tincture of strangeness, eyedropped into the body of an otherwise mimetic story. The payoff for this withholding of weirdness can be a reader's intensified complicity in defamiliarization: a sensation of slippage into the unreal just as we know it ourselves, from our dreams and fantasies. In Millhauser, the effect is often also deeply mournful, as in this devastating slow-fuse emotional tragedy—"The Ghost and Mrs. Muir" rewritten with an exquisite attention to the incommensurateness of loss that's truly worthy of James. (It is also worthy of James that this story of being posthumous-yet-alive can be read against the fate of a living writer who finds himself entombed within a "New and Selected Stories.")

"The Next Thing" describes a super department store of the future, one that undermines (literally, since the store consists of a vast basement) the life of the American town where it appears, having arrived first as a fad and diversion and then increasingly become a new mode of being for the town's citizens. "The Next Thing" forms an explicit dialogue with Millhauser's earlier story "The Barnum Museum," a fantasia of a vast and magical institution that adapts to the desires of its visitors. "The Barnum Museum" is quintessential Millhauser: it exemplifies his interest in microcosms (dioramas, stage shows, dream worlds and so on) that loom into macrocosms, then threaten to rival or even engulf the reality that gave birth to them.

In Millhauser's hands, this recurrent motif is a versatile and suggestive mirror-symbol, fluently alive to interpretation. It glints with aspects of Plato's Cave and Borges's Library of Babel—and now, like those earlier images, it can't help seeming like an emblem of *our* new thing, the virtual life. Millhauser also seems to tease at virtuality in "The Wizard of West Orange," in which an unnamed Edisonian inventor struggles to bring into being a tactile medium to rival the phonograph or Eastman's film apparatus. The effort draws one of the inventor's assistants, the story's narrator, into an aching disillusionment with his former "blind skin": "A new life beckons. A shadow-feeling, an on-the-vergeness. Our sensations fixed, rigid, predictable. Must smash through. Into what? The new place. The there. We live off to one side, like paupers beside a railroad track."

Yet for all the ambivalence Millhauser excavates from his "new" things—the carnivals and aliens, the Barnums and Edisons who blow in to topple our complacencies, to tempt and usurp—he may seem a little too certain of the stability that's overturned by his marvels. "The Next Thing" feels brave and inspired because Millhauser damps his signature romantic luster as he frames the cold costs of enchantment; but the story also made me wonder if his halcyon, bittersweet town—an updated Bedford Falls, from *It's a Wonderful Life*, overrun for the hundredth time by Pottersville—wasn't too much of a default setting. Here on our permanent frontier, we like telling stories in which innocence has been abruptly torn from us, just a day or a decade before. And Millhauser, a controlled writer if ever there was one, mostly adapts this to his own fine uses. Yet every once in a while it might be seen as driving him instead.

Not least because "The Slap" appears to refute this small reservation, the collection's opening story is my favorite among the new offerings, and may even rival "Cat 'n' Mouse" and "A Visit" in my Millhauser hall of fame. A town—a Millhauser town, of course, but a degree more contemporary, less varnished with yearning—finds itself the victim of a serial face-slapper. The story, from there, goes boldly nowhere. Rather than developing or resolving the action, Millhauser chooses simply to portray the brutal daily presence of rage and distrust in a community discovering itself and unsure what to think, yet unable to avert its eyes.

> Looked at another way, the slap doesn't merely withhold: the slap imparts. What it imparts is precisely the knowledge of greater power withheld. In that knowledge lies the genius of the slap, the deep humiliation it imposes. It invites the victim to accept a punishment that might have been worse—that will in fact be worse if the slap isn't accepted. The slap requires in the victim an unwav-

ering submission, an utter abnegation. The victim bends in spirit before a lord.

In "The Slap," this gesture is a Millhauserian mirror of unprecedented ungenerosity: it shows us only ourselves.

—*The New York Times*, 2011

IV

Lost Worlds

The Mechanics of Fear, Revisited

In a piece called "The Mechanics of Fear," published in *The New Yorker* in 1976, Greil Marcus made a case for John Franklin Bardin as a greatly neglected American noir writer—at the time Bardin was being brought back into print by Penguin in *The John Franklin Bardin Omnibus*. Marcus wrote: "Drawing partly on his own mother's madness and the uncertainties of a Depression coming-of-age, he made paranoia his subject: Bardin's protagonists solve the mysteries in which they are implicated or perish in them." Twenty-odd years later, despite Penguin's and Marcus's efforts, Bardin was just as obscure when an editor at Vintage Books and I discovered our mutual fascination with his first three books, those reprinted in the Omnibus. At the time I joked that the way to best reintroduce Bardin would be to republish *The Deadly Percheron* in something I off-handedly called *The Vintage Book of Amnesia*. I argued that Bardin was, with Philip K. Dick and Steve Erickson, one of the greatest and most recurrent practitioners of "amnesia fiction," a hitherto unidentified genre. That joke eventually became an anthology, in which a chapter of *The Deadly Percheron* appeared, though I'd originally hoped to include the entire book. So, perhaps consider this introduction a belated enclosure of Bardin's bizarre and enthralling first novel within the sphere of that project.

Paranoia and amnesia make heavy companions, but the tone

of *The Deadly Percheron's* opening chapters is anything but. Instead, the book comes off like a brisk blend of Damon Runyon and *The Twilight Zone*. At the start, the pedantically reasonable psychiatrist Dr. George Matthews meets a new patient, Jacob Blunt, who, though by appearance young, sane, and clear-eyed, claims ludicrous hallucinations and wears a flower in his hair. On hearing Dr. Matthews's pat explanation of psychosis ("A person who is mentally ill often lives in a world of his own imagining, an unreal world,") Blunt exclaims, "I am nuts, thank God! It isn't really happening!" This contradiction is the first of what will become an obsessive sequence of reversals; Bardin captivates the reader's interest by a flourish of happenings and motivations seemingly impossible to explain, showing a fondness for bald paradox rivaled only by A. E. Van Vogt, G. K. Chesterton, and Borges. Like those others, Bardin arouses everywhere our suspicion that, along with his characters, he's making it up as he goes along.

Hearing Jacob Blunt's exclamation, Dr. Matthews thinks: "This was unusual; I had never before met a neurotic who admitted wanting to lose his mind." *Admitted* may be the key word. For when at Blunt's moonish instigation Matthews finds himself whirled into what seems an innocently hectic adventure, tinged with Bohemian New York whimsy involving Americanized leprechauns and other droll non sequiturs, it is impossible not to detect an occult appetite in the narrator for novelty, crisis, disorder. If George Matthews doesn't knowingly "want to lose his mind," he's nevertheless driven, from the first page, by an unacknowledged yearning to shift into Jacob Blunt's irrational universe. Dr. Matthews is also, from the first, weirdly susceptible to his careening emotions: he likes and dislikes people at the drop of a hat, and has his feelings bruised by the leprechaun's refusal to let him participate in Blunt's shenanigans. He also tends to an abrupt and swooning eroticism, fixated on legs and skirts in a manner that hints at the fetishism of a Bruno Schulz or R. Crumb. In short, Dr. Matthews's existence as a prestigious Manhattan therapist rather begs to be overturned.

The tension here is the familiar and thrilling malign urge underlying all film noir—the sensation that the complacent surfaces of post-war American life were brimming with irrationality, subversion, and vice, ever ready to erupt. Yet for the first few chapters George Matthews's smug certainties seem to be sufficient to the task of containing, or repressing, the book's disturbances. Jacob Blunt's merry paranoia, and the whiff of conspiracy that surrounds him, is kept at a comfortable arm's length, treated with psychiatric platitudes even as it veers into a murder plot. The reader may initially suspect Bardin of purveying a wild goose chase, albeit one with some of the color and brio of Kenneth Fearing's *The Big Clock* or perhaps a minor Hitchcock film like *Saboteur*, or Orson Welles's *The Lady from Shanghai*.

Yet, whether Dr. Matthews was itching for trouble or not, he can't have had in mind the torments for which he is bound. Beginning in Chapter Four, Jacob Blunt and his dray horse vanish from the scene, and *The Deadly Percheron* gets personal. The reader, with George Matthews, is plunged into a classical noir nightmare of dissolution and estrangement, as implausible as it is emotionally vivid. Bardin's genius is for the waking nightmare, lucid, outwardly reasonable, yet vertiginous, with a tinge of hysteria. His only rival in this mode is Cornell Woolrich, but Bardin's a more felicitous writer than Woolrich, and his anarchic commitment to panic is more absolute (even if, like Woolrich, he's drably bound to the implausible logical final explanations that mar the work as the slapdash last-minute happy endings mar so many film noirs).

In *The Deadly Percheron's* consummate middle passage, Dr. Matthews allows himself to be transformed into the homeless drifter, John Brown. First, Matthews conspires with his own unseen tormentors, pretending to accept an outcast identity in order to fool the benighted staff of the sanatorium in which he has been imprisoned (they present him with Freudianism at its most obstinately cryptological, i.e., the more you protest that a certain thing is true, the more certain we are that you are in denial of something else). Then, in the devastating Chapter Five, "In Which a Man Runs Down" (the chapter-title takes on at least two meanings), on earning his release Matthews is confronted, in a shop-window's reflection, with a stranger who turns out to be himself:

> What made him really fascinatingly ugly was the wide, long, angry red scar that traversed his face diagonally from one ear across the nose and down to the root of the jaw at the base of the other cheek. It was an old scar that had knit badly and in healing had pulled and twisted at the skin until the face it rode had the texture of coarse parchment and the grimace of a clown. One cheek, and the eye with it, was drawn sidewise and upward into a knowing leer, the other drooped, and with it a corner of the mouth, as if its owner were stricken with grief. The skin's color was that of cigar ash, but the scar's color was bright carmine. I pitied the man, then was embarrassed to look around at him: surely, he must have seen me staring at his reflection! But as I had this thought I noticed that his glass emptied itself of coca-cola just as I sucked noisily at my straw.

Meeting his disfigurement, Matthews accepts the John Brown identity not as an imposture but as a deeper reality uncovered. His amnesia is a condition of shame, and his former life becomes irretrievable, a kind of bluff that the revelatory logic of noir has called. The presentation of John Brown's life as a cafeteria counterman at Coney Island, including the almost allegorical clarity with which he inventories the carnival folks he befriends while working there, bears all the descriptive gravity the Manhattan psychiatrist's milieu lacked. Here, as Marcus suggests, is the trauma of the Depression leaking up through the veneer of middle-class complacency. Similarly, as noted by scholar Kenneth Payne, the gothic details of torture and flight that slowly emerge out of the fog of Brown/Matthews' amnesia seem a kind of European concentration camp horror come to roost on the American shore.

Everything Bardin presents in these middle chapters persuades. Sonia, Brown's damaged and abject Coney Island lover, is wholly real and poignant, whereas Sarah, Dr. Matthews's wife, is never anything other than an idea, the notion of a desirable life incarnated in a name. By this time the reader has been enlisted in a study deeper than a murder mystery: whatever paltry rationalizations are offered, this book presents a nightmare of affliction and complicity, one unfolding according to the deeper operations of the dreamlife. At one point, attempting to parse the malicious and absurd plot that enfolds him, Bardin's narrator muses, "Murder might be termed the ultimate practical joke; similarly, a practical joke might be called the social form of murder." I was reminded of the British psychoanalytic critic Adam Phillip's pregnant formulation: "Businessmen are criminals disguised as artists; criminals are only failed artists."

The Deadly Percheron and Bardin's next two novels were poured onto the page in a period of less than three years. Bardin himself seemed to understand what he'd accomplished, though he showed no propensity for repeating the trick. Offering Grahame Greene, Henry Green, and Henry James as his influences (I adore the overlapping names, as though even that citation was enslaved to some unconscious punning instinct), he gave in

1980 the following statement: "A novel is a detector of mined experience. As a soldier walks a mined field with a contraption in front of him that buzzes when it's over a mine, so a novelist, such as I, elaborates a contraption that when the reader experiences it may warn him of the mines of his own emotions. I draw no distinction between the novel and the detective novel: there are only good and bad novels." Julian Symons, introducing the 1976 reissue, said: "He belongs not to the world of Agatha Christie and John Dickson Carr, but to that of Patricia Highsmith or even that of Poe." Marcus, perhaps even closer to the mark, insisted Bardin's true affiliation was with the B-movie poets of film noir, most of them European exiles: Robert Siodmak, Edgar G. Ulmer, Max Ophuls (I'd add Jacques Tourneur). In his commitment to a vernacular American surrealism, rooted in the materials of noir, I'd also suggest Bardin points ahead, to Charles Willeford, Paul Auster, and David Lynch. Bardin's contraption is a sturdy one, and more than half a century later, his mine detector shrieks with what it finds.

—Introduction to *The Deadly Percheron*, 2006

On the Yard

The mind flinches from the fact of prisons—their prevalence, squatting in the midst of towns and cities, their role in so many lives, and in the history and everyday life of our country. And when the mind does find its way there, it wants the whole subject covered in hysteria and overstatement. Let prisons be one simple thing—either horrific zoos for the irretrievably demented and corrupt, or inhumane machines which grind down innocent men. Let them stand apart as raw cartoons of black-and-white morality, having nothing to do with the rest of us—we who live in the modulated, ambivalent, civilized world "the novel" was born to depict. We might secretly feel prison doesn't *need* a novel, that it instead needs a miniseries or the Op-Ed page.

Malcolm Braly's *On the Yard*, temperate and unhysterical as its title, is the novel prison needs. It's also a book any lover of novels ought to know, for its compression, surprise, and wry humor, for its deceptively casual architecture, and for characters and scenes which are unforgettable. Of course, readers may be compelled to read realistic novels set in war or plague or prison by uneasy cravings to know particulars of lives they hope never to encounter more directly. And Braly surely has knowledge we don't, tons of it. During a miserable, nearly fatherless childhood, Braly began acting out his grievances through a series of petty and eventually not-so-petty burglaries, until, in the company of some reckless partners in crime, he found himself in an interstate chase which climaxed in a gun battle with police, then capture and imprisonment. Upon his first release he slipped back into a desultory pattern of minor crime; eventually managing to spend a majority of his first forty years of life behind prison walls without having murdered or raped, without having even stolen anything of much value.

Apart from knowledge, Braly possesses an insouciant tone of confidence which causes us never to doubt him, and which is more persuasive than any fact: if these things can be taken as givens, taken almost lightly, then truly the prison is another world as real as our own. But beyond reportage, or tourism, *On the Yard* succeeds because through its particulars it becomes universal, a model for understanding aspects of our self-wardened lives. Inside and outside prison walls human beings negotiate, stall, bluff, and occasionally explode in their attempts to balance ecstasy against ennui, to do more than merely eke out their narrowing days on earth. But Braly skirts allegory: his book is much too lean and local to bother with that. The reader supplies the allegory.

The novel could be said to center on the plateau and fall (we never witness his rise) of Chilly Willy, a prison racketeer who deftly controls a small empire of cigarettes, pharmaceutical narcotics, and petty bureaucratic favors, orchestrated by a routine of minimal violence and, as his name suggests, maximum cool. Despite his name, and the outlines of his career, he's a deeply real and human character, even a sympathetic one. We watch as Chilly manipulates the razor's-edge power dynamics of the prison until a single miscalculation causes him to lash out. It is then that the prison administration undertakes Chilly's destruction, by the simple act of placing a receptively homosexual cellmate in his previously solitary cell. The new cellmate serves as Chilly's mirror—not for a repressed homosexuality, but for the fact that his manipulations had always had concealed within them a grain of solicitude, perhaps even disguised family-feeling. The men Chilly commands are under his care, however apparently dispassionate a form this care has taken. Sex becomes the means of Chilly's self-destruction—but then nearly every character in the book is shown in a second act of self-destruction inside the prison, which recapitulates and confirms an initial act outside.

The novel *could* be said to center on Chilly's fall, except it barely centers anywhere, moving by its own cool strategy through the minds and moments of dozens of characters, some recurrently, some only for a sole brief visitation which nearly always proves definitive. Three or four of these are into the minds of the prison's keepers, including that of the morose, long-enduring Warden. The rest are a broad array of prisoners, some "hardened" repeaters, some newly arrived at San Quentin, some floating in between and trying to measure the rightness and permanence of their placement inside those walls. All but the craziest and most loathsome—like the shoe-sniffing, anal-compulsive Sanitary Slim—are presented at least briefly as potential audience and author surrogates. All of them are rejected, either gently or rudely, by the end.

This is Braly's brilliantly successful game—he's a master at exploiting the reader's urge to identify with his characters. The results are estranging, in the best sense: both funny and profound. Each character undergoes a sort of audition. The first pair of candidates is offered in Chapter One: Nunn, a repeat offender shuffling his way back inside and trying to come to terms with his propensity for self-defeat, his missed opportunities during his brief stint outside, and Manning, a sensitive and observant first-timer who has overturned his innocuous life with a sudden and incomprehensible crime of sexual perversion. The reader begins to squirm in a way which will become familiar—ordinary guilt and innocence will not be our map here. Braly is enormously conscious of the effect of withholding the criminal histories of certain of his characters, while blurting others. His writerly pleasure in this game is tipped in comic miniatures like this one: "He lit his cigarette, then held the match for Zekekowski, noting again how finely formed Zekekowski's hands were, actually beautiful, the hands of a . . . of an arsonist, as it happened."

If the men glimpsed in Braly's San Quentin break into roughly two groups, Manning and Nunn are typical of each: those who are career criminals, and those who've committed single crimes of impulse—the molesters and wife-killers. Braly leads us gently to the irony that the former commit relatively harmless crimes and yet are compulsively recurrent, whereas the latter are morally abhorrent yet less likely to return to the prison after their release. The impulsives are frequently bookish and bourgeois, unlike the careerists in outlook or temperament, and with a tendency to look down on them as lessers. At the extreme we meet Watson, a priggish impulsive: "Watson stood with culture, the Republic, and Motherhood . . . He had killed his two small sons, attempted to kill his wife, . . . all because his wife had refused a reconciliation with the remark, 'John, the truth is you bore me.'" Watson defends himself in a therapy session, claiming, "I see no point in further imprisonment, further therapy, no point whatsoever since there's absolutely no possibility I'll do the same thing again." And he's immediately teased by the raffish, Popeye-like career criminal Society Red, who says, "That's right . . . he's run out of kids."

More sympathetic is Lorin, a fragile jailhouse poet who cringes inside fantasies of Kim Novak and notebook jottings like "*Yet I am free—free as any to test the limits of my angry nerves*

and press the inner pains of my nature against the bruise of time."
Braly doesn't hold such sensitivity up for either mockery or
admiration: like other responses to the condition known as
San Quentin, it is simply presented as one possibility among
many. Nearer to the author's own sympathies—or so a reader
may suspect—is Paul Juleson, Lorin's sometimes mentor and
protector. Juleson at first glance seems the most resourceful
and best equipped of the prison intellectuals, and therefore
both a likely survivor and a good bet for author's proxy. In a
flashback we learn that Juleson killed his wife; the hell of his
short marriage is portrayed with devastating economy and insight, and the violence of his crime doesn't prevent our inclin-
ing toward Juleson's sympathies. Richard Rhodes, in *The New
York Times*'s original review of *On the Yard*, came out and said
it: "Juleson is probably Mr. Braly's alter ego." Yet I don't think
it's so simple as that—and certainly Braly denies us the usual
satisfactions of rooting for this character when, despite all his
wiles and wisdom, Juleson puts himself in the path of Chilly
Willy's contempt by a dumb play for a few packs of cigarettes.

From that point Chilly and Juleson catalyze one another's
destruction. It is as though these two have always been fated
to expose the weakness in the other. So if Braly has an alter
ego in the book, it is split, in an act of symbolic self-loathing, between these two men. Rhodes, in his otherwise admiring review, went on to call the book "curiously ambivalent, as
though the author had not yet sorted out his own attitudes
when he wrote it." I think this ambivalence, far from uninten-
tional, is in fact the essence of Braly's art. The criminal pro-
fessionals are not so different from the middle-class murderers
after all—they are united in self-destruction. San Quentin exists, at some level, because these men need a place to solve the
puzzle of their lives by nullification. It also exists because of
our society's need to accommodate that nullification, giving it

four square walls, a pair of coveralls, and a number, as well as a few perfunctory hours of group therapy a week.

In other words, if it's difficult to discern with whom Malcolm Braly identifies, this is likely because Malcolm Braly doesn't identify with himself. Not exactly. This becomes plain in Braly's *False Starts*, his extraordinary memoir of his childhood, and of his pathetic criminal and prison careers. In this second masterpiece, published ten years after *On the Yard*, Braly marvels extensively at his own tropism for the prison, at those miraculous self-sabotages which led him again and again to the miserable comforts of incarceration. We learn that during one break-in he actually managed to accidentally leave behind a slip of paper bearing his full name and address, as though desperate to forge a path back inside.

Standing outside *On the Yard*'s character scheme is the lanky teenage sociopath, Stick. Leader of a mostly imaginary gang of fascist hoodlums called The Vampires, Stick is a cipher of human chaos, and he eventually brings down an unlikely destruction on the prison. Stick's uncanny near-escape is by hot-air balloon, one painstakingly constructed by his cellmate and stolen by Stick at the last moment. This reveals a vein of dreamy masturbatory fantasy, a childishness, which our fear of criminals and prisoners usually conceals from us, but which Braly doesn't want concealed. The balloon is an unusually direct symbol for any novel, but especially Braly's. It bears evidence of that ambivalence which marks all the characters and their strivings: when examiners consider the crashed balloon they find it scored by excessively reworked sewing, which has weakened the fabric: "[the stitches] suggested an analogy to hesitation marks in a suicide." Stick also, it seems to me, reveals *On the Yard* as being a 1960's California book, and San Quentin in the Sixties as being oddly subject to the same propensity for utopianism and social experiment as the Bay Area within which the prison darkly huddles. In an eastern prison Stick might more likely have been drawn into some preexisting gang or Mafia: thirty years later he'd be a Crip or Blood. Here he's free to self-invent, and so becomes a prognostication of Charles Manson or Jim Jones.

Malcolm Braly's life was sad, triumphant, and sad again. He lived mostly inside for twenty years, until his writing, together with the will and generosity of Gold Medal Books editor Knox Burger, provided a rescue. He died in a car accident at fifty-four, leaving behind a wife and infant daughter—Knox Burger has said he was "fat and happy." His peak as a writer came in the two complementary books, the novel and the memoir, and in the memoir he says about the novel "I was writing over my head." A reader needn't to explore the earlier books to confirm this, for Braly is working over his head in *On the Yard* in the sense that any novelist is when he has moved beyond his tools, or through them, to experience a kind of transubstantiation with his characters. At those moments a writer always knows more than he ever could have expected to, and he can only regard the results with a kind of honest awe. The book is no longer his own, but a vehicle by which anyone can see himself both exculpated and accused, can find himself alternately imprisoned and freed. Braly's novel is something like Stick's borrowed balloon, in the end, a beautiful, unlikely oddment rising from the yard of San Quentin, motley with the scars of its making and no less perfect for showing those "hesitation marks." It rises above the prison walls in a brief, glorious flight, before gravity makes its ordinary claim.

—Introduction to *On the Yard*, 2012

Walter Tevis's *Mockingbird*

Walter Tevis is a maker of fables, and *Mockingbird* is one of his finest, a fable written twenty years ago that you, reading this now, need and want urgently though you don't necessarily know it. Parts of this elegant fable will seem oddly familiar, accidentally and by design, for Tevis was a master manipulator of archetypes, an artist capable of delving into the zeitgeist while nevertheless remaining on his own pure search for himself.

Chunks of books like *1984* and *Brave New World* and *Earth Abides* seem to be swallowed here, likely because Tevis knew those books, but also chunks of movies, movies he knew (and mentions) like *Kong Returns* and movies he might have seen, like *Vertigo*, and movies he couldn't have, like *Blade Runner*—and while we're at it, doesn't *Mockingbird* read like the perfect bridge between Clifford Simak and Steve Erickson, and don't you hear echoes of Bob Dylan's "Isis" in this tale of exile and return? All of these shadows and echoes moving through *Mockingbird* attest to our yearning, graver than we probably know, for fables of this type at the end of the American century, for stories that embarrass us with their desperate hopes, their savage nostalgia, their instinct that precious things have already been destroyed and forgotten—Vonnegut, Bradbury, Bernard Wolfe, *Brazil*, *Alphaville*: we gather stories like these until we thrust them away, appalled by adolescence, divesting ourselves of grandiose and absolute feelings.

But Tevis's book isn't adolescent, it's ruminative and ironic with middle-aged wisdom, richly ambivalent and knowing, because when Tevis reached for images of the grim, dwindled world against which his young lovers would strive, he reached into himself: the flinching eyes, the retreat of his citizens into drugged privacy, the pointlessly repetitive operations of his machines, and especially the nihilistic elitism of Spofforth, the ancient robot at the center of *Mockingbird*, who wishes for the world to die so that he may die—when he limned his world Tevis drew a dark self-portrait to contrast the bright one he drew in his lovers.

And despite the echoes and shadows moving through *Mockingbird* and for all of Tevis's sophistication, he has the unembarrassed courage to write his tale of the future, his paean to memory, with a sort of beautiful literary amnesia: like Orwell and Huxley and George R. Stewart and Bernard Wolfe, he wrote as though no one had ever written a tale of the future before, so that *Mockingbird* stands apart, gawkily refusing genre, instead a novel of character and a fable as singular as the wrecked Empire State Building that looms over Tevis's Manhattan, a fable that, I may already have mentioned, you want and need more than you know.

—Introduction to *Mockingbird*, 1999

Everything Said and Exhausted
(Daniel Fuchs)

Six years ago I wrote:

> There's nothing on my shelf I flip open for inspiration
> as often these days as Daniel Fuchs's three novels about
> Brooklyn, set and written in the 1930's . . . reprinted
> in 1961 in one volume as *Three Novels*, then separately
> in paperback in 1965—a moment of rediscovery now as
> forgotten as the original publication. Fuchs published in
> *The New Yorker*, was a buddy of Cheever's at Yaddo, and
> somewhere Irving Howe compared him to Willie Mays
> for the ease of his effects, but unlike Willie Mays he's
> nearly vanished from the record books . . .

Today, thanks to Black Sparrow's superb one-volume distillation of the latter part of Fuchs's career—in which our hero
flees Brooklyn and, for the most part, fiction, in favor of Hollywood and an uncommonly serene career as a studio screenwriter—contemporary readers are likely to come to Fuchs's
grittily enchanted vision of Brooklyn backward. That brief
volume, *The Golden West*, published in 2005, gathered essays
and a trickle of fiction on the theme of Hollywood, produced

over five decades. However lovely—and any paragraph Fuchs put to paper is lovely—*The Golden West* records a disconcerting abandonment. The present bulging volume, *The Brooklyn Novels*, three books produced in little over five years, presents the commitment—to fictional voice and fictional form—that was to be abandoned. And, since Fuchs was a man of compulsive scruples, the book also records the dilemmas, artistic and personal, that made Fuchs's flight from the material of his splendid early fiction so needed, as well as the terms by which abandonment was to be enacted.

I discovered Fuchs at Yaddo, while browsing idly on the shelves reserved for the works of previous occupants of the place. I was there trying to find a way to write about Brooklyn. You can imagine my surprise at opening *Summer in Williamsburg* and discovering Fuchs's secret Dickensian tapestry depicting a coming of age among immigrant dreamers and scoundrels. Fuchs's voice—tender, antic, vernacular—struck me as essential, a compass for my own work, and his collected works a missing piece in my interior bookshelf. Here was something like the milieu I'd glimpsed in Malamud's earliest fiction, in Vivian Gornick's memoir *Fierce Attachments*, in the tenement stories of Will Eisner, depicted in full and from the inside, with absolute and sometimes claustrophobic authority, yet without the air of decrepitude and undropped grudges, of mingled bitterness and sentimentality, which had so often discouraged my curiosity about Jewish Proletarian fiction. The material evoked, specifically, my experience of my mother's family (my uncle Fred, a numismatist, author of several volumes on American coins, who tattled on a mobster and lived in fear of reprisal, was, just for instance, a perfect Fuchs character). Fuchs's voice was so fresh and enticing that I felt a disbelief at the 1930's copyright dates—yet if I could accept the sense of contemporaneity I located in the dialogue in Fitzgerald and in Howard Hawks movies, maybe I should accept Fuchs's.

Summer in Williamsburg ("written," Fuchs said, "in a state of terror") is a first novel if ever there was one: a "dictionary" or "encyclopedia" of the Brooklyn precinct that formed Fuchs's awareness, and encapsulating almost despite itself the writer's meditation on the development of his own puzzling sensibility, despite the fact that the central figure, Philip Hayman, never declares himself a writer-to-be. Rather, he seems to accept the collapse of any dream of escape from the pragmatic logic of Depression life. The tone is one of endurance, but never stoical, always yearning. *Homage to Blenholt* reworks the same turf with new writerly tools: comic compression, ironic distance, and rattletrap dialogue. Fuchs's characters jabber in poetry, compressed and glinting, warmer than Don DeLillo's Bronx argot in *Underworld* but worthy of the comparison. *Low Company* (set not in Williamsburg but in Brighton Beach) distills Fuchs's instinct for the comic-grotesque even further from the earlier tone of autobiographical reminiscence. Here it's schemer versus schemer, with nary a dreamer in sight. Or rather, dreams have been now sublimated in schemes, a perfect model of American arrival. *Low Company*, of the three, might even be called a crime novel (though *Summer*'s little plot concerns Catskill bus-route gangsters), except that Fuchs's tone is resolutely soft-boiled, and his bullies' brief outbursts of violence tend to fall like weather, or fate.

This third novel, so chewily grim, exasperated at least one critic who might have wished Fuchs to go on exemplifying if not exalting the Proletarian dilemma: Irving Howe, who called it "slick." It may also have somewhat exasperated another, peculiarly harsh critic: Fuchs. "I was tired of making fun of the people in my stories, hitting them off, as I did, easily and without conscience. I was, in the end, in the peculiar position of a writer whose forte was a quality he secretly disliked and wanted to lean on less and less and not at all, and who, on the other hand, had no other special talent or great idea to offer in its place."

All this was in long retrospect: Those comments come from a 1987 autobiographical essay, extensively and seductively justifying his migration from fiction to screenwriting. One could also point out that all the vernacular elements that attracted him to Hollywood (and vice versa), abundantly present in the fiction from the start, found culmination in *Low Company*: the rapidly sketched milieus of tawdry Americana, the scraped wit, the ferociously humane dialogue, the unfussy emotionality, the love of "types." Soon enough Fuchs would become one of the myriad voices expanding, if not originating, what would later be called film noir. In the Hollywood sun and in the scenarist's craft he seems to have found the escapes he desired: out of the guilty traps of a Jewish-ghetto cultural inheritance; out of the political duties of a Proletarian novelist, from which he instinctively flinched, to the great benefit of his prose, but which he nevertheless seems to have felt weighing on him implicitly; from the solitary woes of a public-school substitute teacher writing novels on the side and measuring his value by "four hundred copies sold." The movies, which he plainly loved—and why not?—presented him with his own American arrival. The dream-turned-scheme out west was the greatest scheme of all: the production of dreams.

John Updike was right to identify Fuchs's "admiration of energy, however ill expended," and his "acceptance of people as the troublesome, messy spirits they are" as reminiscent of Saul Bellow. There's no doubt that had Fuchs stuck around the fiction game he coulda been a contender for that Jewish-American pantheon, a founding father. Another point of reference is Henry Roth, Joycean poet of Yiddish-American childhood—

yet Fuchs is so much less neurotically Modernist than Roth. It's even fair, oddly enough, that 1930's critics groping to explain the energy of Fuchs's tragic farces compared him to the Marx Brothers: Fuchs's characters draw on that same reservoir of panic, that clawing for attention, that fueled comedians who never completely left the vaudeville stage no matter what fame they attained.

Yet what's Jewish about a writer when he only happens to be a Jew? Unlike, say, Philip Roth, Fuchs never toils in Talmudic consideration of his immigrant families' dual allegiances, Old World piety versus New World secularism. For Fuchs, as for so many others, that's what running to California was for: guiltless escape from entrenched identity (California being in this sense America, squared). Blenholt, the commissioner of sewers in *Homage*, is celebrated for his ethnic mutability, for playing to the expectations of whatever constituency he addresses. Blenholt's only religion being power, and money. Setting aside cultural particulars (we're all from *somewhere*), the best comparison for Fuchs's affectionate nightmares of underclass striving may be Thomas Berger's roiling Midwestern small-town farces *The Feud* and *Sneaky People* (Berger, however affectionate, also fled his Midwest). Like Berger, Fuchs touches every character with sympathetic irony and, while infusing the human sphere with a visionary wholeness, eschews redemption in favor of a benign shrug.

Describing *Homage to Blenholt*, Fuchs said "I devoted myself simply to the life in the hallways, the commotion at the dumbwaiters, the assortment of characters in the building, the tenement scholar, the horse-bettor, the tenement aesthete, their strivings and preoccupations, their troubles in the interplay of the sexes. There was always a ferment, slums or no slums." Fuchs is as native a voice as we've got, at least in Brooklyn, where it was not only during the Great Depression that the

American dream uncovered a choice between surrender to the grind or to collusion with the grinder, between aspiring to the murderous practicality of Fuchs's mobsters or the hunger-artist sublimity of Philip Hayman's father in *Summer in Williamsburg*: "honest, good, and kind, but poor . . . he's old, he's so skinny, and all he has after all the years is a cigarette and a window." Deliverance, if it comes, may only be in a storyteller's craft: "the timing; the devices and felicities; the insistence on style, to throw the story according to the guise that properly belonged to it; the instinct for material and content, to choose what would ensnare; the instinct for form, to give the piece its full workout so that at the end everything has been said and exhausted," wrote Fuchs in 1990. "The best is when you write and *know* what you're doing, that you've got it." Of course, he was by then speaking of his work in Hollywood. That he'd had it fifty-odd years earlier Fuchs never allowed himself fully to know.

—Introduction to *The Brooklyn Novels*, 2006

How Did I Get Here and What Could It Possibly Mean? (Bernard Wolfe)

Bernard Wolfe's *Memoirs of a Not Altogether Shy Pornographer* comes into your hands as a book-out-of-time. Such republication efforts as these always collapse the shallow literary present into a more complicated shape, making a portal through history—who is this lost writer, we ask ourselves, and what is this lost book? But also: what views of a lost cultural landscape might be available through the portal this particular lost writer and lost book represents?

Make no mistake, the case of Bernard Wolfe is an especially interesting one, not least because, even in 1972, in the pages of his memoir when it rolled fresh off the presses into the hands of god-knows-how-few readers, Wolfe already presents himself as a man-out-of-time, in ways both helpless and defiant. Wolfe's career was bizarrely rich: from time as Leon Trotsky's personal secretary to stints in the Merchant Marine, as ghostwriter for Broadway columnist Billy Rose and author of early-TV-era teleplays, as editor of *Mechanix Illustrated*, and as exponent of the theories of dissident psychoanalytic guru Edmund Bergler (whose homophobia was obnoxious, but whose discarded theories strongly anticipate later thinking, and who could be seen as a kind of "lost American Lacan," if anyone was digging for one), to his glancing participation in the realm of American science fiction, and his role as amanuensis, to jazzman Mezz Mezzrow, in writing a memoir depicting a prescient version of "hipsterdom" and which became a kind of bible of inner-urban American slang—Wolfe was practically everywhere in twentieth-century culture.

Yet Wolfe was also *nowhere*, in the sense that the present interest attaching to him doesn't stem from the notion of "reviving" a writer with an earlier purchase on either popularity or the embrace of literary critics of his time. Wolfe had neither. A few of his books sold a bit; *Limbo* has kept an obscure reputation within science fiction and bobbed back into print a few times. Yet for his hyperactivity, Wolfe had little traction, and in 1972 was hardly a writer whose memoirs any publisher were likely to be clamoring for. Wolfe, restless, fast-producing, and seemingly impervious to indifference, wrote one anyway. When he did it was surely the "pornographer" of the title that drew Doubleday's interest in publishing the result.

What the reader meets here is both fascinating and truly eccentric. The book is a writer's-coming-of-age narrative, but a highly unsentimental one, describing Wolfe's location of a habit and a craft and a discipline and a capacity, much more than it details his discovery of any definite sense of purpose as a writer. Wolfe's vibrant intelligence, which picks up and turns over any number of vital subjects as if they were rocks concealing scuttling insect life, rarely settles on introspection, let alone seeks a tone of confession or remorse or self-doubt, such as we'd expect from nearly any memoir lately. Despite this, there's a terrible poignancy to the material concerning his father's spiraling mental illness, and the bizarre ironies attaching to Wolfe's own role as a New Haven-townie-gone-to-Yale who gets a psychiatric fellowship at the same institution in nearby Middletown where his father is a semi-comatose inmate. Of course, a commissioning editor, nowadays, would have insisted that Wolfe punch this material up, goose it emotionally, and put it in the foreground (a contemporary point of comparison might be Nick Flynn's fine *Another Bullshit Night in Suck City*). The same imaginary editor would surely, I think, have asked Wolfe to excise so much of the fading political context from the book, but for various reasons one can guess this book wasn't so much edited as it was simply written and published. It's in the politics that one can feel how deeply, and restlessly, Wolfe was, by 1972, testifying from an already-lost world. His passionate and still unresolved commitment to Marxism, a commitment betrayed (of course, and in so many different ways) by twentieth-century historical reality, remains the lens through which he views the "labor" of writing, and the social relations into which he projected himself as a hungry young writer in the wartime years.

Despite his engagement with history, there's no attempt to make a wide-screen historical panorama of his book—what enters of political and cultural context does so through individual experience. Wolfe also doesn't trouble much over the question of censorship, despite the great battles over *Ulysses*, *Lolita*, "Howl," and others that he'd certainly be capable of drawing into the mix. Apart from Henry Miller, and one other generationally important writer who comes in as a bizarre punch line, late in the book, Wolfe doesn't drop names. He doesn't situate his writer's life in terms of movements or generations, apart from dividing his future efforts from the drab proletarianism he sees as the Marxist writer's obligated legacy.

That the "labor" young Wolfe found for himself was to create exotic, gussied-up porn novels for the private delectation of gentlemen-collectors, or maybe just one gentleman-collector— talk about your lost worlds!—is a perverse irony of which the book makes its primary meat. Not that the memoir is salacious in any way (in fact, Wolfe can seem prim), but the situation forms a puzzle for the young writer, one the older Wolfe's still captivated by: how did I get here and what could it possibly mean? The book is a portrait too, a poison-pen portrait, of the disappointed, pretentious, and disingenuous publisher/go-between for the porn novels, who Wolfe calls "Barneybill Roster." In his luxuriant and fascinated distaste for this man, Wolfe himself resembles Henry Miller in the grip of one of his long denunciatory ranting episodes, like his great novella *A Devil in Paradise*. This brings us to the matter of the book's style—the weird, cavorting, punning, ruminative, aggrieved and deeply humane style that was Wolfe's own. Like many things in the book, Wolfe's astonishing and peculiar voice is deeply individual, but also historically characteristic. It shows, to me, the way Joyce's influence, but also Henry Miller's, was essential in the development of so much colorful "voice" in mid-century writers as seemingly otherwise unallied, or even divergent, as Mailer, Kerouac, Brautigan, Pynchon, Philip Roth, and so forth. Wolfe, in his novels, never quite rose into that company—his restless and motley enthusiasms may have catapulted him in too many directions, and he may simply not have had the luck or even the desire to apply such fixity to the novelist's art—he's almost a monologuist, a stand-up man, like Lenny Bruce or Lord Buckley. But the fellow who writes, here, "Words are problem-prongs" was a great man of language, and it's a gift to be able to read him again. Wolfe lives.

—Introduction to *Memoirs of a Not Altogether Shy Pornographer*, 2016

'Twas Ever Thus (Tanguy Viel's *Beyond Suspicion*)

One hesitates to do more than part the curtain and step aside, or perhaps strike a pensive single piano note repeatedly for overture, in the way of introducing a performance as delicate, complete, and fierce as Tanguy Viel's *Beyond Suspicion*. The book's reader will meet its opening pages with an intake of breath destined not to be completely released until its last lines have been reached. (You can certainly read it in one sitting, yet like certain novels of James M. Cain or Nathanael West or Paul Auster it demands recognition, in form and proportion, as a novel, rather than novella or story.)

The mode can be called classical, by now: Suspense, subclass: Hitchcockian-Highsmithian. The lineaments of the tale echo a thousand others, creating a narrative spell trafficking less in surprises or shocks than in an undertow of doomy inevitability, inciting a reader's perverse craving to understand how the ancient fates will exactly be distributed among this latest cast of the damned. Noir is above all in the details, and Viel unfolds his with the restraint and confidence of a stage-magician mastering an auditorium with a mere deck of cards; but he does something more: by distilling his noir through an air of almost cosmic remorse, he dares to soft-boil the hardboiled, to tip it back in the direction of the romanticism the mode traditionally denies. The double-benefit is to humanize his story while also etching it into a kind of mythic frieze: *'twas ever thus*. Much in the manner of Francois Truffaut adapting Cornell Woolrich in *Mississippi Mermaid*, or for that matter Camus adopting Cain's *The Postman Always Rings Twice* as a model for *The Stranger*, as well as Boileau and Narcejac deepening Hitchcock's own themes in offering him *Sueurs Froides: D'entre les Morts* as a source for *Vertigo*, this looks to be a particularly French response to noir: to purify it in the mode of a dream, to stalk its alienated essence. The most marvelous trick is that this pursuit, this distillation, uncovers noir's continuity with novels as apparently distant from this strain as Ford Madox Ford's *The Good Soldier*, or Henry James's *The Wings of the Dove*—James's Morton Densher and Kate Croy, schemers destroyed at the crossroads of love and money, are not so far from James M. Cain after all. *Beyond Suspicion* is a tiny novel, but it is like an X-ray of an enormous one.

—Introduction to *Beyond Suspicion*, 2008

Russell Greenan's Geniuses

It may seem like a fairly lame point, but follow me: a symphony can't extensively describe a brilliant—and nonexistent—work of architecture. Nor can a building, or a painting, or a play, or a song (or a mix tape or a video game or a designer dress) ever do very much in the way of persuading you of the existence of a fictional work of art in another form. It's only the novel—the baggiest, most elastic and inclusive of forms—that really has a chance. A novel can seem to envelop time and space, and with them the varieties of human experience, inside its borders. So, among its many unique opportunities (and booby traps) is the possibility of enclosing within its descriptions a fictional work of genius—an unheard symphony or an unseen painting.

Film, fiction's nearest cousin in its variety and relationship to time, may also appear able to enclose other forms. But photography's fatal literalism means film needs to prove what it asserts—and so a piece of, say, choreography depicted in a film must either be real and persuasive or else kept teasingly offscreen. The novel, with its mesmeric capacity to engage the reader's complicit imagination, can actually dwell on another art form, or artifact, or performance, until the item seems to hum into existence, and become a part of the larger-on-the-inside-than-on-the-outside magic spell of a book. The pitfall is only the vast risk of failure—see those dozens of rock and roll novels featuring "legendary" bands no one would ever have wanted to listen to, or novels in which "famous" movies are described and sound only unbearably trite.

Russell Greenan's *It Happened in Boston?* is a magic spell of a book—phantasmagoric, lushly written, full of unforgettable characters and devious twists of plot, traditional and even in some senses old-fashioned, but making delightful use of modernist touches, with hints of unreliable narration and wryly self-conscious structural devices. It's a riotously silly and engaging "entertainment" that is nevertheless at times both devastatingly sad and existentially terrifying. If the descriptive lushness of the prose recalls Patrick Suskind's *Perfume*, the conflation of mythical realms of art and history with an acute portrait of a sensitive psychopath losing traction in the everyday world suggests the result if a Borges or Cortázar had tackled the tale of Norman Bates, or the Unabomber. Greenan's debut is one of those in which the writer has offered a smorgasbord of every notion he'd ever hoped to transmit, as if in fear that he'd never have a second opportunity. Above all, the book achieves its distinction by presenting, by my count, not one but two characters of *unmistakable* genius as painters. I mean of course the narrator and his friend Benjamin Littleboy. That the talent of these two men is anachronistic, impractical, and, by the end, tragically misused, only makes the reader more certain that it could have been real. And the buttery opulence of Greenan's descriptions only makes our appetite to see the invisible masterpieces with which he decorates the novel more ravenous. In the words of the critic Ed Park, Greenan's painting scenes are "even better than Gaddis's *in The Recognitions.*"

Too, *It Happened in Boston?* contains a tender depiction of male camaraderie, among the narrator and Littleboy and a third, more ordinary and more successful painter, Leo Faber. The sweetness of the triumvirate's friendship remains unpoisoned by professional jealousy—or by the naïve and increasingly dangerous fantasizing of the narrator. This in turn renders the swirl of corrupt commerce around them even more stark, and makes the disasters of chapters 54 and 89 genuinely tragic. It would be criminal not to also mention the joke- and riddle-loving ghetto urchin, Randolph, who serves as a kind of earthly sprite or spirit-guide at the entrance to the novel's chamber of horrors and wonders. Late in the book the narrator muses, "Is there more to the child than meets the eye? His precocity is almost weird," and the purity and innocence of the remark, given the weirdness and precocity of the narrator himself, is heartbreaking and hilarious proof of the narrator's good faith with his companions, and Greenan's with his creations. The narrator loves Randolph, and Faber, and Littleboy, and we love them and the narrator too, and we wish to preserve them all from disenchantment, from the rapacity of a modern world which discounts their reveries and shortsells their masterpieces as forgeries.

Cheapened by his descent into that world of forgeries, the narrator of *Boston?* then further dilutes his own angelic purity by shifting his efforts from the glorious white magic of the making of beautiful objects, and of his dreamlike voyages to distant times, to the paltry, venal black magic of arcane spells and ancient curses. Most bitterly, those prove more effective than art can ever be. The book's unnamed angel is Lucifer, and like that angel, everything in the book is fallen: art and art patronage and love and late 1960s inner-city Boston are all fallen from grace by the end, and redeemable only by the faith required to assent to the book's last few paragraphs. However deep into reverie you are able to follow *Boston*'s pathetic and splendid narrator—I reach a different conclusion each time I read the book—I guarantee you will not be sorry to follow him to the juncture where you must part ways. What a pleasure it is to introduce to you, reader, this little masterpiece on the subject of the world's neglect of masterpieces! I feel almost as though I had single-handedly pulled Benjamin Littleboy's "Birth of Death" from the flames of destruction, painstakingly restored the damaged portions, and then hung the canvas where it so clearly belongs: in the lobby of the Boston Museum of Fine Arts.

—Introduction to *It Happened in Boston?*, 2014

V

---

*Ecstatic Depictions of
Consciousness*

Consumed

I seem to be in the middle of a minor "Cronenberg moment" this summer. I pinned my thumb in a car door, so tightly that I had to click the door open again to get it out. Days later the pain had faded, but the nail had turned black. After a few weeks' growth, a feeble dividing edge of torn nail crept from my cuticle, as the dead nail begins its crawl out, to be replaced by—what? A new nail, I hope. (Stay tuned).

What makes this experience Cronenbergian, however, isn't simply the grossness. It's the obsession. Each morning I check the advancing nail as if self-Googling, or hitting "refresh" on a website. Whether Nail.2 is eventually a disappointment ("One of five stars: derivative of the earlier nail, not worth the wait"), I'll nevertheless have been as enraptured as repulsed by the little allegory of death-and-regeneration my body is enacting—specifically by the mechanistic distance this slight mutilation has inserted between my sense of self and a new orientation towards my thumb as a foreign object, as a suffering machine stuck to my hand.

Our present is full of entrancing but rapidly-decaying media prosthetics: your new iPhone is hot, sure, but that's partly because it's also *dying*. In some 20 feature films, Cronenberg's specialty has been a meticulous probing of the juncture where the resemblance between illness and sexuality becomes a metaphor for our relationship to our technologies—including the arts. Though we're usually drawn to one and repelled by the other, sex and disease both amplify awareness of the mechanistic nature of our bodies, the obliviousness of their imperatives to our delicate selfhoods. That we work this out through our proxy devices—films and novels included—is helpless.

Now, if my black thumbnail wasn't your cup of meat, you'll likely wish to spare yourself even the rest of this review. On the other hand, if you found yourself leaning forward, I've got a book for you, and don't say you weren't warned. Nathan and Naomi, in Cronenberg's first novel, *Consumed*, are a very contemporary couple. They're media junkies who peddle the junk themselves, making a living as internet journalists feeding their own and others' rabid appetites for sexual scandals or true-crime confessions presented in intimate and lurid detail. Their frantic pursuits are framed by intellectual references to thinkers including Foucault, Beckett, and Sartre, and mediated through the very freshest electronic sensors, camera lenses and computer apps.

Nevertheless, and as one would expect, such investigations plunge them into timeless and primal matters of sex, death, and mortal illness. Specifically, the book presents a locked-room mystery of sorts: Can it be possible that a woman said to be dying of cancer, and whose philosopher-cannibal-husband was seen devouring parts of her body on a YouTube video, is still alive? Or was she a consensual accomplice to her own murder? This core plot is elaborated in a highly traditional (and satisfying) way: twin investigations, apparently unrelated, which gradually entwine. Amateur detectives who become complicit— and, of course, involved sexually—with their suspects. As in a majority of his films, Cronenberg's approach to narrative is sturdy and direct, the opposite of avant-garde. His originality is in what he's driven to show you, the fierce sculptural intensity of his details and his willingness to linger. The tableaus in *Consumed* attain the same level. Taking just one for-instance, a 3-D printer constructs a model of a penis disastrously warped into the shape of a boomerang by Peyronie's Syndrome (which exists; as many of Cronenberg's ailments are real as conjured).

Whether to your taste or not, it really shouldn't be shocking. In fact, such particulars are most likely routinely matched, or surpassed, in the work of thriller and horror writers in the post-Thomas Harris era, when monsters must trump Hannibal Lecter or else go home. What's vertiginous in Cronenberg's book is that such matters are presented in the absence of a reliably bourgeois moral framework. Instead, Cronenberg details them with a clinical curiosity. Try this:

> When a slim-hipped naked young man entered the frame, Naomi immediately knew it was Hervé, even before he walked around the side of the table to place his hooked penis in Célestine's coolly accommodating mouth. He brought with him something metallic that looked like a ray gun from a 1950s sci-fi movie, pale-blue and silver and trailing a black cable behind it . . . The naked young woman who entered from frame right, however, she did not immediately recognize, even after the woman had knelt at the head of the table in order to kiss and lick Célestine's mastectomy scar . . .

Or this:

> Nathan zoomed into the photo in front of them. That was ecstasy on her face as she cut herself, not self-pity, not masochistic pleasure . . . Nathan was shaping the article as he reacted. He would have liked to record these thoughts, just say them to GarageBand so that he wouldn't forget

them, but he was not yet comfortable enough with Roiphe to collaborate in that intimate way, to leave himself vulnerable to the old man's sarcasm and irony.

These passages are typical of the book's descriptive exactitude and flatness; its use of banal signifiers like "GarageBand," and the constant germane citations of psychoanalytic or philosophical brands. The book seems to desublimate itself for you: No sooner does the reader think "This is like the case of Louis Althusser's murder of his wife" than some character makes the comparison for you. The result is provocatively comic, and surreal in the manner of a Max Ernst collage. As Zadie Smith recently wrote, commenting on J.G. Ballard's *Crash* (a book adapted by Cronenberg to film, and an unmistakable influence on *Consumed*): "Some of the deadening narrative traits of pornography can be found . . . but surely this flatness is deliberate; it is with the banality of our psychopathology that Ballard is concerned."

Such a tone prevails except when illuminated by the characters' own reactions, and Nathan and Naomi are haphazard guides in this Bosch landscape. Their attitudes are distracted, craven, naïve, and occasionally rapturous. They're rarely caught judging themselves or anyone else. A flash drive full of crime-scene evidence and a newly acquired venereal disease are equally examined for use-value: Could this new thing win me followers on Twitter? Is there a chance it might turn me on, or make my lover helpfully jealous?

In this, Nathan and Naomi are worldly, media-savvy innocents, and innocents are always waiting to be schooled. In the later chapters, and quite unexpectedly, *Consumed* gives way to a monologue confession by Aristide Arosteguy, the aging philosopher-cannibal-suspect of Naomi's investigation. His testimony becomes, among other things, a tender paean to romantic love, to its persistence, its adaptability, its necessity in the face of death. Of course, Cronenberg being Cronenberg, this also necessitates a tender paean to another subject: elder sex (its persistence, its adaptability, etc.), especially elder sex of a non-vanilla sort. This may be, for readers the ages of Naomi and Nathan, a taboo more unsettling than cannibalism. Certainly it goes on in far more of your neighbors' homes. After all, it isn't only the young and tech-fetishizing among us who are fated for cyborg interfaces. Ever considered the perverse erotic potential of hearing aids? *Consumed* has.

—*The New York Times*, 2014

Dog Soldiers

Robert Stone's second novel, after announcing himself (and winning the Houghton Mifflin Literary Fellowship Award) with the Algren-esque bad-trip picaresque of *A Hall of Mirrors*, was a ruthless diagnosis of the Vietnamization of the homeland. The book works as a bait-and-switch: set first in Vietnam, *Dog Soldiers* reverts to Berkeley, Los Angeles, and SoCal Desert milieu that inevitably recalls Charles Manson's, yet never for an instant do the characters succeed in leaving the war behind. Browsing amid porn theaters, "Hippie" cops à la Serpico, tabloid newspapers ("Housewife Impaled By Skydiving Rapist"), drug culture, and—most presciently for the U.S.A. we know today—prison culture, the book surveys both Joan Didion's and Tim O'Brien's nightmares and concludes that The Two Are One.

Yet for all that it is topical to Vietnam and the counterculture, to that moment when the early '70s became the receptacle for all that had curdled out of the '60s, *Dog Soldiers* is also a mercilessly doomy, and timeless, crime novel. Particularly as it concerns Danskin, one of American fiction's greatest psychopaths, *Dog Soldiers* comes as near as The National Book Award's ever gotten to the domain of someone like Jim Thomson or Charles Willeford.

And then there is the sheer fried density of the language,

where clots of military and druggie jargon and early-'70s pseudo-philosophy ooze through Stone's tight, clean, driven voice, which derives, it seems to me, from Hemingway, from the Faulkner of "The Bear," and from Graham Greene, and which ought to speak to any fan of Don DeLillo or Denis Johnson. Stone's certainly as much a master as Greene of the intentional Pathetic Fallacy, in which the natural environment or world of inanimate objects is made to throb with the psychological matter of the humans moving through it. Check this out:

> In the course of being fragmentation-bombed by the South Vietnamese Air Force, Converse experienced several insights; he did not welcome them although they came as no surprise.
>
> One insight was that the ordinary physical world through which one shuffled heedless and half-assed toward nonentity was capable of composing itself, at any time and without notice, into a massive instrument of agonizing death. Existence was a trap; the testy patience of things as they are might be exhausted at any moment.
>
> Another was that in the single moment when the breathing world had hurled itself screeching and murderous at his throat, he had recognized the absolute correctness of its move. In those seconds, it seemed absurd that he had ever been allowed to go his foolish way, pursuing notions and small joys. He was ashamed of the casual arrogance with which he had presumed to scurry about creation. From the bottom of his heart, he concurred in the moral necessity of his annihilation.

A great American masterpiece.

—The National Book Foundation website, 2009

Bizarro World

What more do we want from Will Self? To make the obvious pun, are we after more Will, or more Self? In *Tough, Tough Toys For Tough, Tough Boys*, his third collection of short fiction to be published in less than a decade—or fourth, depending on how you count the paired novellas of his American debut, *Cock And Bull*—Self provides more, much more, of his vibrantly caustic prose and his anarchical and florid satiric premises. If Self isn't funnier than he's been before, it's only because it would be impossible. He is flaunting his distinctive gifts again, with riotous, if inconsistent, results. And again Self hasn't much bothered to deepen his engagement with character—that customary virtue of serious fiction—or temper his outrage with a smidgen of empathy.

It's fair to suppose that Self has become the writer he means to be—a truly odd one, frozen in a rich collision with his culture, his influences, perhaps even himself. Blurbists have compared him to both William Burroughs and J.G. Ballard, which certainly captures his aggression as well as his suburban surrealism. His erudite, onomatopoetic prose is often compared to Martin Amis's. Yet none of these comparisons quite encompass the stubborn strangeness of Self. No, strip away his generically British body-disgust and anti-P.C. rants, and the contemporary writer Self most resembles is Nicholson Baker—the Baker of the outlandish fiction, not the tasteful essays. Both writers couple a fractal intensity of attention to the texture of the everyday with a fierce commitment to bizarre conceits that render everyday reality plastic and silly. Sometimes he achieves this in a single passage, as in "Flytopia," where he fantasizes fly-killing expanded into a Hemingwayesque blood sport involving miniature needle-guns:

> The quarry has broken from behind its cover of lint and fluff. It's in the air! And the guns lead the flies, their muzzles moving sharply up, down, obliquely, tracking the erratic paths. A slight pressure on the trigger and the needle flies fast and true, skewering the droning bluebottle precisely through one wing and its bulbous abdomen. Crunch! It falls to the twistpile, bounces, settles down into death, like a slo-mo film of a wildebeest dropping on the veldt.

At best, Self's struggle with these opposed gifts conjures up fiction that alternately boggles, amuses, and horrifies with strobe-like rapidity. At worst it offers punchlines laboriously stretched on a rack of realist detail. *Tough, Tough Toys* has plenty of both.

But what about the disgust, contempt, and alienation that pervades Self's fiction? In his world humans of all classes, professions and races are little more than walking compendiums of the most garishly-unappealing physical and mental characteristics, their emotional responses manifested largely in bodily fluids, their ordinary strivings ludicrous, sad and corrupt. These premises are too heartfelt in Self's work to seem received, yet they're so uniform and, finally, unenlightening that they recede into backdrop. In the foreground is Self's maniacal engagement with his own terrifying imagination. This, rather than his "darkness," is the generator of the real energy in Self's work.

The book opens with "The Rock of Crack As Big as the Ritz," a perfect example of a tale overwhelmed by its premise. Self labors to produce a story under the shadow of this outrageous title, offering a gritty tale of black Londoners intoxicated by money and drugs; it's never much beyond a showcase for his prodigious descriptive powers. "A Story for Europe" also suffers from conceptual overload. It's about a British toddler who speaks his first words in what Self calls "business German," and grinds interminably toward its payoff.

"Flytopia," on the other hand, is a gemlike biological horror story, resembling a desublimated version of Patricia Highsmith's story "The Snail-Watcher." Self never flinches from connecting the dots between repulsion and desire, and he's likely to put the squeamish reader off sex until they've shaken the memory of his special effects.

"Caring, Sharing" is even better: Self unveils an alternate reality where oversized personal golems of pure comfort, called "emotos," have taken the place of sexual partners, eradicating the dangerous highs and lows of real encounters. This deadpan allegory is not startlingly new—science fiction satire experts like Frederik Pohl and Robert Sheckley were delivering similar stuff in the 1950s—but it's performed with tremendous gusto and a peculiar sweetness.

In "The Nonce Prize," the short novella that closes the book, Self revives a black drug dealer featured in "Rock of Crack" for an elaborate and strangely tender tale of a prison short-story-writing contest. Danny, a criminal and addict with a gentle disposition, is framed for a horrific pedophilic murder. In prison Danny is introduced to literature—"Reading burst through his mental partitions, partitions that the crack had effectively shored up, imprisoning his sentience, his rational capacity, behind psychotically patterned drapes"—and is offered the chance to distinguish himself from the sex-offender population by winning a literary competition. As in his novel *Great Apes*, Self reserves his sympathy for the characters he's written into the grimmest and most hopeless corners. Danny's plight, as well as his unexpected spark of literary ambition, provides a merciful hint of human possibility that's missing from the other stories—not that Self forgets to also provide calamitous humor, acidic lit-crit satire and the sound of iron gates clanking shut at the end.

That leaves "Design Faults in the Volvo 760 Turbo" and the title tale: linked stories concerning driving, sex, drugs, and self-hatred. "Design Faults" has all the Ballardian flash but it's this collection's title story which toughens and, yes, even darkens Self's previous vision. The least fantastical tale in the book, it is essentially the interior monologue of Bill Bywater, a drug-abusing psychoanalyst on an insomniacal drive across England. Bill's ruminations are interspersed with his perfunctory inquisition of Mark, a hapless hitchhiker Bill has picked up and whom he is predisposed to loathe. "Tough, Tough Toys" retrieves one of the themes of *Great Apes* and strips it of the camouflage of Swiftian goofing: namely, that misanthropy might just be in the eye of the beholder. This hint of auto-critique (Self would forgive the pun) should fool no one: Self is unrepentant in his own misanthropy, and Bywater is punished for displaying the heretical weakness of self-knowledge.

So, *Tough, Tough Toys* offers the mixture as before. Self is still funny, brilliant, uneven; he still dares you to think him heartless. The only promises he makes have been delivered: fury, hilarity, and chaos. If you're looking for rounded characters in a substantial moral framework Will Self is not your man. He remains, as the name suggests, his own.

—*The New York Times*, 1999

On Two Sentences from Charles D'Ambrosio's "Screenwriter"

With her malady, the ballerina wasn't really into fooling around, but I hoped her new medication, Manerix, which was supposed to dampen some of her desire to burn herself, might also lead by inverse ratio to an upsurge in her passion for old-fashioned sex.

The sentence itself starts out old-fashioned, "malady" confessing the narrator's sentimentality and "lady" doing double-duty to echo "ballerina." Then "into fooling around" turns both jocular and abject—into the story's psych-ward milieu, it introduces a seedy frat boy. This story features cascades of pharmaceutical proper nouns; the one it picks to frame as central, "Manerix," impeaches the narrator's curliqued style of denial as mannerist while also saddling the ballerina-lady with a Man. The ebbing, faintly lush "supposed/dampen some/desire" runs poetical hopefulness up against the shock cut of "burn" but "herself" halfway restores the bogus lyricism, at least as far as the ear's concerned. Then "inverse ration/upsurge" admits a scientific-cum-business-culture bottom line in the narrator's calculations, incompletely repaired by "passion"—especially as "old-fashioned sex" turns smirkily to the language of a hotel room-service menu (old-fashioned double chocolate malted?). Everything in this sentence predicts the speaker's grievous inadequacy to the challenge his cutter-ballerina will soon present: "I'm a screenwriter and my movies gross millions and when I write 'THE CAR BLOWS UP' there's a pretty good chance a real car will indeed blow up, but I wasn't particularly keen on the idea of roasting this woman's cunt over a hot coal." The problem, though he doesn't know it, isn't whether he's "keen" but whether he'd ever know the difference between a real car and the words "THE CAR"; nor would he distinguish a real cunt from "CUNT" (or coal from "COAL" for that matter). This second remarkable sentence implodes: The startling but fatuous comparison between movie violence and the ballerina's mutilation fetish indicts only the speaker inserting it between himself and his anxieties—and he can't keep from bragging about "millions" in the meanwhile.

—*The Stranger,* 2006

Remarks Perhaps of Some Assistance to the Reader of Joseph McElroy's *Ancient History: A Paraphase*

1. At the center of Henry James's writings, forming a sort of hinge in James's shelf, perhaps, stand a handful of tales in which someone contemplates and abides with the mysterious and supervalent absence of a dead or dying writer: "The Lesson of the Master," "The Figure in the Carpet," "The Aspern Papers," "The Middle Years." Joseph McElroy's shelf is double-hinged (at least), with two narratives that resonate with this archetypal plot, in *The Letter Left to Me* and *Ancient History: A Paraphase*. In *Letter*, as in the examples from James, the narrator/protagonist is a vulnerable recipient, a would-be interpreter or medium, left to contend with an opaque address from the dark side. *Ancient History* reverses these charges. It takes the form of an eloquent, garrulous, obsessionally digressive, tender and yet rebuking address to a dead genius.

2. I've just heaved out my effort at categorical description—"a reverse-engineered Jamesian address to the dead"—at great cost. For, like most—all?—of McElroy's fiction, *Ancient History* stymies the categorical impulse to an extreme degree. McElroy's prose, coming on less like a street-gang than like a storm cloud of evocations, intimations, and signifiers, robs the reader of his guidebook and compass. McElroy doesn't shirk clarity, or particularity; he's a great bestower

of intensely clear descriptive and conceptual moments. His writing consists of almost nothing else. But there are few writers less interested in standing to one side, in the role of ringmaster or stage manager, to interject with comparisons, framing remarks, or encompassing descriptions. For a reader hungry for announcements as to what he or she is experiencing, before, during or after the experience of it (and we are all this reader, sometimes, most especially at the fraught start of a new relationship to what fiction can do, the kind a first encounter with a master necessarily entails), a plunge into McElroy can be vertiginous.

3. It is worth it.

4. Another Advertisement for McElroy, while I'm risking those: like most writers who throw up such explosive challenges to ordinary narrative "sense," McElroy's at heart an adamant realist. A realist, that is, in the sense that his discontinuities generate, it seems to me, from a single pure impulse: to sort out what consciousness—our interval as minds trapped inside bodies on planet earth—really feels like, when pushed through the strange machine of language. *Like this, damn it, not like you've been told before!* It is with such self-appointments, rather than any desire to innovate in narrative or language *per se*, that a writer like McElroy sets out on a life's work. And that, in turn, is what makes it (see #3, above) worth it: McElroy is demanding that his machine of language *think*, with each sentence it sets down, about what life on earth really consists of (*hint*: it can be vertiginous).

5. Anyone seeking further such general encouragement ought to consult, as I have, Garth Risk Halberg's eloquent "The Lost Postmodernist" (on *Women and Men*), and the invaluable McElroy festschrifts in both *Electronic Literature* and *Golden Handcuffs Review*—perhaps most especially Mike

Heppner's defiant *envoi* "The Courage of Joseph McElroy," which itself gives a reader courage, too.

6. *Ancient History* consists of an address, then—to whom? The famous dead writer, a suicide, bears a striking resemblance to Norman Mailer (in as much as he gives speeches in put-on accents, runs for office, writes about outer space, divorces spectacularly, punches and bleeds in public, etc.). The narrator, Cy, lives in the same New York apartment building as the Great Dean Man; he's snuck into the famous writer's rooms during the police investigation, there to deliver the text as a monologue both written and spoken, with a brief interruption during which he hides, like Hamlet, behind a curtain. Monologue consisting of what? Of centrifugal meditations on Cy's coming of age in the company of two friends, one—like the narrator—a native of Brooklyn Heights, a city boy. The other, a friend from summers spent fleeing the city, a country boy. The two friends have never met, but may be on the verge of doing so; this possibility is for the narrator strangely destabilizing, and supercharged. So: two sets of men in erratic conjunction. Around them: women, children, careers, fame, public events, the world, outer space. McElroy is a specialist in matters of spatial relation: neighbors upstairs and down, passersby on the street, the eerie distances contained inside nuclear families—generally, he makes a subject of the power of adjacency and proximity in our intimate lives. Yet why should the Mailer-like writer be made to listen—if the dead can listen—to Cy's stories of his two friends? The answer is that for all the intellectual and political force of the addressee's public career—and these forces are respected by Cy as considerable in themselves—this monologuist may be seen to believe that the addressee has missed something. Missed something of life as it is actually lived, missed a

thing as elusive as it is essential. It might even be supposed that it is this absence, this oversight, which has driven the addressee to his suicide.

You thought only the thirsty media cared for you, Dom—to drink you down and piss you out: the meteoric you at San Gennaro taking a flap in the face from one of those flag-exposing twin guinea hens who run Empire Hardware while yours truly watched through the fence with Joseph and Mary and their boy behind me; or you not quite upstaging sweet Seeger on the Hudson babbling huskily over your bourbon to a black news-chick while the skipper and his banjo sang us down the stinking tide; you bleeding right onto a hand-mike a raincollared TV reporter darted to you like an electric prod, against a field of dark Barrio stone the edge of live gunshots one summer night when you were supposed to be not in Spanish Harlem but giving a big birthday party for Dot in Edinburgh; you getting mugged all alone on Brooklyn Bridge a month ago by three kids who it turned out didn't know who you were then or even by name later in some station house; you vomiting on a TV talk show, pointing at the eggy pool and calling it "Magma," and after mopping your mouth and tongue-tip, answering the host's original question straight and mild.

And those excuses posted in the kitchen for any and all callers? And what about "EARTH = SPACE-CRAFT"? That addendum hardly seems an excuse for anything. Would you use it to put off a media representative? Or is it a hot-line excuse for the President of the United States to whom if he phoned you to congratulate you on being you you could say, "Sorry, can't talk now: the earth is a spacecraft." I'm losing you, Dom . . .

7. So, maybe *Ancient History* is a kind of secretly-not-too-late intervention: Mailer was, after all, still alive. McElroy's argument with his titanic soulmate (for I believe McElroy may have felt Mailer to be his rare equal in curiosity about the existential implications of the new technology and media that had altered the scope of our planetary understanding, and, assuming I'm right, I believe he would have been right to feel this). One Brooklyn boy calling to another to reconsider his "Manichean" (the word is McElroy's) exaggerations in favor of a view more grounded in awarenesses of bodies in time, bodies in their places, in rooms and in streets and in nature, and most of all as bodies in relation to others rather than existing in solipsistic outer-space vacuums of ego:

> As on the educational channel last week my small Emma was watching the thin man Mr. Rogers from his own private outer space end his kids' show "You make each day such a special day. You know how. By just your being you," the gossip column Eagle Eye said that your wife Dorothy had got her final decree but that you were sitting around these days enjoying life in your "vast elegant" living room running your slide collection round and round your Carousel projector—mostly "candid news shots involving himself."

McElroy's narrator persistently feels the uncanny call of his life as both a child and a parent, as well as a resident of the specific and intimate cultural space of midcentury Brooklyn: "I take the measure of my Heights street's space partly by my two-sewer line-drive which Hugh Blood backpedaled to catch without coming within thirty yards of the harbor-view dead-end whose lamp-post and black-iron fence were roughly in the same plane as the street window of my parents' third-floor bedroom . . ."

8. A speculation, doomed to be incomplete for many reasons, not least my insufficient grasp of literary theory: Joseph McElroy, with his ecstatic depiction of consciousness as a thing incarnated in the unstable but gorgeous *relations between* humans and their companions here on spaceship earth may be exactly the great writer who most needed— most *needs*—the terminology of what is currently called "Affect Theory" to come along and account for what he's getting at.

> *Ancient History*, then, because of the clarifying urgency of its mode of address, is possibly McElroy's manifesto, a master key, even—the hinge, I called it earlier, of his shelf. At the least, a precursor to his two most daunting (and divergent) masterworks: the densely economical *Plus*, that outer-space deconstruction of the absolutes of solipsistic estrangement, and *Women and Men*, McElroy's symphonic and encompassing depiction of the vast field of human proximities. The way such proximities bind us to the permanent mystery of *presence*—in our bodies, and in time—despite how consciousness and recollection seem precisely designed to escape such limits, much as a space voyager escapes the field of earth. The way our thinking, no matter how abstract, takes place inside, not outside, our lives.
>
> —Introduction to *Ancient History: A Paraphase*, 2014

VI

Thomas Berger and I Have Never Met (Ishiguro, Berger and PKD)

Kazuo Ishiguro

The Remains of the Day, the story of an English butler in pains-taking denial of both his employer's Nazi collusion during World War Two and his own lost hopes for emotional fulfillment, is a stately and melancholic diagnosis of tragic reserve, and a book now taken for granted as a masterpiece by a writer still just in his mid-forties. The plot is negligible: The butler Stevens drives his master Lord Darlington's car across England and ru-minates on the past glories of Darlington Hall, on the death of his father, himself a great butler, and on Miss Kenton, the housekeeper whom he might have once dared to love. The voice of Ishiguro's butler is arduously deferential—perhaps as a Jap-anese émigré raised in British schools, the author was uniquely placed to know how servility infiltrates self, culture, and history. *Remains* is an essay in the use of unreliable narration—not in this case to show a gross comic disparity between the narrator's observations and the reader's perceptions, but instead to detail the workings of self-abnegation.

Few American readers knew how specifically Ishiguro's first two novels, each depicting postwar Japan, were dry runs for *The Remains of the Day*. *A Pale View of Hills* and *An Artist of the Floating World* are brief, elliptical, and precise. *Pale View* is told by a Japanese housewife now living in England, *Artist* by a retired painter and patriarch, but their voices, as they recount lives pierced by hesitation and regret, are similarly mournful, digressive, and finally, unreliable. *Pale View* is the more striking of the two for its barely glimpsed images of horror—but both books disappeared beneath the shadow of Ishiguro's third.

Perhaps, though, *Remains* was not only a consummation, but a dead end. Perhaps Ishiguro felt misunderstood as a historical realist, or was sick of awards—he'd won one for each of his first three books, climaxing in the Booker for *Remains*. Whatever the reason, he threw off the shackles of expectation and acclaim with the sprawling, brilliant, and exasperating fabulation *The Unconsoled*. The dreamlike epic of Ryder, a celebrated composer struggling to pull off a concert tour stop in a surreal European city, *Unconsoled* forcibly insists on comparison to Kafka. The amnesiac Ryder meets with every possible frustration as he attempts to check into his hotel and find a quiet moment to practice for his performance: accusatory relatives, manipulative journalists, and drunken rival musicians. Dozens of minor characters are given five- and ten-page speeches, in set pieces alternately hilarious, harrowing, and stultifying. *The Unconsoled* is at once a great psychological dystopia and the most hilariously distended entry yet in the "booktours-are-hell" genre. It's also a riveting instance of a highly controlled writer challenging his own methods at every level of his narrative—though aligned with Ishiguro's previous work as a study in regret and complicity. One is tempted, finally, to call *The Unconsoled* promising, for it shows its author pushing towards another, completely different kind of masterpiece.

—*The Salon.com Reader's Guide to Contemporary Authors*, 2000

The Butler Did It

Kazuo Ishiguro is much weirder than I think you think he is, and I want to find a way to say how, since *When We Were Orphans* is his weirdest book yet. I'm not sure it's as unified a conception as *The Remains of the Day* or *The Unconsoled*, but then, when I had a chance to weigh in on *The Unconsoled*, I leaned back from that book's brilliance a little—a year later I think it's a masterpiece. *The Unconsoled* was infuriating in many ways—imagine Henry James and Franz Kafka collaborating on a seven-hundred page description of a painting by Giorgio Di Chirico—but it aches in memory like a ruined monument.

But wait, you say: Wasn't Ishiguro the Anthony Hopkins-stuffy-butler-Booker-Prize guy? That's him. And didn't everybody ignore the book that came after? Not exactly. *The Unconsoled*'s defiance of follow-up expectations—and its exhausting where-are-the-paragraph-breaks too-late modernism—earned some tepid reviews and (I'm guessing) disappointing sales, but I know a lot of patient readers who've taken to it. The book felt like a repudiation of *The Remains of the Day*'s popular reception—Ishiguro may have been irritated that he'd been taken for a realist, that the feebly tragic love story and historical particulars had gotten the attention instead of his meticulous use of unreliable narration to explore a relentlessly, if almost subliminally, fantasizing consciousness. Denial's habit

of decorating the world with splendid but pernicious nonsense—
that's his subject. I also think the butler's problems with his dad
were more important to Ishiguro than the thwarted romance
the film adaptation underlined. In the two books that follow
he's exhibited a belief that romance and sex are tiny, helpless
figures dancing on a precipice beside a sea of familial and parental craziness.

I go on about the difference between *The Remains of the Day*
and *The Unconsoled* because *When We Were Orphans* feels like an
attempt to bridge the two. We're returned from the Mitteleu-
ropean shadows and fog of *The Unconsoled* to the ostensibly real
and historically fraught cities of London and Shanghai between
the World Wars, recalling not only *The Remains of the Day* but
also J. G. Ballard's *Empire of the Sun* and Ishiguro's two earliest novels. *Orphans*'s narrator and lead, Christopher Banks, has
a Ballardian Shanghai childhood, playing with an expatriate
Japanese kid against a backdrop of strife. He's orphaned at nine
by his parents' vanishing, then whisked to England, where he
makes good on childhood fantasies by becoming a "celebrated
detective" (impossible, you'll see, not to put that in quotes).
Later he returns to Shanghai to rescue his parents and punish
their kidnappers. The Detective's voice is as agonizingly seemly
as the butler's was in *Remains*, and, like the butler's, is full of
awkward hesitations and ellipses that suggest unconfronted
emotional and factual material. Only the material may be a little stranger in the Detective's case.

Orphan's closest parallel to *The Unconsoled*, to put it simply, is
that the events in the narration *don't make sense*. This realization
comes gradually, as the novel's unruffled surface disguises any
lapses in logic. The Shanghai Boy Detective's story is strewn
with gaps, but after all it is *a kid's memory*, hanging first on a
fantasy about a scary manservant who collects monkeys' hands
and magically transforms them into spiders, second on a series

of *What Maisie Knew* hints that Mom is having an affair with the mysterious Uncle Philip. Flash forward: Back in England, the Grown Detective is gathering accolades and pining, ever so politely, for love. Prewar London here has a very Anthony Powell feel, full of cocktail parties and abrupt marriages. Among the adults, the narration's solipsistic undertone is harder to ignore.

What the hell kind of detective is the Detective, anyway? He's got Sherlock Holmes's gift for effortlessly making sense of baffling crimes and a Holmesian obsession with ferreting out the insidious, evil secret that links all crime and—who knows?—perhaps all human misery. But he's as humble and normal as Dr. Watson. And about as plausible as the two rolled together. Which is to say, as likely as a boy's fantasy that "detection" can control or dismiss the chaos of adult experience—in this case, war, parental sexuality, parental death. Ishiguro might almost be satirizing Andrew Vachss, whose detective rescues abused children with a protests-too-much regularity that begs for Freudian interpretation. Or remember *The Seven-Percent Solution*, where a fictional Freud carefully guides Holmes to the realization that his nemesis Moriarty is really only his mother's secret lover?

The fact that the book is a phantasmagoria becomes undeniable after The Detective's return to Shanghai. Ishiguro's at his best here, uncorking the seamless but wild shifts of emphasis, and the gently titled camera angles, which made *The Unconsoled* such a fastidious piece of surrealism. The Detective is caught behind enemy lines in the Sino-Japanese war in a ludicrously garbled quest for the "house of the blind actor, Yeh Chen," where, he's come to believe, his parents are still being held, over twenty years after their kidnapping. He's also on a hunt for the mysterious Japanese POW known as Yellow Snake. Throughout he's dogged by a sycophantic officer named Grayson, whose confidence in our hero is such that he's preemptively arranged a public festival for the celebration of the parents' rescue. Holy doppelgänger, Commissioner! Grayson is the civilian name of Batman's sidekick, the Boy Wonder. And Batman, come to think of it, is another analogue—a parent-avenging detective living in a world tailored to function as his personal psychodramatic morality play.

I'm spoiling the plot next, so put your fingers in your ears and hum real loud if plot's your thing. Any last doubts as to the grip of childhood material on adult experience—or dream—are trashed when the Japanese expat playmate reappears in a soldier's uniform, Yellow Snake is revealed to be a close family friend, and the Detective's mother turns out to have been kept as a sex slave of a barbarian warlord, like Barbara Stanwyck in Frank Capra's *The Bitter Tea of General Yen*, or Natalie Wood in *The Searchers*. Even if I've got the sources wrong, I'm namedropping to suggest what Ishiguro's upper-crusty tone and pedigree seem to deny: that pop-cultural archetypes murmur under the surface of *When We Were Orphans*. And that a smoothed-over intertextuality in Ishiguro's last two novels is part of what's made them hard to get, and part of what makes Ishiguro weirder, as I said, than you might have thought. I'm still not sure whether or not I think the book completely works, but I'll say for certain that I don't know of another famous novelist I so wished worked faster, or who I think is moving in a more encouragingly odd direction.

—*Bookforum*, 2000

Footnote on Ishiguro

Some of these pieces embarrass me. Mainly the book reviews. I think they're scrupulous critical forays, and I certainly never took shortcuts in the required reading, or falsified my assessments— and that's why I'm proud enough to help Chris Boucher assemble them here for reprinting, rather than letting them evaporate into the ether. What embarrasses me is the tone, especially in the earliest pieces, those dating back to 1999 and first years of the new millennium. The two entries written for the *Salon.com Reader's Guide to Contemporary Authors*—Ishiguro and Berger— are good examples. I was new to writing literary criticism, actually new to non-fiction of any kind, and the tone I located came from my earliest impressions of what criticism should sound like. It was borrowed from reading Anthony Burgess's *99 Novels* and *But Do Blondes Prefer Gentlemen?*, and Kingsley Amis's *New Maps of Hell*, and Colin Wilson's *The Outsider*, and to a certain extent from growing up reading Updike's book reviews in *The New Yorker* and Andrew Sarris's film reviews in *The Village Voice*. It was a pretty stuffy borrowed tone, to be honest.

Writing about Ishiguro and Berger a second time you see me groping my way to something a bit more relaxed. Whether I overtly introduce a personal anecdote or make reference to a personal obsession, my approach is anyway more personal, more willingly subjective. My thinking is also, mercifully, couched in a (somewhat) less posh and tortured syntax. On the whole, that's the approach that pleases me most, and the one that prevails eventually. While the casually-sidling-up-to-you-on-the-barstool approach can certainly become wearisome (did I really have to talk about my smashed fingernail to review Cronenberg's *Consumed*?), it has the permanent and renewable virtue of dissipating any air of bogus objectivity. Books are reviewed as they are written, by individuals on or off their game, in or out of their comfort zone, kidding or not kidding themselves about what they understand and control (always some of both, of course). The difference is that the review is written very quickly. You know how college students write papers? Yeah, like that. I think you can count on this. Whereas the book is beneficiary (ha!) of years of rumination, stalling, reservations, well-manicured self-loathing, and the layering-on of gloss, as on the hull of a sailboat.

Despite gloss, sailboats sometimes sink. Maybe the gloss was too heavy. But I digress.

The thing I wanted to say about Ishiguro is this: the tone is better in the second piece, but the piece is demonstrably silly. Why should dissipating an air of bogus objectivity be such a good idea? Because objectivity is bogus: reviewers bring stuff to the table. Blindspots, baggage, peeves, leanings, agendas— selves. What I brought to *When We Were Orphans* was a pet theory, about Batman. The reason I know it is wrong is because one day in London, years later, I sat at Kaz Ishiguro's dining room table, and brought up the theory I'd aired out in this piece (which he sort-of recalled, or pretended to). Then Kaz told me he'd never had Batman in mind, and had no special interest or fondness for Batman. He was very nice about it.

Why, then, you ask, am I reprinting a piece that I have now called silly and wrong? Because I still feel that in writing the piece, I arrived somewhere I like, and like sharing: it is a layer of gloss I laid on someone else's boat.

High Priest of the Paranoids

Philip K. Dick is a necessary writer, in the someone-would-have-had-to-invent-him sense. He's American literature's Lenny Bruce. Like Bruce, he can seem a pure product of the 1950s (and, as William Carlos Williams warned, *pure products of America go crazy*), one whose iconoclastic maladaption to the conformity of that era seems to shout ahead to our contemporary understanding. And, as with Bruce, the urge to claim him for any cultural role—Hippie, Postmodern Theorist, Political Dissident, Metaphysical Guru—is defeated by the contradictions generated by a singular and irascible persona. Still, no matter what problems he presents, Dick wielded a sardonic yet heartbroken acuity about the plight of being alive in the twentieth century, one which makes him a lonely hero to the readers who cherish him.

Dick's great accomplishment, on view in the twenty-one stories collected here, was to turn the materials of American pulp-style science fiction into a vocabulary for a remarkably personal vision of paranoia and dislocation. It's a vision as yearning and anxious as Kafka's, if considerably more homely. It's also as funny. Dick is a kitchen-sink surrealist, gaining energy and invention from a mad piling of pulp SF tropes—and clichés—into his fiction: time travel, extrasensory powers, tentacled aliens, ray guns, androids and robots. He loves fakes and simulacra as much as he fears them: illusory worlds, bogus religions, placebo drugs, impersonated police, cyborgs. Tyrannical world governments and ruined dystopian cities are default settings here—not only have Orwell and Huxley been taken as givens in Dick's worlds, so have Old Masters of genre SF like Clifford Simak, and Robert Heinlein and A. E. Van Vogt. American SF by the mid-1950s was a kind of jazz, stories built by riffing on stories. The conversation they formed might be forbiddingly hermetic, if it hadn't quickly been incorporated by Rod Serling and Marvel Comics and Steven Spielberg (among many others), and become one of the prime vocabularies of our age.

Dick is one of the first writers to use these materials with self-conscious absurdity—a "look at what I found!" glee which prefigures that of writers like Kurt Vonnegut, George Saunders, and Mark Leyner. Yet having set his characters loose inside his Rube Goldbergian inventions, Dick detailed their emotional abreactions with meticulous sympathy. His people eke out their days precariously, never knowing whether disaster is about to come at the level of the psychological, the ontological, or the pharmacological. Even his tyrannical world dictators glance neurotically over their shoulders, wondering if some higher authority is about to cause their reality to crumble or in some other way be exposed as fake. Alternately, they could always simply be arrested. Dick earned his collar as High Priest of the Paranoids the old-fashioned way: in his fiction, everyone is *always* about to be arrested.

The second set of motifs Dick employed was more prosaic: a perfectly typical 1950s obsession with the images of the suburbs, the consumer, the bureaucrat, and with the plight of small men struggling under the imperatives of capitalism. If Dick, as a bearded, drug-taking Californian, might have seemed a candidate for Beatdom (and in fact did hang out with the San Francisco poets), his persistent engagement with the main materials of his culture kept him from floating off into reveries of escape. It links him instead to writers like Richard Yates, John Cheever, and Arthur Miller (The British satirist John Sladek's bulls-eye Dick parody was titled "Solar Shoe Salesman.") Dick's treatment of his "realist" material can seem oddly cursory, as though the pressing agenda of his paranoiac fantasizing, which would require him to rip the façade off, drop the atomic bomb onto, or otherwise renovate ordinary reality, made that reality's actual *depiction* unimportant. But no matter how many times Dick unmasks or destroys the Black Iron Prison of American suburban life, he always returns to it. Unlike the characters in William S. Burroughs, Richard Brautigan, or Thomas Pynchon, Dick's characters, in novels and stories written well into the 1970s, go on working for grumbling bosses, carrying briefcases, sending interoffice memos, tinkering with cars in driveways, sweating alimony payments, and dreaming of getting away from it all—even when they've already emigrated to Mars.

Though Dick's primary importance is as a novelist, no single volume better encompasses his accomplishment than this collection, which doubles as a kind of writer's autobiography, a growth chart. From *Twilight Zone*–ish social satires ("Roog," "Foster, You're Dead") to grapplings with a pulp-adventure chase-scene mode which was already weary before Dick picked it up ("Paycheck," "Imposter"), the earliest pieces nevertheless declare obsessions and locate methods that would serve for thirty-odd years. In "Adjustment Team" and "Autofac," we begin to meet the Dick of the great sixties novels, his characters defined by how they endure more than by any triumph over circumstance. "Upon the Dull Earth" presents an eerie path-not-taken into Gothic fantasy, one that reads like a Shirley Jackson outtake. Then, there is the Martian-farmer-émigré mode, which always showed Dick at his best: "Precious Artifact" and "A Game of Unchance." Later, in "Faith of Our Fathers" we encounter the

Dick of his late masterpiece *A Scanner Darkly*, working with the *I Ching* at one elbow and the *Physicians' Desk Reference* at the other. "Faith of Our Fathers," together with "The Electric Ant" and "A Little Something for Us Tempunauts," offers among the most distilled and perfect statements of Dick's career: black-humor politics melting away to Gnostic theology, theology to dire solipsism, solipsism to despair, then love. And back again.

If Dick thrived on the materials of SF, he was less than thrilled with the fate of being *only* an SF writer. Whether or not he was ready for the world, or the world ready for him, he longed for a respectable recognition, and sought it variously and unsuccessfully throughout his life. In fact, he wrote eight novels in a somber realist mode during the 1950s and early 1960s, a shadow career known mainly to the agents who failed to place the books with various New York publishers. It's stirring to wonder what Dick might have done with a wider professional opportunity, but there's little doubt that his SF grew more interesting for being fed by the frustrated energies of his "mainstream" ambition. Possibly, too, a restless streak in Dick's personality better suited him for the outsider-artist status he tasted during his lifetime. Dick was obsessed with stigma, with mutation and exile, and with the recurrent image of a spark of life or love arising from unlikely or ruined places: robot pets, discarded appliances, autistic children. SF was Dick's ruined site. Keenly engaged with his own outcast identity, he worked brilliantly from the margins (in this regard, it may be possible to consider the story "The King of the Elves" as an allegory of Dick's career). "Sci-Fi Writer" became a kind of *identity politics* for Dick, as did "Drug Burnout" and "Religious Mystic"—these during the period when identity politics weren't otherwise the province of white American males. Here, from an introduction written for *Golden Man*, a collection of stories assembled in 1980, Dick reminisces:

In reading the stories in this volume you should bear in mind that most were written when SF was so looked down upon that it virtually was not there, in the eyes of all America. This was not funny, the derision felt toward SF writers. It made our lives wretched. Even in Berkeley—or especially in Berkeley—people would say, "But are you writing anything serious?" To select SF writing as a career was an act of self-destruction; in fact, most *writers*, let alone most other people, could not even conceive of someone considering it. The only non-SF writer who ever treated me with courtesy was Herbert Gold, who I met at a literary party in San Francisco. He autographed a file card to me this way: "To a colleague, Philip K. Dick." I kept the card until the ink faded and was gone, and I still feel grateful to him for this charity . . . So in my head I have to collate the experience in 1977 of the mayor of Metz shaking hands with me at an official city function, [Dick had just received an arts medal in France] and the ordeal of the Fifties when Kleo and I lived on ninety dollars a month, when we could not even pay the fine on an overdue library book, and when we were literally living on dog food. But I think you should know this—specifically, in case you are, say, in your twenties and rather poor and perhaps becoming filled with despair, whether you are an SF writer or not, whatever you want to make of your life. There can be a lot of fear, and often it is a justified fear. People do starve in America. I have seen uneducated street girls survive horrors that beggar description. I have seen the faces of men whose brains have been burned-out by drugs, men who could still think enough to be able to realize what had happened to them; I watched their clumsy attempt to weather that which cannot be weathered . . . Kabir, the sixteenth century Sufi poet, wrote, "If you have not lived through something, it is not true." So live through it; I mean, go all the way to the end. Only then can it be understood, not along the way."

The conflations in this passage are so perfectly typical—SF writer and uneducated street girl, Dick's suffering and yours. His self-mocking humility at Herbert Gold's "charity" is balanced against that treasured, ink-fading file card: a certainty that value resides in the smallest gestures, in scraps of empathy. Dick was a writer doomed to be himself, and the themes of his most searching and personal writing of the 1970s and early 1980s surface helplessly in even the earliest stories: the fragility of connection, the allure and risk of illusion, the poignancy of artifacts, and the necessity of carrying on in the face of the demoralizing brokenness of the world. Dick famously posed two questions—"What is human?" and "What is real?"—and then sought to answer them in any framework he thought might suffice. By the time of his death he'd tried and discarded many dozen such frameworks. The questions remained. It is the absurd beauty of their asking that lasts.

On a personal note, I'm proud to make this introduction. Dick's is a voice that matters to me, a voice I love. He's one of my life's companions. As Bob Dylan sang of Lenny Bruce, *he's gone, but his spirit lingers on and on.* In that spirit, let Phil have the final word here. Again, from the *Golden Man* essay:

What helps for me—if help comes at all—is to find the mustard seed of the funny at the core of the horrible and futile. I've been researching ponderous and solemn theological matters for five years now, for my novel-in-progress, and much of the Wisdom of the World has passed from the printed page and into my brain, there to be processed and secreted out in the form of more words: words in, words out, and a brain in the middle wearily trying to determine the meaning of it all. Anyhow, the other night I started on the article on Indian Philosophy in the *Encyclopedia of Philosophy* . . . the time was 4 A.M.; I was exhausted . . . and there, at the heart of this solemn article, was this: "The Buddhist idealists used various arguments to show that perception does not yield knowledge of external objects distinct from the percipient . . . The external world supposedly consists of a number of different objects, but they can be known as different only because there are different sorts of experiences 'of' them. Yet if the experiences are thus distinguishable, there is no need to hold the superfluous hypothesis of external objects . . ."

That night I went to bed laughing. I laughed for an hour. I am still laughing. Push philosophy and theology to their ultimate and what do you wind up with? Nothing. Nothing exists. As I said earlier, there is only one way out: seeing it all as ultimately funny. Kabir, who I quoted, saw dancing and joy and love as ways out, too; and he wrote about the sound of "the anklets on the feet of an insect as it walks." I would like to hear that sound; perhaps if I could my anger and fear, and my high blood pressure, would go away.

Thanks to Pamela Jackson, whose 1999 dissertation "The World Philip K. Dick Made," helped clarify my thinking in writing this introduction.

—Introduction to *The Selected Stories of Philip K. Dick*, 2013

The Man Whose Teeth Were All Exactly Alike

If literary history has an undertow in the form of neglected works, then the undertow of the undertow is unpublished writing: How many hundreds of interesting novels live only in attics? Yet how could we ever lay hands on such material, let alone sort it for value?

During his lifetime, Philip K. Dick's wrenching and hilarious science fiction novels earned him cult status. After his death in 1982, his work leapt into the pantheon of American literature, bringing with it biographies, letters, dissertations. Now comes *The Man Whose Teeth Were All Exactly Alike*, one of a staggering *eleven* naturalistic novels Dick wrote and shelved from 1955 to 1960, before turning completely to genre writing. Set in Marin County, California, the book is a gently savage minor-key comedy of small-town manners, against a backdrop of middle-class malaise and real estate values. At a time when our culture seems transfixed by yearning projections of '50's life—*Mad Men* and the slick adaptation of Richard Yates's *Revolutionary Road*—here's an uneasy tonic brew of the real thing.

The relations between Dick's husbands and wives are unbearably vivid and sad; the sense of an old set of manners giving way to the new, a harbinger of the decade to come. Dick captured middle-class conformity just as its neurotic undercurrent sizzled to the surface. The counterculture that rose in reply was one Dick—like Pynchon and Donald Barthelme and others—would require surrealistic means to depict. Yet this book shows that before Dick was the "poor-man's Pynchon" he was the poor-man's Richard Yates, though no one could possibly have known it at the time.

—O, 2009

To *Ubik*

Ubik, short for ubiquity, a kind of medicinal eternity
Available in pharmacies, an aerosol product,
Ubik, you yourself play at being little more than a discontinued
       item.
Though disguised as a clown or a jape, as ephemera, an eruption
From the pop-junk stratum,
you're an American Book of the Dead.
You embarrass your readers and get under their skins forever—
You embarrassed your author!
It was he who disguised you as a clown,
Your characters in costumes unbearably larkish,
Your women all described tits-first, yet—
Your author found himself condemned to wonder
Whether this book, above all his others, might hold the key
To his lifework, to his life, to the universe.
Your hero's an everyman—Joe Chip,
A good egg, stolid and homely as they come.
Your basic motif's as sturdy, as hoary! even,
As Bierce's "Occurrence at Owl Creek Bridge," or
O'Brien's The Third Policeman. *Yet unfolded, as it is,*
Within your satiric consumer paranoia,
Of rival corporate psychic-spies dependent
On over-the-counter entropy-reversal balm

You're positively Pataphysical!
(In fact, were ratified as such, by the French,
A nation better at theorizing the surreal
Than at creating it themselves,
That best left to Austrians, Swiss, Russians,
Or American pulp writers—nearly anyone else.)
Ubik, in our hour of need, you restore our sense
That the living and the awakened dead
have more in common than not:
Both lost in time, and permeable
To selves not ourselves.

—Black Clock, 2015

Life After Wartime

When I first moved to Berkeley in 1984 I was driven to walk in the footsteps of my recently-departed hero, Philip K. Dick. Of course, as a lifelong New Yorker, I had my Californias a little mixed up. Dick had for the last decade of his life been living five hours south in the other California—in an anonymous apartment complex in the Republican suburban and tract house haven of Orange County, not far from the birthplace site (and now the museum) of his bête noire, Richard M. Nixon. In southern California, in 1984, I could have easily searched out members of the circle of writers and other friends who'd surrounded him in those last years, in lieu of meeting the man I'd originally meant to visit in person when I planned to go to California in the first place, a chance I'd been cheated of by his death.

In eccentric, paranoid, radical Berkeley, Dick's natural spiritual home, and the place to which I was drawn for a variety of personal reasons, Dick's traces were fainter. They were the traces of his childhood and early adulthood, his apprentice years as a writer. These I sought avidly, though they were hardly legible shrines, more the random markers of an only slightly out-of-the-ordinary existence. I lived for five years just a few blocks from the first home Dick owned, in the early 1950s: a tiny, ramshackle house in an unglamorous neighborhood near the waterfront, known as the Berkeley Flats. It was there that Dick wrote his first stories and novels while still employed at the only respectable occupation of his life, unless you count writing: working at a store called University Radio, a busy hive of a place, which sold and repaired radios and record players and early televisions, as well as records. Dick's employer there was a sort of surrogate father, a beleaguered figure of kindly but irascible authority, who became a model for many of the sometimes gruff but always well-meaning small business owners Dick's readers find scattered throughout his novels.

Dick's lifelong love of not just music but of the ephemera of record collecting began in that shop, as did his admiration for repairmen and tinkerers, the sort of guys who worked in the basement of University Radio. Dick himself was just a shopkeeper's assistant—a shelver of records, he also swept the Shattuck Avenue sidewalk in front of the store, just like Stuart McConchie, the character he introduces in the first lines of *Dr. Bloodmoney*. The building was still in evidence there on Shattuck, though the business was closed. Two doors away a rival music shop was still in operation, one with long old-fashioned display windows much like the ones described in *Dr. Bloodmoney*. It was easy, visiting there, to picture those scenes of Dick's early life.

Still in business as well on nearby San Pablo Avenue was the Lucky Dog Petshop. There, Dick confessed in an essay, he sometimes bought horsemeat intended for animal use, to feed himself and his wife, during his starving writer days in the tiny one-bedroom house. Berkeley is of course home to a famous university—where Dick took a few classes and then dropped or was kicked out—and the Bay Area more generally encompasses several institutes of scientific research and weapons development, places like Livermore, where a Doctor Bruno Bluthgeld might be expected to work. Dick distrusted academics and expatriate scientists and weapons developers, along with pretty much all authority figures, and in his writing he consistently plays these types against the sort of common-man protagonist he adores—the Stuart McConchie type of worker, striving to get ahead, or the ingenious artisans, like Andrew Gill with his hand-rolled cigarettes.

Finally, across the Bay and north of San Francisco, is Marin County, a geologically lush peninsula dotted with small towns, which provides the pastoral post-apocalyptic setting for the latter two-thirds of *Dr. Bloodmoney*. Dick himself lived in Marin in a kind a rural fantasy for a few years, during which he suffered a violently unhappy marriage to an intellectually remarkable woman, and wrote the greatest sequence of masterpieces of his career in an exceptionally brief time. *Dr. Bloodmoney* is one of those masterpieces, and his churning ambivalence about Marin County informs the book at every level. No surprise there, for Dick was an artist who transmuted his ambivalent feelings into metaphor and paradox with the obsessive ingenuity of a prisoner devising repeated escapes from a prison whose walls he'll never see the outside of.

Many of these fragments of Dick's Bay Area life contribute to the setting for *Dr. Bloodmoney*, which is at once one of the most realistic and the most absurd of Dick's non-realist novels. Like *Time Out of Joint* and *The Man in the High Castle*, two novels that precede it, *Bloodmoney* contains elements of the unpublished realist novels Dick was writing around the same time, a relationship exemplified by Dick's use of the prosaic details of the Bay Area settings, including the names of streets and buildings. It is typical of Dick that he located his capacity to write about Berkeley, San Francisco and Marin most affectionately in a novel in which he first destroys these places (along with the rest of the world) in nuclear war.

Dr. Bloodmoney stands apart from all Dick's other novels in addressing this fear of atomic or nuclear destruction directly, rather than leaving it implicitly or explicitly hanging over the heads of the characters, as it was hanging over the heads of all Americans, all human beings, during the Cold War era in which Dick's sensibility was formed. (Never mind that we ought to be equally worried now; collective global anxieties have drifted to other metaphors). Nuclear fear both haunts and activates Dick's imagination, as it did Bob Dylan's, and Rod Serling's, and Stanley Kubrick's, and so many others. It must have taken a leap of courage for Dick to depict the bomb, as he has, unmaking the streets of the city of his youth. These early chapters are delicate, scrupulous, and painful. Yet it must also have been a relief to go ahead and at last have it done, to not have the terror hanging over his head. Despite the threat still represented by Hoppy Harrington's power-drunk murders and manipulations, and by Dr. Bruno Bluthgeld's continuing uncanny ability to bring disasters into being by confusing his inner torment with outer reality, the book depicts a post-apocalyptic Marin County world that is relatively sunny. The radiation-spawned freaks are regarded with a gentle curiosity which again conceals an eternally unresolved ambivalence—are the highly-intelligent mutant rats better hunted down as a Darwinian threat to man, or should they be employed as bookkeepers in offices?

In Marin, Dick portrays a community which is as tattered and fragile as his Martian colonies, yet never as desolate or nihilistic. Perhaps this is because he was in those years in that very same place exploring the possibility of a connection to a natural environment—to dogs and sheep and trees and mushrooms—which, while indifferent to man, might contain some measure of the grace of the music and writing he previously regarded as his only solace and redemption. As for music and writing, those are embodied in the novel in Walt Dangerfield, the lonely disc jockey circling the earth in his satellite, his broken transmissions offering samples of the solace of culture, of wit and irony and savoir faire to the dismembered world below. Dangerfield, whose wife died earlier, leaving him isolated in his satellite, is a flattering and self-pitying portrait of the artist, and he's also for Dick a characteristic image of a man riven forever from his natural female companion. Dick was born a twin, but his sister died at birth, and he would be forever haunted by the thwarted possibility of completion by a feminine other. In later books this yearning would take on galactic or theological overtones, but as embodied in Dangerfield it remains humbly mortal.

Of course, if you suspect his ambivalence about this possibility of male-female symbiosis, look no further than the mutant twins Edie and Bill Keller, one, the male, embedded in the other, the female, and bitterly wishing for escape. These twins, while hardly the villains that Hoppy and Bluthgeld represent, are certainly a repository for Dick's uneasiness about birth, childhood, symbiosis, and much else that is common in nature, including earthworms and owls. I'll say it again: Dick's self-contradicting tendency is his genius for paradox, and it is everywhere in *Bloodmoney*. Take Stuart McConchie, a black man in racist America, who is himself first distinguished by his fear and prejudice of Hoppy Harrington. Yet Dick will turn this irony on its head by justifying Stuart's suspicion of Hoppy: he's certainly aware of Hoppy's potential for corruption. Another instance is Bluthgeld/Bloodmoney himself, who makes the mistake, early in the book, of believing that he in his sickness is responsible for the catastrophe: we share Dick's horror that Bluthgeld solipsistically takes the explosions personally when everyone else is suffering too. Yet on a symbolic level, Bluthgeld types are the architects of the war economy that terrorizes the world. And anyway, Dick contradicts himself in the later chapters, when he shows us that Bluthgeld somehow does have the ability to create explosions with his mind. Which is true? Either way, on rereading, Bluthgeld's delusion that he is helping to heal the city when, after the fallout settles, he stands at Berkeley's waterfront and directs the movements of the straggling swimmers, becomes unbearably poignant instead of merely ridiculous. What's more, Dick slightly undermines his commitment to his post-apocalyptic premise by hinting that the bombs might not have even fallen, that we might instead be dwelling in some twilight world of collective subjective catastrophe, all manipulated by a warped dreaming brain. In this hint, Dick forecasts *Ubik* and *A Maze of Death*, his late masterpieces of collective solipsism—and glances back to his earlier novel of Berkeley's destruction, *Eye in the Sky*.

Dr. Bloodmoney is very much a novel about fear, and like the game of Rocks/Scissors/Paper that the settlement's children are shown playing, fear has infectious fluency in the lives of the characters: Gill fears McConchie, McConchie fears—and loathes—Bluthgeld, Bluthgeld fears Hoppy, Hoppy fears Bill Keller, who speaks to him in frightening voices. Barnes, the newcomer who has become Bonnie Keller's latest lover, fears Bill Keller too, and so in a way, does Doctor Stockstill. Anyone who learns of him fears Bill Keller, and yet who does Bill Keller, who can speak with the dead, fear? He fears Bonnie Keller—his momma.

By the time he wrote his own afterword to *Bloodmoney*, Philip K. Dick had forgotten his empathy for Bruno Bluthgeld. He declares Bluthgeld inhuman. This is another contradiction, but in this case you should trust the song, not the singer. Dick also claims that Stuart is the novel's main character, and the character he feels closest to, because of their alliance as sweepers of Shattuck Avenue's sidewalk. This is touching, but Dick's wrong again (I suspect he only read the opening chapter before writing his afterword, trusting his faulty memory to reconstruct the plot). The novel's main character, if it has one, isn't Stuart or Hoppy or Bloodmoney—nor is it the admirable and charismatic Walt Dangerfield or Andrew Gill. It's Bonnie Keller, whose irritable sexual vitality both frightens and thrills Dick, and whose fitfulness about the agrarian paradise that Marin promises to become probably closely matches that of her creator. Dick was, ultimately, a city boy, an apartment dweller, and despite the dreamy pastoral possibilities glimpsed in *Bloodmoney*, the prospect of a full recovery from Bloodmoney's bombs is only gained with the return to San Francisco and Berkeley, to the stridency and chaos and risk of a life among those who wanted to build and invent and create a new culture, one capable of constructing universities to drop out of and deplore, one capable of binding words into books and pressing music onto vinyl discs and perhaps even one capable of designing weapons and advertising. If the majority of Dick's novels prove he's not on the side of capitalism, *Bloodmoney*, charming as it may be, proves he's not wholly on the side of the mushrooms and earthworms either.

Leonard Cohen sang: "There is a war between the rich and poor/a war between the odd and the even/there is a war between the ones who say there is a war/and the ones who say there isn't." In *Dr. Bloodmoney*, Dick decided, with typical lack of resolve, to take a side: For once, he'd declare for certain that there was a war. And yet, maybe there wasn't. And anyway, maybe if there was it would lead to something beautiful. By unleashing his written violence on the streets of his own city and killing the boss he loved at University Music and then puzzling sincerely over the results, by allowing Bonnie Keller to fuck every guy who walked into town and not punishing her as he might have wished to, by letting Walt Dangerfield and Edie and Bill Keller and Stuart McConchie and Andrew Gill all survive their brush with Bluthgeld and Hoppy, Dick was as generous as he was likely ever to be in the 1960s: generous with his world, and with himself. By the time he was as hopeful again, it was a mystical hopefulness, enlivened by the strange and terrifying glimpses of a higher power he'd begun to experience in the early '70s. In

1964, he was still able to see the galaxy in a grain of fallout, or in the prospect of a mutated rat playing a noseflute.

—Afterword to the Italian edition of *Dr. Bloodmoney*, 2008

Thomas Berger

What if there were a great American novelist with a vision so diverse, timeless and hilarious that he'd been mistaken by literary culture for an irrelevant virtuoso? That's the fate of Thomas Berger, apparently. Though his popular and critical heyday was the '70s, when he was meaninglessly grouped with the "black humorists," Berger's focus grew through the '80s. But by the end of that decade he'd mostly lost his audience and been taken for granted by critics, his image blurred somewhat by two film adaptations, one good (*Little Big Man*, faithfully Bergeresque but credited to the director and star), and one awful (*Neighbors*, with John Belushi and Dan Aykroyd a casting trainwreck—Donald Sutherland and Alan Arkin might have worked).

No summary can do justice to the extraordinarily various assignments Berger has given himself: to visit each genre in turn (Western: *Little Big Man*, Detective: *Who is Teddy Villanova?*, Dystopia: *Regiment of Women*, Arthurian legend: *Arthur Rex*, etc.), to span his career with an anti-Updikean sequence featuring a lumpen protagonist at different life stages (the four Reinhardt novels), to understand and demolish existentialist justifications for murder (*Killing Time*, *Meeting Evil*), and, whatever else, always to advance his lifelong exercise in deadpan eloquence. The fact that Berger is often painfully funny isn't incidental, but central to his accomplishment. Scenes in

Berger's fiction never unfold logically, but instead are warped this way and that by the fleeting and paradoxical responses of his main characters who, though tormented by guilt and experience, remain yearning and gullible and oddly angelic.

Three of Berger's first five novels featured his hopeless alter-ego Reinhart—the books are brilliant, each encompassing a new aspect of American life—but typical of Berger, Reinhart seemed a different character each time out. The two non-Reinharts were *Little Big Man*, the encyclopedic Western most usually acclaimed by readers unfamiliar with Berger, and *Killing Time*, which was poorly received but now seems Berger's early masterpiece—Jim Thompson noir as done by an American Flaubert.

Neighbors, in 1980, was a watershed book (as well as a comic summit). There Berger refined a theme of malice, guilt and victimization that had been emergent in his work. This exploration produced dark masterworks in *The Houseguest* (1988) and *Meeting Evil* (1982). *Houseguest* refracts the hostility of *Neighbors* through multiple viewpoints, culminating in that of a female character. Berger had too often previously denied his women the misanthropic, contradictory depths of his men.

Special mention should also be given to Berger's "small town" books—*Sneaky People* and *The Feud*. Without abandoning his trademark mordancy, these are perhaps Berger's tenderest books, and covertly autobiographical of his Cincinnati childhood. Elsewhere in his late career Berger is slight, and droll—*Nowhere*, *Changing the Past*, *Robert Crews*, *Being Invisible* and *Reinhart's Women* (the fourth and last of the Reinharts) are best savored by initiates.

Berger's giddy program of writing a different book every time out, coupled with the curlicues of his style and his obsessional approach to character, make him a sort of auteur within the space of his own career: no matter what genre or mode or scale the "studio" of his vast imagination dictates, the sensibility of the "director"—Berger's uniquely sweetbitter vision of life—is unmistakable. One can only hope that the ballyhooed sequel to *Little Big Man* currently in the works will provide the occasion for a major boom.

—*The Salon.com Reader's Guide to Contemporary Authors*, 2000

Letters from the Invisible Man: My Correspondence with Thomas Berger

Thomas Berger and I have never met. Yet I also count Thomas Berger, a veteran of World War II and the (insufficiently) celebrated author of 23 novels, among my best friends on this earth. Can this possibly be true? And if so, might it be pathetic, something better kept to myself? My question has some general currency, since lately some of us befriend, or "friend," whole armies of discorporate beings. Yet long before virtuality made this gesture prosaic and compulsive, readers were in the habit of making disembodied friendships with authors. I mean, of course, in the sense that J.D. Salinger had in mind when Holden Caulfield, after reading a book, expressed the wish to call its author on the telephone.

That this variety of intimacy is usually unknown to its target is a fact authors, even those less fan-averse than Salinger, have considered merciful. Yet that doesn't mean it isn't a valuable human feeling. Though stalkers make everyone rightly nervous, feelings that cannot be reciprocated—love of artists dead and distant, hatred of governments, etc.—are one of the unacknowledged legislators of the world. We derive the word "fan" from "fanatic," yet to make ourselves fans of the right things, and to do so with unashamed abandon, can be an exalted mode of being. Fannish feeling, like laughter or tears, is one of those things that make us human.

It was this form of phantom kinship I felt for Thomas Berger when, at the age of 18, I discovered his writing. Reading his novels, I felt not only amazed and entertained, but more alive and less lonely, confirmed in my presence as a member of my species by the commingling of some of the strangest parts of my brain with the strangest parts of another person's. Being amazed and entertained made me Berger's fan; I have been so ever since. I recommend his uniquely eccentric and erudite tales everywhere I go; Berger's books are accessible and funny and immerse you in the permanent strangeness of his language and attitude. He also offers a book for every predilection: if you like Westerns, there's his classic *Little Big Man*; so too has he written fables of suburban life (*Neighbors*), crime stories (*Meeting Evil*), fantasies, small-town "back-fence" stories of Middle American life, and philosophical allegories (*Killing Time*). All of them are fitted with the Berger slant, in which the familiar becomes menacingly absurd or perhaps the absurd becomes menacingly familiar. You have very few excuses for not reading Berger. And anyway, I don't want to hear them.

The books made me Berger's fan; my sense of kinship with the person behind them—the sensations of feeling "more alive and less lonely"—made me want to become his friend as well. For those are the sorts of thing one usually looks to friendship to deliver, no matter the height of expectations one brings to books (mine tend to be outlandishly high). So it was that, a few years later, I started pestering Thomas Berger with letters.

However, to begin writing to Berger, which I did in 1989 at the age of 25, I felt I needed an excuse. I couldn't unstop gouts of fannish emotion into my missives—not only because these might have inspired Berger to contact the police, but because I wasn't much good then at unstopping gouts of emotion into my prose. This aspiring writer was at the time also a baroquely brainy kid, busy disguising feeling behind all manner of clutter. My excuse for contacting Berger, then, was that I wanted to write a biographical essay or appreciation on his friend, the now-forgotten writer Bernard Wolfe (I surmised Berger's and Wolfe's acquaintance because they'd dedicated books to each other). I wasn't completely bogus in this pursuit: in fact, somewhere in my juvenilia are scraps of an attempt at a book-by-book "guide" to Wolfe's fiction. I'm sure I told myself this was the reason I'd written to Tom—for, once he'd begun writing droll and generous letters in reply to mine, he'd become Tom to me. After all, I was a fan of several other living writers, and I hadn't contacted them, had I? I was thrilled, if a bit daunted when Berger wrote in response: "I might have quite a bit to say about Bernie, . . . but first I'd like to hear your bona fides, for reminiscing takes a lot of energy and I have little to spare." *Bona fides!* How I wished to have some of those—assuming I could figure out what they were.

In retrospect, it's unmistakable that I was attempting to prove to myself that I existed. For, within a year of making contact, I'd shamelessly sent Tom copies of two of my own earliest-published stories and received the sanctification of his letter of November 20, 1990: "You are a gifted writer!" Which verdict, I need no one to point out, may merely have been polite. (More than twenty years later, I'm not going to trouble Tom for confirmation that he genuinely admired the little stories I was managing at twenty-five.) In fact, Tom might have given nearly equal satisfaction if he'd written: "You are a lousy writer, but a writer nonetheless!" I had no one in those days giving me any confirmation that I was a writer at all besides myself, certainly not someone I regarded as one of the living titans of American fiction.

If I'd begun seeking confirmation, and received the gift of

encouragement, I got much more than I'd bargained for. Exchanging letters with Tom regularly for several years, I found I'd fallen down a marvelous rabbit hole, where my self-appointed tutor revealed himself as a figure akin to one of Lewis Carroll's perverse mentors to his Alice. Most if not all my Mock Turtle had to teach me about my own aspirations was how silly they were, how insupportable and perverse and unlikely to be rewarded by any clear result—and, at the same time, how I was likely stuck with them.

Perhaps I fantasized that by contacting a figure in "the literary world" I'd discover the hidden entrance to that world, so I might pass through myself. Yet Tom's "literary world" seemed to consist of rereading Frank Norris's *McTeague*, working his way through Kafka in the original German and watching Laird Cregar movies; I still remember my astonishment when he replied to my mention of Don DeLillo by saying he'd never heard the name. I sometimes joked that writing letters to Thomas Berger was like sending them into a time machine, or an alternate literary reality. Yet that analogy didn't catch the full oddness of my experience. Writing letters to Berger was, and is (for I still do it) most of all like sending them into a fictional space, to be replied to by a member of the Pickwick Society.

Reading over them, I find us talking a lot about dachshunds and Jack Russell terriers, Maine and Germany, peppering our correspondence with the names of character actors and dead authors, those both canonical and sliding from view. I also find Tom gently deflecting my suggestions that we meet in person; I spent a decade or so bringing the subject up, and receiving his demurrals, before I quit. I was obtuse in persisting with this suggestion, not grasping how Tom was patiently assembling a performance-art project in slow motion over nearly a quarter-century, that of an unreal friendship more real than most things. As he wrote to me, a few years ago: "Who can prove I'm still alive?" By the time Tom presented this teasing paradox, I'd grown accustomed to the regular sensation of his teasing the ground out from under my feet. The reply I wish I'd thought of on the spot, and that I offer him now: "Who cares one way or the other, so long as you keep writing?"

—*The New York Times*, 2012

Footnote on Berger

Thomas Berger died in 2014, at 89. He'd published a short novel, *Adventures of the Artificial Woman*, in 2005; another novel, completed after, went unpublished. (It'll turn up in his papers, but also in mine, since he sent me a copy of the manuscript, with no Max Brod request that I destroy it.) In our letters, Tom had always bragged of his indestructibility, while giving hints of the physical suffering he and his wife Jeanne increasingly endured. She was older than he was, significantly sicker, and both were bedridden and suffering dementia at the end. I don't think Tom was writing at all in his last year or two, but instead caring for her, cooking and cleaning, maintaining their house as well as he could. I was surprised he died before her (she followed less than a year later). I imagine he was too.

Our thirty-year friendship, conducted exclusively in letters or e-mails and phone calls, then took a peculiar turn to the material realm. It began with furniture. Tom left me a desk and a trunk. A lawyer described these to me: a seventeenth-century Spanish vargueno traveller's writing desk, with inlaid-ivory and hidden drawers, and an eighteenth-century carved trunk from Madagascar. Tom had also specified that I was to have my choice of the books in his library, which couldn't be dissolved until I appeared at the house to make a selection—would I please appear at the house? I was bewildered. I'd never been

204 • MORE ALIVE AND LESS LONELY

left anything in a will before. And now I was to invade the mysterious address Tom had never even revealed, having preferred a nearby P.O. box for receipt of his letters.

After some appropriately Bergerian confusion and dismay (long silences, missed calls, a change in lawyers by the estate), a year or so later I appeared, with my mother-in-law Sally as my back-up (She knows furniture, and can talk to anyone.), at a tiny house perched on the river side of a street overlooking the Hudson, just south of Nyack, New York. This wasn't a long trip, just across the George Washington Bridge. Tom, that semi-famous recluse, had been forty-five minutes away from the action all that time.

It was a cool day in March; I think it had rained. Tom's executor Charles arrived. Charles was tall and elegant, a retired actor and a friend of Tom's and Jeanne's from their days in Greenwich Village in the 1950s. He was in his nineties, and overwhelmed by the tasks before him. (Pick an executor younger than yourself—you might live a while.) He was driven by Michele, a younger friend who'd been helping a great deal. The house was in poignant disarray. Jeanne had been cared for by a visiting nurse in the weeks following Tom's death, then moved to a nursing home. But the books, and Jeanne's paintings, were intact on the walls. Here were the desk and the trunk—I decided to arrange to have the desk, which was gorgeous, shipped to California. The trunk I declined on the spot. Tom will forgive me for saying it looked like a large sculpture of a dog turd.

Charles and I talked while I looked over the books. They were perfectly organized, and made a version of Tom's brain for me to climb around inside. I selected about three cardboard boxes worth of them—probably less than five percent of what was there. I took Tom's copies of Kafka in English and in German, a few of which were those early editions he'd bought to read while stationed in Germany after World War Two (He'd

written the year and the city of their acquisition on the flyleaf.).
I took Tom's ancient edition of Malory's *Le Mort d'Arthur*, the
source for his own *Arthur Rex*. I took my embarrassing gush-
ingly-inscribed copies of my own books, which I'd sent over the
years to that P.O. box. One of these I presented to Charles, who
appeared pleased. It was Berger who'd introduced me to my favorite quote of Nietzsche's: "The thinker or artist whose better
self has fled into his works feels an almost malicious joy when
he sees his body and spirit slowly broken into and destroyed by
time; it is as if he were in a corner, watching a thief at work on
his safe, all the while knowing that it is empty and that all his
treasures have been rescued." Now Tom had—perversely?—cast
me in the role as a scavenger at the site of his departure.

Charles had been tentatively reminiscing about Tom and
Jeanne, and gratifying me by saying how much our correspondence meant to Tom in his last years. He and Michele also
worried aloud about the problem of properly dispensing with
Jeanne's paintings and drawings and prints; there was no gallery,
and no one who still cherished her work, that they knew of. I
began thinking of ways I could help, beyond just claiming my
desk and pillaging the bookshelves. I began talking of how I
knew a friend of Tom's and Jeanne's, the Pakistani-American
writer Zulfikar Ghose, in Texas, who might very much like to
have one of her canvases—would they like me to try to arrange
a gift? They would.

As we warmed to one another, it seemed Charles had been
feeling me out for another task. Or perhaps it was only a sudden impulse. Anyway, he gripped my arm and pointed into
the kitchen. On the counter, amid the clutter, stood a distin-
guished-looking black package with a typed white label. "That's
him," Charles said. I didn't understand. "His ashes." I understood, but couldn't speak. "He asked to have them scattered in
the Hudson River," said Charles. "I haven't been able to do it.

You have to do it, please." I worked to rearrange my grasp of reality quickly enough. Did he mean today? "Yes," said Charles. "It's perfect. We'll do it. You'll help me."

With that, with nothing more than that, we were on our way outside. As Charles held my arm, we proceeded down the steps inlaid in the hill at the side of the house, to the stone embankment where the back porch overhung Jeanne's painting studio at the water's edge. (Charles and Michele pointed out how her studio had been flooded during Hurricane Sandy, and never reclaimed.) Michele and Sally stood by. I unscrewed the container. Charles and I both said a little something, not much; I don't remember what I said. I got Tom into the water pretty efficiently, without getting too much of him on my coat or pants, only a little. Then Sally and I drove back to Manhattan.

VII

OK You Mugs

Heavy Petting

It's hard to read a compilation as genial and whole-hearted as *O.K. You Mugs: Writers on Movie Actors*—edited by Luc Sante and Melissa Holbrook Pierson—and not wish it to go on a bit longer, or to be followed immediately by a sequel. The book's premise is as easily-grasped as it is irresistible—*Wasn't there such a book already?* you wonder as you browse, searching for favorites on each side of the ledger, the adoring and the adored. After compulsively gobbling down, say, Greil Marcus on the late, great character actor J.T. Walsh, you want to know what he thinks of *M. Emmet* Walsh, or, for that matter, Paul Dooley. Geoffrey O'Brien on Dana Andrews, Jacqueline Carey on Margaret Dumont, David Hadju on Elmer Fudd: all quite brilliant, yes—now where's Diane Johnson on Peter Lorre, Michael Tolkin on Laurence Fishburne, Jack Womack on Godzilla? I want to read them, too. More than that, I'm ashamed to say that I can't keep from petulantly wishing that I'd been invited to this dinner party myself (confidential to Sante and Pierson: Anyone have dibs on Robert Ryan? I could do you a great Robert Ryan), and not just allowed to eavesdrop. Maybe *O.K. You Mugs* should be a magazine instead of a book - I'd get a lifetime subscription.

However much sweat went into these essays, the results pleasingly mimic those adrenaline conversation one overhears or engages in coming out of a revival house after a showing of this or that auteurist masterwork or cult gem—that rush of speech after the long silence of a meal at Hollywood's cornucopian table. Like a lot of good conversation it offers a form of healing from everyday wounds: first, and most obviously, for the "neglected" performers given their due here after careers in the "shadows." (There are probably millions of us who prefer Warren Oates and Thelma Ritter to anything else in the films in which they appear, yet they retain their magical function as tokens of obscurity, so that it's thrilling to see them enshrined here.)

Healing in a more profound sense is proposed by Stuart Klawans's terrific "Shined Shoes," a meditation on LeRoy Daniels, the dancing bootblack who performs a brief number with Fred Astaire in *The Band Wagon* (1953). Klawan's detective work reveals that Daniels was a real dancing bootblack, scooped off the streets of L.A. and never to appear in film again. Klawans then widens his frame ever so slightly, recalling the homeless man with a paper cup who functions as a de facto doorman for his apartment building, and the world—our real world—floods in. The book also provides the same rush as David Thomson's *Suspects*, Marcus's "Real Life Top Ten" column, and certain homespun Internet fan sites (find Ray Davis's Tuesday Weld homepage for a particularly fine example) can, by vigorously and cheerfully exploding our mute acceptance of pop culture's ideas about what parts of itself are lasting or important, by continuously swapping spit and other bodily fluids with the gods.

Sante and Pierson include a handful of reprints to round out the commissioned essays. To my eye these provide the only speedbumps. John Updike's 1983 paean to Doris Day remains too much the review of Day's autobiography it presumably was, and its highbrow defensiveness is dated—the rest of these writers take for granted the cinematic ocean in which we swim. Manny Farber's "The Decline of the Actor" (1971) is an odder case. Farber's a descriptive genius ("Sinatra's romantic scenes with Miss Leigh are a Chinese torture: he, pinned against the Pullman door as though having been buried standing up, and she, nothing moving on her body, drilling holes with her eyes into his screw-on head") and hugely deserves revival. But his thesis here—that overloaded visual frames and over-conceived shot designs have calcified individual performances—is nicely contradicted in the discussions of Oates and Walsh, as well as by the steady arrival of new performers like Steve Buscemi and Janeane Garofalo, who seem capable of doodling in the margins of even the most hypertrophied spectacles.

I suspect that Updike and Farber are included here as legitimizing paternal figures, precedents to show how these particular million flowers were seeded. This display of bona fides isn't necessary, but then it isn't necessary that this be a tidy book. It isn't telling a tidy story, and personally I'm grateful for its breadth. As I said, I'd love to see *O.K. You Mugs* turn into an open-ended series. And listen, Luc and Melissa: after you've enjoyed my take on Robert Ryan I'm sure you'll be eager to know what I think of Agnes Moorehead and Val Avery and Lily Tomlin and . . .

—*Bookforum*, 1999

More Than Night

In my neighborhood the best local video store is aimed at the twenty-something college-educated hipsters who set the local tone, and it's eerily deficient in "Classic Hollywood." Japanimation and blaxploitation and concert documentaries rule these shelves; Marilyn Monroe, John Wayne and Greta Garbo might not have ten vehicles between them in the whole place. The perfunctory "directors section" forms an inverted auteurist pyramid that would make Andrew Sarris nauseous with vertigo: Cronenberg, Lynch, Coen Brothers, Tarantino, Jarmusch and Hartley resting on Altman, Penn and Kubrick, who in turn rest on Hitchcock, Welles and Nicholas Ray, who rest on—nothing. No sections for Ford, Hawks, Capra, Lubitsch, Sturges or Cukor. No Lang, no Huston, no Wilder. Whenever I rent there I recall the title of George Trow's classic '70's essay on the ahistorical diffuseness of post-television culture: *Within the Context of No Context.*

The exception is the store's film noir shelf, which proudly overflows with titles good, bad, indifferent and camp. Here's where Lang, Wilder, Hawks and Huston sneak into the shop—just so long as they play by the rules, working in black and white and casting Bogart or Edward G. Robinson in a story with guns, trenchcoats and plenty of shadows. Here are dozens of 1940s and '50s titles which would be forgotten without the consecrating force of film noir's permanent vogue. Here too, otherwise jaded clerks lean forward, eager to offer the consolation that if *Odds Against Tomorrow* is already rented, Gloria Grahame and Robert Ryan also appear together in *Crossfire*. I once pointed out to one such clerk that *In a Lonely Place* should be moved from "film noir" to "Nicholas Ray" and he seemed crushed that a perfectly good black-and-white Bogart movie should have to go sit beside the squarely technicolor *Rebel Without a Cause* and *Johnny Guitar*.

This isn't exactly a depthless view of film history, but the depths it suggests aren't auteurish or historical, they're stylistic and iconographic—fiercely so. Such fetishization surrounded noir from its inception, suggests James Naremore in his brilliantly grounded *More Than Night: Film Noir in Its Contexts*. His argument is nicely paradoxical, since he begins by convincingly disrupting cherished myths about when and how that inception took place. Sure, it was French critics who teased out of certain Hollywood products the tendrils of noir style, but Naremore shows that it was Surrealists, as much or more than usual-suspect Existentialists, who set the terms. And noir may have been erected on a platform of the American crime novel, but the key writers were themselves not primitives. Rather, Cain, Hammett and Chandler were Europeanized aesthetes, responsive to High Modernism, with strong resemblances to their Nobel Prize–winning contemporaries Faulkner and Hemingway, as well as to a Brit whose noirish "Entertainments" may have cost him the Nobel—Graham Greene. Naremore's restoration of Greene's place among noir progenitors is one of the book's virtuoso sequences.

Naremore's program is to insistently complicate the long-standing debate over the boundaries and characteristics of Hollywood's most infiltrative and self-conscious genre. His book works, though, because this program is anything but nakedly theoretical. In fact, it's often barely visible for being subsumed in the pleasures of original, thorough and un-programmatic research into the making and makers of films. Some of the noirs he scrutinizes so fondly are legends residing at the center of the canon, others pleasingly widen that canon's margins, which, by the time Naremore is finished, can seem to embrace anything from *Citizen Kane* and *Leave Her to Heaven* to, yes, blaxploitation.

More Than Night is structured like Kurosawa's *Rashomon*, as a series of views onto aspects of an impossible, elusive story—as Naremore is quick to point out, each chapter might have been worked up into an entire book. The structure invites and rewards browsing: allowing oneself to be allured by a still (the book is generous with stills) from a favorite neglected film like Irving Lerner's *Murder by Contract* or an unexpected reference to contemporary videographer Mark Rappaport, or to Welles's unmade first-person-camera *Heart of Darkness* results in immersion in stirring discussions of the influence of censorship and McCarthyism on key noirs, or a welcome refutation of the myth of the "B" movie (a majority of the essential noirs were anything but). Only a chapter entitled "The Other Side of the Street," which gestures towards noir's love/hate compulsion towards the racial Other, seems too brisk. "Asia" and "Latin America" are cursory, and "Africa"—up to and including Charles Burnett's *The Glass Shield* and Carl Franklin's *Devil in a Blue Dress*—is only a little more than cursory. Here I wished for that entire book on the subject Naremore didn't manage to write. Maybe next time.

Elsewhere Naremore dissects the lighting tricks, camera-angles and costuming styles which became the common denominator of noir image, parodied by Fred Astaire and Bob Hope a decade before French critics had made their identification widely known. Our culture seems to have recognized that noir was both silly and crucial, even threatening, without any help from Surrealists *or* Existentialists. "The Noir Mediascape," *Night*'s final chapter, gracefully extends Naremore's argument to celebrated contemporary films. In a few deft pages he shows how *Pulp Fiction*'s strengths work within an almost suffocatingly narrow range, demolishes *L.A. Confidential*, and proposes a reconsideration of the overlooked *Lost Highway*—in each case persuasively. That persuasiveness is a side-benefit of Naremore's generosity with his historical research, and the contextualizing force it lends.

In his updated reissue of *Within the Context of No Context*, George Trow suggests that the cure for the cultural amnesia induced by the mediascape is individual and specific. "Perhaps you will need a motto," he says. "I suggest this one: Wounded by the Million; Healed—One by One." *More Than Night* is a splendid offer of such healing. Naremore permits us to understand that film noir's iconographies and stylistics exist to be appropriated endlessly (and too often hollowly) by advertising and "high art" alike because they continually and energetically issue not from a single center of real meaning, but a whole host of them.

—*Bookforum*, 1998

You Talkin' to Me?

Are we satisfied with Martin Scorsese as "the greatest living American director?" Not until Billy Wilder enjoys his last cigar, thank you. Still, in the context of his *Easy Riders* and *Raging Bulls* generation he's looking pretty respectable, even if it's partly due the relatively high floor on his failures. There's no *Peggy Sue Got Married* or *Bonfire of the Vanities* on his résumé, let alone a Robin Williams vehicle. His compromises and flops bear contemplation as mistakes only he could have made, lame in an auteurish way. And his masterpieces hardly bunch at the start of his career—*Goodfellas* (1990) gets him into the '90s, while *Casino* (1995) and *Kundun* (1998) may come into better focus on repeat viewings, as have *New York, New York* (1977) and *The King of Comedy* (1983). So where's that nagging voice coming from, persistently suggesting that we should have wanted more? Why, it's Martin Scorsese himself, in the University of Mississippi Press's latest entry in their "Conversations with Filmmakers" series, here edited by Peter Brunette. "I think a lot of the pictures I've made are good," he tells *Premiere* in 1991. "But they're not *The Searchers*. They're not *8½*. *The Red Shoes*. *The Leopard*."

Elsewhere in this unvarnished and overlapping compilation of magazine interviews spanning Scorsese's career, the director pokes holes in the reputation of all but his most seminal films.

Catch him in the right mood and he'll defer completely to audience disregard for commercial flops like *After Hours* (1985) and *New York, New York*—while in the same breath distancing himself guiltily from successful commercial tradeoffs like *Alice Doesn't Live Here Anymore* (1974) and *The Color of Money* (1986). An undisguised fan of classic Hollywood, he pines for the traditional storytelling skills he reveres in Hitchcock, Samuel Fuller, and Jacques Tourneur, but concludes, "as far as a straight narrative story, I came close to that in *Cape Fear* . . . I really tried and I found that I don't really have the talent for it."

Great American film directors, those who make long careers in (or out of) Hollywood, usually conform to the John Huston/ John Ford/Howard Hawks personality type: big, encompassing egos, willing to dominate circumstances and engulf collaborators, prone to brushing off analysis or introspection. Not so Scorsese, who surpasses even Woody Allen for torment and self-doubt, and whose modesty, far from seeming a blind for a raging self-regard, is actually pretty persuasive. A director's biography is usually a catalogue of slighted screenwriters, cinematographers, editors, wives, and others whose contributions have been steamrolled by the myth of omnipotent genius. But here Scorcese does to himself what Pauline Kael did to Orson Welles: "*Taxi Driver* (1976) is really Paul Schrader's. We interpreted it." Then, "*King of Comedy* and *Raging Bull* (1980) really stem from Bob [DeNiro]." As Scorsese chips away at himself, it's possible to lose sight of how singular and vibrant his better work really is, and how many personal and obsessive themes reverberate through even his weakest films. (One tonic is to recall how cloistered and dry Schrader's self-directed movies can be, and how many of DeNiro's performances for other directors seem perfunctory or cloned.) The early interviews, before Scorsese had curbed a tendency to confessional ranting, show evidence of some unsurprising sources: childhood sickness, neighborhood violence and racism, and that old white-hot fuel rod of creative expression, Catholic religious training.

Handwringer or not, Scorsese is a very pure filmmaker at his best, one who's progressed from the somewhat Cassevetian lo-fi expressionist of *Who's That Knocking at My Door* (1968) and *Mean Streets* (1973) to a technically obsessive anthropological muralist in *Goodfellas*, *The Age of Innocence* (1993), *Casino*, and *Kundun*. The question his most recent films raise—whether Scorsese has misplaced the autobiographical impulse that powered his early work—isn't answered in the last few interviews in the compilation. Scorsese's still babbling long replies to questions, but he's drowned the confessional impulse in formal analysis—180-degree pans, dissolves, and source music. Even a discussion of a shot containing hundreds of slaughtered monks centers on his choice of a digital camera. Then, as Scorsese politely credits various screenwriters, editors, technicians, Philip Glass, and the Dalai Lama for their contributions, come tantalizing mentions of projects you really hope he'll get to: a Gershwin biopic and a period epic called *Gangs of New York*. If Scorsese squeaks by as our greatest living *active* American director, it's on the chance that his *The Searchers* or *The Leopard* still lies ahead.

—*Bookforum*, 1999

New York Characters

It's all about what Dr. Zizmor and Bobby Short and The Real Kramer have in common—but before that, it's about Mister Clean. Mister Clean was a guy on our street in Boerum Hill when I was growing up; he lived in a rooming house, one of several still functioning on the block in the early '70s. The rooming houses were presumably established when the neighborhood was dominated by steamfitters and longshoremen working on the docks at the end of Atlantic Avenue, and by the Mohawk Indians who built skyscrapers and had chosen this part of Brooklyn to live in, but they were now mostly filled with Puerto Rican bachelors, and Puerto Rican drunks. Mister Clean wore a porkpie hat and had a chipper, vibrant style of hailing his friends on the block. He was legendary for his love of his car—this likely was the source of his name, though I never heard it explained—which was a fancy Dodge Dart with colored side panels, if I remember it right. Mister Clean would, right, clean and polish the car: the hood, the hubcaps, the windshield. And when it was too clean to clean again, he'd stand outside or sit on the stoop and regard it pridefully: Mister Clean's car. It was weird that he even had a car. Certainly nobody else on the block cleaned theirs. Mister Clean was everybody's eccentric, everybody's neighborhood star, but he was a little more mine than anyone else's after I cracked his windshield with a thrown baseball. Though I was terrified, I confessed to my parents. When my father and I went together to apologize, and to offer to pay for a replacement, Mister Clean not only forgave—he immediately began taking my brother and me to Yankees games. To the bleachers. He'd make us wait by a pillar eating hot dogs while he rushed across to the bars under the subway to place bets; then we'd sit and root for Mickey Rivers and Reggie Jackson. That we were Met fans, Mister Clean couldn't seem to be made to understand. He spoke little English. Maybe he'd never even understood that I'd ruined his windshield, only that my father was trying to tell him something about baseball.

Even if Mister Clean were still out there polishing, he'd be a little too local (and too outer-borough) for photographer Gillian Zoe Segal's sterling little collection of *New York Characters*, but the point of her book encompasses and implies Mister Clean's meaning: New York is bloated full of local fame. More than that, in a city founded on a make it here, make it anywhere premise and on an ethos of taking celebrity for granted, local fame often dwells on an uninterrupted continuum with the shrug-worthy, Hollywood Squares celebrity junk-stratum, where 15 minutes is being stretched to forever all over the place. *Sure, everybody knows that guy, he's the one who used to— whatever.* My brother and I wouldn't have been that shocked to see Mister Clean show up on *Real People*, or *The Gong Show*.

What makes this book of photograph-and-blurb portraits brilliant is the insight that crushes together Spike Lee, Ed Koch, Yogi Berra, George Plimpton, Comden and Green and the aforementioned Bobby Short with figures like the Oldest Cabbie, Sister Marlane (the Bird Lady), Radio Man, the President of the Polar Bear Club, and the aforementioned Real Kramer. Not to mention Dr. Z. Sure, those in the former group once could (or still can) play Peoria, but basically they're our own loathed and beloved eccentrics as much as the latter group. By noting that New Yorkers hold a certain clan of luminaries in that special combination of "to their bosom" and "at arm's length" which characterizes a familial or neighborly relationship, Segal has, seemingly effortlessly, described a rare and elusive aspect of New York City culture. And the proof, the clincher, is in the middle-range figures she also rounds up. Quick, to which camp belongs Al Goldstein? Speed Levitch? Don Imus? Elaine Kaufman? Henry Stern? In another part of the country, would all these figures be only local flakes or charmers—odd uncles or aunts who, when they came for the holidays, could stir up an entire block or neighborhood? Does anyone outside the city really know the name Ron Kuby? Patrick McMullan? Poet-O? Gotcha.

Plimpton, who is depicted in this volume and also provided a Foreword, squirms at seeing himself put "jowl to jowl . . . with the likes of David Blaine, who not long ago enclosed himself in a huge block of ice and put himself on display in Times Square." But George, what did you do except enclose yourself in a huge block of literary celebrity—and a Detroit Lions uniform? The splendid willfulness that wrenched them into the public eye is what links Lauren Ezersky, Curtis Sliwa, John MacEnroe and the Egg Cake Lady (stringing these names together produces poetry every time). That's true even if, like subway dermatologist Dr. Zizmor, they claim they were only trying to make a buck. Dr. Zizmor explains that he designs those hideous ads himself—a clear, if unconscious, confession of the lust for fame. He also mentions that he treats a lot of cheating husbands who fear they've picked up sexually transmitted diseases, which puts a new spin on all those rainbows and "before" and "after" photos in his ads. Which, being a glimpse of the dark side, reminds me of who was, for me, the only outstanding missing piece in Segal's book (apart from, of

224 • MORE ALIVE AND LESS LONELY

course, Mister Clean). Segal explains in her afterword that Woody Allen shined her on, and that she feuded with the Soup Nazi, but I didn't really miss that overexposed pair. No, my candidate is perfectly typical of the Ed Koch model, the New Yorker who comes home to local prominence after a brief shot into the wider stratosphere: Where's Bernhard Goetz?

—The New York Observer, 2001

Lost and Found

Classic, film-noir amnesia—bewildered victim awakening in a hospital room with no sense of self, no memory of a name or of the events leading up to the present, dependent for clues on nurses and policemen and others claiming (but surely only pretending) to be family members: This sort of amnesiac state is almost completely a fiction. It is the stuff of movies and novels, a reliably suspenseful narrative device and a metaphor richly evocative of human experience but in fact hardly a human experience at all. Amnesia in the clinical sense is usually something much less absolute (and often quite temporary) even at its worst.

Odd, then, that *Past Forgetting*, a gemlike, seductively readable and quietly moving memoir recounting that great rarity, a truly encompassing and persistent loss of memory—in this case caused by a swimming-pool accident—should be written by a woman whose life involves so many fairy-tale elements and is populated by so many movie stars that if it were fiction it would seem ludicrously trashy. The novelist Jill Robinson (*Perdido*, *Bed/Time/Story* and many others) is the daughter of Dore Schary, who, when he replaced Louis B. Mayer at MGM, became legendary as the only screenwriter ever to be handed control of a movie studio.

Robinson spent her childhood and early adulthood at court with Hollywood royalty. This is a woman who grapples for memories of her childhood and comes up with snippets of conversations with Cary Grant. She conveys an impression that celebrity is a way of life—a given, like sky or water, to be puzzled over only in philosophical asides. When she reconstructs a crucial period of dissolution in the 1960s and early '70s (she writes with great insight on the texture of the counterculture), her partners in crime are Dennis Hopper and Bob Rafelson, Los Angeles art stars David Hockney and Ed Kienholz, and so on.

None of this stargazing detracts from the center of her narrative: the amnesiac writer's poignant groping, with her husband's patient, infinitely caring assistance, for an understanding of who she is, of how her children have grown and her parents have died and of how she came to be living in England when she knows she's never been on an airplane. Her struggling brain has crushed together her two marriages and mingled her children's childhood and her own. She cringes daily in anticipation of chastening phone calls from parents long dead. Her strongest remaining impressions are of the '70s.

Most strikingly, she recalls the vast emotional importance in her life of the act of writing, without remembering anything of the methods or the discipline writing requires, nor of what she would write about if she could. It is of course through her writing that she eventually recovers not her memory but her self. In a language at once conversational, aphoristic and deeply nuanced, Robinson shows herself coming to understand that even before her amnesiac rupture she was really only constructed of postulates, of stories, of moments; that memory is an illusion and a dance—one she can rejoin if not reconstruct.

Two-thirds of the way through the book, she is lured out of her introspective convalescence by an assignment from *Vanity Fair* to search out the victim of a famous Los Angeles rape. The sequence at first threatens to derail the book but grows in interest until it becomes an analogical double for her memory quest and an exploration of the meaning of Los Angeles in the long aftermath of the '60s. It reads like a collaboration between Dominick Dunne and Steve Erickson; if, in Ezra Pound's famous dictum, literature is "news that stays news," then Robinson's accomplishment here might be described as gossip that stays gossip.

The emotional peak of her story comes late in the book, when she arranges a reunion with a certain grade school acquaintance, a boy who, despite his kindness, was daunting, distant, impossibly attractive and stirring in some way she has never quite resolved. She isn't certain he'll remember her at all—her amnesiac condition is so absolute and infiltrative that she constantly attributes it to those around her and to the world at large—but he greets her on the phone with familiarity and warmth. They meet and speak of childhood and self with vast sensitivity, and when Robinson finds a part of herself restored, the reader thinks: It isn't only amnesiacs who need to commune brilliantly with the most beautiful person of the opposite sex from grade school—I need this, too!

The friend in Jill Robinson's book is Robert Redford.

—*Salon,* 1999

The Original Piece of Wood I Left in Your Head: A Conversation Between Director Spike Jonze and Critic Perkus Tooth

Wildcat pop-culture critic Perkus Tooth and Being John Malkovich *director Spike Jonze met, at Tooth's insistence, at Yonah Schimmel's knishery on Houston Street in New York City. A small digital tape recorder was placed between them. After some small talk on a smattering of subjects, including Mervyn Peake's Gormenghast trilogy, Mark Feeney's* Nixon at the Movies, *and the resemblance between Sun Ra's "Nuclear War" and LCD Soundsystem's "Yr City's A Sucker," Tooth drew from his pocket a few grubby, coffee-stained pages of notes he'd taken in advance of their conversation, and their attention turned to the upcoming Criterion reissue of* Being John Malkovich. *What follows is an unedited transcript of the results.*

TOOTH: *Being John Malkovich* is a film that inverse-recapitulates—precapitulates?—its own future concerns to a nearly fractal extent. Not only does the "Heloise" puppet already resemble Catherine Keener before it logically ought to, but at 4:15 John Cusack sits on his couch beside Elijah the chimpanzee, desultorily paging through the *New York Post*, an edition celebrating New York Yankees pitcher David Cone's July 18, 1999, perfect game. The front-page headline reads, "Awesome!" while the rear sports page indulges the woeful pun "Conegrats!" "Awesome" and

"Conegrats" together can be anagrammatized to "Get across name woe," "Came onstage worse," while "Conegrats" by itself translates to "Angst core"—perhaps a tad unsubtle there? David Cone's special rooting section was known as the Coneheads—derived, of course, from the Dan Aykroyd–Jane Curtin franchise *Saturday Night Live* sketch—and they often wore the plastic head costumes, thereby in totality conveying the rebus: alien visitor (alienation) plus head plus cone (or funnel, or tunnel) plus *Post* (delivery, i.e., birth canal). For the more alert viewer, you barely needed carry on with the film beyond that point, its payload had been so satisfactorily conveyed. The rest, I imagine, was merely a matter of following through.

JONZE: Actually, it's the *Daily News*. Otherwise, you're completely on target here. Mea Culpa. Do you remember that incident where David Cone was caught masturbating in the New York Mets' bullpen? Also, was there really an off-broadway show called *Puppetry of the Penis*? Or was that a dream I had?

TOOTH: It's well known that if you pitch for the Mets, you've got a 70 percent chance of throwing a no-hitter for another team later in your career. Whereas the percentage of masturbators who make it to the Great White Way is surely what a statistician would call "vanishingly small." But back to *Being: John Malkovich*.

JONZE: You pronounced it like there's a colon in the title. There's no colon.

TOOTH: Sorry?

JONZE: It's not like a catalog of stuff in some alien survey of Earth—City: New York, Species: Human, Being: John Malkovich. It's a gerund. Like *Being There* or *Breaking the Waves*.

TOOTH: Sure. Or *Breaking: Away*. Or *Eating: Raoul*.

JONZE: That's so freaking annoying I can't even begin to say.

TOOTH: Ahem. The film develops an extraordinarily intricate series of nestings and inversions on the theme of puppetry, masks, acting and authenticity, which in turn are made to resonate with notions of one body's sexual possession of another body—attempted or briefly and tantalizingly achieved. This occurs to such an extent that relatively innocuous language becomes enlisted in an obsessive motif. Catherine Keener analyzes herself as a disjointed assemblage of characteristics, saying, "My voice is probably the least intriguing thing about me." And when she teases John Cusack that his observation about the "orientation film being bullshit" is just one of "fifty ways to get into a girl's pants," we reflect on the resemblances between hand-puppets—which only find animation when someone has, to use the film's phrase, "gotten into their pants"—and the meat puppetry of the flesh. Similarly, when the cab driver, guessing at John Malkovich's so-called *real* name, comes up with "Mapplethorpe," one can hardly keep from having brought to mind certain photographs of the human hand and forearm farther up—

JONZE: That's enough of that, I'd say.

TOOTH: Being oneself is simultaneously never remotely enough to satisfy, and yet a wearisome and absolute inevitability. Cameron Diaz, on exiting Malkovich the first time, exults incoherently: "Being inside did something to me. I knew who I was." When Malkovich demands access to his own portal, Cusack attempts to dissuade him, saying: "I'm sure that would pale in comparison to the actual experience." That's to say that the so-called experience of *being* oneself has become eligible to be measured against the experience of *playing* oneself, which, after Malkovich denounces it as hellish, is defended by Cusack's surprised remark that "for most people, it's a rather pleasant experience." At the same time, Malkovich's unpersuasive habitation of his own unpopulated real life presents a convergence of his rehearsals into a tape recorder—of Chekhov's *The Cherry Orchard*—and his ordering of new towels and bath mats into a cordless telephone, into which, after discovering that his first color option isn't available, he says, "I'll go with the loden"—a line-reading that may arguably be the single most enervated and soul-crushing moment in cinema history. Conversely, his greatest performance, and possibly this promising yet failed actor's own, is as Cusack's flesh puppet in Craig's *Dance of Despair and Disillusionment*. Yet it is one that finds itself entirely preempted by the precredit sequence and upstaged by a creature of wood and string!

JONZE: I'm getting the feeling you found the film unnecessary.

TOOTH: Beautifully so. Please don't take this the wrong way.

JONZE: Oh, never. Do you want to talk about some other film? *Eating: Raoul? Walking: Tall? Finding: Nemo?*

TOOTH: Really, the film's entirety is nothing more than a dream or nightmare on the part of Derek Matini, the obnoxious rival puppeteer who's barely glimpsed in the film. Or is that an unfair supposition?

JONZE: If by unfair you mean ludicrous.

TOOTH: Think again. The characters in your little puppet show never break through to the quote-unquote real world in the television clip showing Matini's triumphant mounting of the Emily Dickinson spectacle from the bridge span. That film clip may be our only glimpse of an outside to the theatrical fantasia of your so-called diegesis. This can be proved in the simplest possible way: After the "Eight Months Later" title card (an absurdly short duration, incidentally), John Malkovich, ostensibly, is widely understood to have introduced an era of massively popular serious-art puppetry; Matini's celebrated and widely televised spectacles are entirely effaced in this self-evident fiction. And, of course, Matini's own tendencies toward paranoid, self-ratifying fantasies of engulfment by the outside world are inscribed in his choice of the hermetic Emily Dickinson as his subject. Like Elijah the chimpanzee, Dickinson never broke free of the cage of her room. Like Elijah the prophet, Derek Matini declines to appear in a world made ready for him.

JONZE: I don't think I can go on with this.

TOOTH: At the one-hour-and-twenty-minute mark, you give the game away again, with an overt reference to my favorite film—of course, I speak of Hitchcock's *Vertigo*—when, after arriving soaking wet at Orson Bean's door, Cameron Diaz is given something dry to wear: "You look so lovely, my dear, standing here before the fire in my oversized man's robe." As with James Stewart's character in the Hitchcock film, Catherine Keener is in the position of loving not one single person, nor two, but a sort of hologram, a *virtual third* presented by the impersonation of one by the other. Cued by this reference to the instability and dread of male desire, an instant later the film uncovers the motif of performance anxiety: the difficulty with being John Malkovich is, in effect, the problem of *staying in*—i.e., the fleeting duration of sexual intercourse. We understand this when Cusack exclaims, to Keener's great delight: "I figured out how to hang on as long as I want." This is then immediately intercut with Orson Bean's explanation of the risks of being diverted into a newborn vessel and of the goal of achieving a conscious rebirth in Malkovich instead. So we understand that to stay in is to be born again; fantasies of male sexual stamina immediately give way to the procreative urgencies of the sexual act. As, indeed, we witness in the arc of Cusack's consummated relationship, which skips from sexual yearning to pregnancy and cradle with barely a blip of satisfaction between. And the baby isn't even his—which prefigures the necessity of his eternal return to immaturity-in-reincarnation.

JONZE: [*Silence*]

TOOTH: When I e-mailed my colleague Sophocles Jones to tell her that I'd be discussing the film with you, she wrote back to say she'd be forever haunted by the scene—and I quote—"when Cameron Diaz is fucking that life-size puppet underwater." I pointed out that no such scene occurs in the film; she then realized that she must have dreamed the scene. I wonder if you're aware that a film such as yours goes on proliferating in such ways in the collective unconscious—in a sense, they are like the original piece of wood that Cusack leaves behind in Malkovich's head, but that in the film he at last retrieves. I'm curious to know whether you feel any responsibility for outcomes like my friend's—or, to put it another way, does Spike Jonze have the obligation to return to Sophocles Jones's head and retrieve the piece of wood?

JONZE: Please, for god's sake, stop.

TOOTH: Last thoughts, before I lose the opportunity. At 45:11, what did you intend with the marble sculpture of the bare foot in a sandal on Malkovich's side table? A reference to Mercury, Achilles, or Dr. Scholls? I did appreciate the fact that, at 55:52, Keener picks up the chaldron from the coffee table in his apartment, just after she speaks the line "So do you enjoy being . . . an actor?" And, again, the unmistakable reference to Marlon Brando in *Apocalypse Now* when Malkovich unveils his shockingly round stomach, a marvelous prosthesis—

JONZE: That's his stomach. It's the actor's stomach. It's not a reference to another stomach.

TOOTH: You'd been notably able to restrain yourself from any bumping-head-on-the-low-ceiling gags until, suddenly, at the one-hour-and-thirty-seven-minute mark, you succumbed. Why? Pressure from the studio?

JONZE: [*Silence*]

Perkus Tooth is the author of Fool's Gold Mouthpiece *and* The Hollow Horn: Admixtures of Contemporary Plight *(forthcoming). His liner notes appear in Criterion's editions of Werner Herzog's* Echolalia, Von Tropen Zollner's *The City Is a Maze, and Fritz Lang's* Prelude to a Certain Midnight, *among others. He lives in Manhattan.*

—from the Criterion Collection edition
of *Being John Malkovich,* 2012

Johnny's Graying Teenaged Sense of What Isn't Boring (*Da Capo Best Music Writing* 2002)

. . . Johnny made up his own job, varying the tasks to suit his eternally teenaged sense of what was and wasn't boring.

—Robert Christgau

Wait, before you flip to the contents page looking for a Christgau piece—the line quoted above isn't from this year's volume, wasn't even written in 2001. It's an attempt to characterize Johnny Thunders's guitar-playing, from Christgau's essay on the New York Dolls in *Stranded: Music for a Desert Island*, a volume edited by Greil Marcus in 1978. So, what's the quote doing there? Here's the thing: This book, the one you're holding in your hands, is haunted, for me, by the ghost of *Stranded*. That volume, a batch of commissioned pieces pegged on the beautifully dumb question "Which Single Rock-and-Roll Album Would I Take to a Desert Island?," not only sets a fine standard for any gathering of essays on music—though it certainly does that. *Stranded* is more: To my seventeen-year-old self in 1981, the book was itself a message in a bottle bumping ashore on my own little ahistorical teenage island. The message read something like this: *Hey, kid, listen. The music you've heard is just the tip of an iceberg.* The book was an overwhelming introduction to the idea of a Rock 'n' Roll Pantheon, one which might intelligibly sweep the Cream and Joni Mitchell albums

I knew from my mother's collection into a continuum with the Talking Heads and Clash I was then so passionately making my own. The message on the other side of the bottle's slip of paper might have been: *What's more, my friend, there's a bunch of really hot-shit writers who've been arguing about this stuff for longer than you've been listening.* Those assembled in Marcus's book included many of the founding fathers (and a couple of mothers) of Rock Writing, itself a pantheon: Christgau, Dave Marsh, M. Mark, John Rockwell, Lester Bangs, Nick Tosches, Ellen Willis, Paul Nelson, etcetera, etcetera. Even without the contextualizing hints in Marcus's introduction, it was easy to infer the sustained (and sustaining) conversation these writers had been in with one another and the music. It was also more than evident that the writers saw this conversation as an opportunity for the conscious practice of an art form, the essay. For a nascent music-nerd and wannabe writer, this was heady stuff. In one shot I'd learned that real writing could alchemize with a passion for music, that some people had made this precious fool's gold an avocation and even a sort of career, and that there had been Kinks' records before *Low Budget*—several of them, in fact.

So, in editing *Da Capo Best Music Writing*, it's been impossible for me not to wonder how the results might fare as a message in a bottle—or, to change the metaphor slightly, as a time capsule of 2001—or, to change the metaphor wildly, as a kind of hologram of popular music culture, a microcosmic Sim City to represent in shrunken proportion every facet of the larger World of Pop. Could a Martian reconstruct our era solely from the evidence contained in this *Best Music Writing* volume, as I had reconstructed the Founding Fathers' worldview from the sole existence of *Stranded*? The answer's no, absolutely. Popular music's history, like its present, is vastly more complex in 2001 than in 1978. Not least because, as Nick Hornby ably described in his introduction to last year's book, that history is now intricately woven into its present, from samples to reissues. Besides, even *Stranded* only intimated the world to my teenage-Martian brain, it didn't actually contain it. I needed record stores and hundreds of further books, as well as thousands of magazines and liner notes and conversations, to enact the full reconstruction. In truth, that project is still in progress, a life's work, though now it's been muddled by the attempt to comprehend everything that's happened since 1978.

Oh, and I've tried to live in the present, too. Pop purists and Buddhists concur, it's best to live in the present. I'm doing my best: *must parse new record reviews, must get ass out of the reissue section in the record store: Be Here Now.* I've so far skirted the whole looming question of *fuddy-duddyism*, destined to be wrestled with eternally in this field of study where the maximum impact between subject and object is ordinarily made somewhere in adolescence, say around age thirteen or fourteen. So, full disclosure: I'm thirty-eight. Though that's poor excuse for a paradigm shift, Da Capo ought to be congratulated on their progress: without actually consulting with a mathematician, I've calculated that the arc from Peter Guralnick (editor of the 2000 volume) through Hornby (last year), and now to me dictates that the editor of the 2004 *Da Capo Best Music Writing* will need to be thirteen years old, while the editor of the 2006 volume hasn't been born yet.

The point? I'm the first editor in this series who can fairly claim to be *faking it in both directions.* Sure, I've got a twelve year-old niece who understands the radio better than I do—who doesn't? But I'll also admit that the first Rolling Stones song I heard on the radio *as a new single*, instead of an "oldie," was "Emotional Rescue" (I thought it was wonderful), a confession sure to chagrin anyone who's endured my discourses on the virtues of *Sticky Fingers* or *Exile on Main Street*, never mind *Aftermath.* My generation, such as it is, is the one jolted into solidarity in mourning Joey Ramone, and we were born into a world the giants, those both writing and written about in *Stranded*, had already made. What did our glorified punk-ineptitudes and leather-jacket poses mean if not this: To seize this music for ourselves, to seize a life for ourselves, was to embrace *faking it*, brazenly.

Not to say the giants have abandoned the field. A quarter-century later, four of *Stranded*'s contributors are collected in the first two volumes of this series (including the undead Lester Bangs). Also Richard Meltzer, who, by the appearance of his *Rock Aesthetics* in Paul Williams's early mimeographed issues of *Crawdaddy*, has a share of the claim to have invented the rock-crit form. What are the chances for the egg-sucking mammals of this planet when the dinosaurs are still so crafty, alert, and strong? It's as unfair as . . . well . . . as the tyranny of Bob Dylan's *Love and Theft* over the *Village Voice*'s Pazz and Jop Poll this past year. Muttering can be heard through the land: When will these guys take their jewels and binoculars and go home and take a nap?

No time soon, I hope. Let any revolution be incomplete while I'm in charge—that thirteen-year-old can clean house in 2004. Much of my favorite music writing last year was by the Usual Suspects, as was much of my favorite music. It happened, for instance, that 2001 was The Year Bluegrass Broke. Go figure. Besides, if picking a big fat pile of writing I loved was pure pleasure, the responsibility to create a snapshot of 2001 was mostly as distracting as it sounds. This is my chance to mention all the things this book could have been, and isn't: Rock Obituaries 2001, The Year's Best Dylan Writing, or Fifty Thousand Music Fans Array Themselves Like Iron Filings in Postures of Attraction and Repulsion Vis-à-vis The Strokes (though I did find a useful distillation of this element in an excerpt from the Ilovemusic online forum, where much of the impromptu chatter is as good as the best magazine writing). The book also isn't The Year's Best

Capsule Reviews, Sidebars, Top Ten Lists and Photo Captions. Though that stuff forms the regular work of a large number of talented writers, and is often smashingly clever, I'm helpless in my general preference for essays and profiles when it comes to re-reading, which is the point of binding this compendium with something more durable than staples. I've let Carl Wilson's poignant references to *which cool bands are coming to town this week* stand as a tribute to the yeoman work done by weekly columnists and listings writers everywhere, whose frontline efforts keep us all fresh and hopeful in our quest for a good show: Good show. Nor is this book What I Was Listening To and How Little It Mattered In September and October, though it easily could have been. 2001 was a year with a crater in it, and it seemed nearly every music writer, nearly every *writer* (myself included), contributed something to the vast collective howl of despair. But to include more than a few references was to feel the void open again under my feet, and then suddenly the subject wasn't music at all. The conclusion of many of the writers, anyway, was my conclusion in editing the book: 2001's music answered the needs of that moment better than music writing ever could. O Death, indeed.

So, welcome instead to Johnny's Graying Teenaged Sense of What Isn't Boring. I promise no objectivity: My tastes in music played a part here, as did my bullshit detector. I spent some money on new CDs to road-test claims for alluring new acts I hadn't heard. If the piece was a rave, I felt I ought to play official taster. Nice work, really, easier than trying to write about music from scratch or crashing vacuum cleaners for *Consumer Reports*. I also vetoed pieces, many of them appealingly written, even rhetorically strong, which were nevertheless pegged on listener's assertions I couldn't abide: Sorry, but if you want to claim that The Spinners' records don't hold up, do it on someone else's watch. Faking it and getting it wrong aren't the same thing. All we've got on this island—all anyone has in this archipelago of islands, here in this sea littered with urgent and impulsive communiqués, both musical and written—are two ears and the truth as we know it.

"When I found Steve Young, I had been heartsick a while," begins David Eason in his piece on the country singer, "and he was singing songs that told stories about a world I knew. It's a world where you go somewhere and aren't sure how you feel about it, where you feel the past pushing you away and pulling you back, where you cover sad feelings with crooked smiles and bitter words, where you make tough choices and always pay the price for them." In trying to explain the pull of Young's voice, Eason offers his own, and there's nothing more a writer can do. Music writing is an art of substitution, but perhaps so is any art. What we seek is the voice, and what's behind it. What we want is to be with ourselves, but not alone. This book, I hope, is a book of encounters, none of them predictable, whether the names are as familiar as the Beatles or Louis Armstrong or Jennifer Lopez, or as new to you as Kelly Hogan or Opeth were to me, or as unfamiliar and *unlikely* as Korla Pandit (I'll admit I searched the name on the Internet to be sure I wasn't being hoaxed by this account of a fake fakir). Take it as an invitation to an impossible, gabbling conversation, a party line, where every voice is unfor-gettable—vivid with a freight of confession, advocacy, sarcasm, dismay. The characters in these pieces are musicians and fans, sometimes also disc jockeys or producers or family members, but above all the characters in these stories are the writers them-selves: chasing leads, pitching angles, making lists, constructing impossible gossamer theories, sprawled wrecked in depression on their couches, envying their heroes, arguing with their friends, changing stations, listening, listening, always listening. Faking it. We're all faking it, even Greil Marcus. Thank God, too. It's literally the best, and most human, thing we can do.

—Introduction to *Da Capo Best Music Writing 2002*

Close Reading (Ricks on Dylan)

Christopher Ricks and I share a privilege. It's one you share too, assuming you join in our almost fathomless esteem for the songs and performances of the *sui generis* poet-singer Bob Dylan. That is, to have had our lifetimes overlap with an artist whom stone fans like Ricks and I suspect future generations will regard, in his visionary fecundity, with the awe reserved for Blake, Whitman, Picasso and the like. This concurrence of our lives with his is a privilege that shouldn't be taken for granted: forty or fifty years from now, one of the questions younger people will surely ask of elderly witnesses to the twentieth century is, "Did you ever go to a Bob Dylan concert?" If the reply comes: "You have no idea what a hassle Madison Square Garden could be," it will be met with shaming incredulity.

That Christopher Ricks? Yes, that one—the great British literary critic, exemplar of the art of "close-reading," explicator of Milton, Keats, Tennyson and Housman, praised by none other than W. H. Auden as "the kind of critic every poet dreams of finding," and now the author of the tome-like *Dylan's Vision of Sin*—a volume perhaps *ipso facto* to be regarded as either the most intimidating rock-critical treatise ever published, or the silliest, or both. Or, as one friend blurted when I'd said I was reviewing the book: "Does that mean you have to read all the way to the end?"

I did, with escalating ease and pleasure. Ricks, surely aware of the oddness of his enterprise—the elevation of a member of the Traveling Wilburys to a place among the greatest poets in the English language—has anticipated not only the possible resistance of his usual readership to his subject at hand, but also the probable unfamiliarity with his aims and methods in the potential new readership he will have attracted. "Most people who are likely to read this book will already know what they feel about Dylan, though they might not always know quite why they feel it"; this is how he opens the book, with typical brio and warmth. Ricks quickly addresses concerns that Dylan might not be properly treated as a poet: "The case for denying Dylan the title of poet could not summarily, if at all, be made good by any open-minded close attention to the words and his ways with them. The case would need to begin with his medium, or rather with the mixed-media nature of song, as of drama." Translation: if the lines in Shakespeare's plays, written for and much enlivened by (sufficiently inspired) performance, make a legitimate object of reverence and study, what's your problem? Might it really only be that you never had to see Shakespeare sing on "We Are the World," or accept an Oscar by live satellite feed from Australia? If so, get over it.

Perhaps thinking of potential new readers, Ricks makes the book a seductive primer in his own methods. Take a look, he seems to say, at the pleasure in juxtaposing one poet with another (he abuts Dylan with Lowell, Marvell, Tennyson, Eliot, Herbert, and many others): see how they seem to read one another, while you and I, reader, stand back and watch. Or consider the rewards of parsing what you've taken for granted even in songs you praise as masterworks: a lyric's exact strategy and means, what it has in common with other human utterances, and what sets it apart. Such clockwork dissection never seems to drain Dylan's work of its vitality (a tribute to Ricks and Dylan both, I suspect), but rather to renew a listener's amazement. By the end of one such disquisition Ricks may persuade you that rhyme, that corny tool, is the central receptacle for not only Dylan's wit but for the moral and emotional brilliance of his art.

Close reading, on close reading, turns out in Ricks's hands to be a lively sport, full of beguiling allusions, teasing asides and free philosophical musings, and bursting with groanworthy puns. See, or rather hear, Ricks analyze Dylan's use of pronouns in "Like a Rolling Stone":

> The pronoun "you" is the song's pronouncement, this being a song in which, although "they" may for a while be hanging out with "you" ("They're all drinkin', thinkin' that they got it made") and "he" may be doing so, too (even if "He's not selling any alibis"), "you" will never, Miss Lonely, enjoy the company of "we" or "us," and never ever the company of an "I." Of all Dylan's creations this is the song that, while it is one of his most individual, exercises the severest self-control when it comes to never mentioning its first person. Never say I. Not I and I: you and you.

Elsewhere, Ricks riffs on one of Dylan's latest offerings, the song "Sugar Baby" (2001):

> Two idioms were the parents of this Sugar Baby, parents who—despite not exactly getting on with one another— were determined to make a go of it. They are the idioms to go without ("You went years without me") and to keep going ("Might as well keep going now"). Their child would be keep going without. Meanwhile, lurking in the brains behind ma and pa is the thought of getting going, which is why the words "get" and "got" get to usher in "went without" and "keep going."

Ricks's lighter-than-air allusion to an earlier song—"the brains behind ma and pa" is a near-quote from "Maggie's Farm"—reminds us of another lyric about quitting and setting off down the road. There's madness in his method, but Ricks's confidence in his reader's willingness to follow him derives from the willingness to follow displayed by Dylan's listeners.

Readers may be disconcerted by Ricks's sheer goofiness, a tendency not constrained to his writing on this new, pop-culture subject: Ricks's *Beckett's Dying Words* is equally antic, even as it worries at Beckett's graveness. Punning is less an ornament on Ricks's critical prose than one of its central methods, one alive with the kind of linguistically embedded meanings he wants to excavate in the first place. Bent on tormenting into view the recalcitrant intention hidden in a writer's vocabulary, syntax and rhyme, Ricks will stop at nothing to extract the information he craves, even tickling. Happily, he's got an ear for a tune as well as a trope. The songs he discusses, taken as the contents of a mix tape, would consist neither of Dylan's greatest hits (though many are here), nor of a bunch of stuff rewarding to parse but musically dull. Rather, Ricks has picked a lot of "sleepers"—those Dylan songs that emerge as favorites on long listening, not purely for their lyrical sophistication but for their depth in that mysterious conjunction of lyric, music, and performance. Ricks's book leads you back into Dylan's music, no small virtue.

Dylan's Vision of Sin seems a conscious attempt to forge a post-biographical context for Dylan's art, to sweep away in one gesture the defensiveness, gossip, and, perhaps worst of all, proprietary distortions too often imposed on an artist's legacy while it is still in the making. There are those who, like Kinbote in Nabokov's *Pale Fire*, ask us to believe their approach to Dylanology, pegged on Woody Guthrie, heroin, or the Kabbalah, is exclusively correct. Ricks, on the other hand, has no stake in persuading his reader that his particular taxonomical trick, which consists of reading Dylan's songs against the seven deadly sins, four cardinal virtues, and three heavenly graces, is anything more than what William Empson calls "the right handle for picking up the bundle," i.e., a reasonably adequate stance from which to begin contemplating the artist's accomplishment. (In fact, he forgoes his chapter on Greed, concluding blithely that Dylan hasn't written any songs on the subject.) Ricks grants art's ultimate indifference to criticism—so, despite a tone of vast assurance, his book is agreeably humble.

In attempting to set, almost single-handedly, the course for the future of "Dylan Studies," Ricks has a counterpart in Greil Marcus. An American critic who began as a "rock writer," Marcus brings to consideration of Dylan's music a freight of vernacular knowledge as weighty as Ricks's academic discipline. Beginning in the classic *Mystery Train*, and then, more recently and extensively, in *The Old, Weird America*, Marcus has placed Dylan deep in his American context, the same swamp of indigenous voicings that gave rise to alchemists like Walt Whitman, John Ford, and Chuck Berry.

Marcus is both Ricks's twin and his opposite. He provides the corrective to Ricks's seeming disinterest in America, or in Dylan's magpie appropriations from folk and pop traditions, as opposed to his relationship to canonical poetry. Certainly there are moments, reading Ricks, when you want to shout: *The sixteen year-old Robert Zimmerman didn't want to be Lord Tennyson, man, he wanted to be Muddy Waters!* But Ricks wouldn't argue; that's the strength of his book. The critic has merely wished to test the songs he loves against his own pre-existing context, which happens to be Philip Larkin and Matthew Arnold, not Blind Willie McTell. In doing so he's found them all the more extraordinary, not wanting in any measure. Any critic's a blind man, faced with an elephant as formidable as the collected works of Bob Dylan. But some blind men have extraordinarily sensitive hands, and it is possible to imagine an elephant's pleasure at their touch.

—*The New York Times*, 2004

Rod Serling

I've never seen a photograph of Rod Serling that wasn't black and white.

In fact, I doubt color photographs of Serling exist. Oh, there may have been family Kodachromes, but let me respectfully submit for your approval the notion that if one were to examine the Serling family albums one would discover standing amidst any number of bright-cheeked picnickers or beachgoers clad in Pop-Art-hued loungewear a lone figure in video grey and black, holding a styrofoam cup of coffee and a cigarette. Like Edward R. Murrow and Humphrey Bogart, fellow icons of narrow-lapelled masculinity, Serling just wouldn't register on color film.

Rod Serling was so many things, and many of them are now hard to keep entirely in focus: Master of a brief, much-lamented era of live plays on television, and paradigmatic figure of that monstrous new medium's potential and decline. Assimilated Jew whose vision of grey-flannel alienation helped define postwar American discontent, and a writer so distracted by celebrity that he never mastered his craft to his own satisfaction. In the end, Serling, much like his big-screen model Orson Welles, was a polymath showboat whose instinct for hamming led him increasingly in front of the camera, to end his days sadly renting out his charisma as a game-show host, documentary narrator, and commercial pitchman for

Schlitz Beer and Famous Writer's Correspondence School.

All these identities have been subsumed and forgotten, need-less to say, behind Serling's one great and defining accomplish-ment, the one that begins: "There is a fifth dimension beyond that which is known to man . . ." I remember very clearly—though perhaps *clearly* is not the word for a memory so freighted with fear, with intimations of an adult world I wasn't sure I wanted to discover—my first glimpse of *The Twilight Zone*. In the 1970s, Channel Eleven in New York would show an hour of *The Twilight Zone* episodes at midnight. I must have been seven or eight and I was up alone watching television, I can't say why. The episode was "Mirror Image"—which in lucid adult retro-spect I know as one of Serling's most pure, stark and dreamlike. I had no such perspective at the time, no perspective of any kind.

In "Mirror Image" the jittery Vera Miles—a favorite actress of Hitchcock's in the same period—attempts to pick up her ticket and check her suitcase at a bus depot; she's informed by the ticket taker that she's *already* checked in. The situation is shrouded in night and gloom, in low-budget black and white as spare and rigorous as an X-ray. In the washroom mirror Miles glimpses her exact double, outside in the waiting room. She pursues her double, who vanishes. She seeks the advice of an-other traveller, a man who, first sympathetic, eventually betrays her to the authorities. Miles is dragged off to the nuthatch. By the remorseless paranoiac ethics of *The Zone* this betrayal seals the man's fate: *his* double appears to usurp him. Then Serling passes the magical hand of his narration over the affair: "Ob-scure metaphysical explanation to cover a phenomenon . . . call it parallel planes or just insanity . . ." My eight year-old self called it terror, and I remember fighting to push it out of mind. How could an image be so unresolved and yet so absolute? Of course my double waited somewhere to slip into the world and replace me! And what a dreadful mistake to have watched this

television show which was like a missive in the night and by doing so to accidentally have learned the truth—for now I'd have
to live with the certainty of doom.

Later it got easier, and a bit more fun, to watch *The Twilight
Zone.*

In America when a writer gets famous, not just slightly but
truly famous, he or she always seems like something other than
a writer. In Serling's case, it turns out that when fame arrived he
seemed like something other than a writer even to himself; this
was a disaster for his morale. Of course, to teenagers dwelling in
reruns of *The Twilight Zone* as my friends and I did, Serling was
anything but a writer—he was a tone of voice, a raised eyebrow,
an attitude of amused tolerance to life's inarguable strangeness,
irony, and danger. He was a semi-fictional creation, an ema-
nation from his own *Zone*, and we learned to mock his clipped
cadences to prove to ourselves that we were as comfortable there
as he was, that we were even able to afford to find him a bit silly.

We were only following a trend, late. *The Twilight Zone*, like
other '50's pop cultural revolutions—method acting, beatnik
culture, and rock and roll—had triumphed and failed simultaneously through the sixties: triumphed by transforming the
culture and failed by being absorbed and defanged through
over-exposure and parody. Later we might come to take the
Zone less for granted, to recognize it—partly with the help of
Marc Scott Zicree's groundbreaking *The Twilight Zone Companion* and Arlen Schumer's sublime coffee-table-sized *Visions
From the Twilight Zone*—as an outbreak of surrealist invention in
the bland, fantasy-resistant center of our culture, as a crossroads
where Edgar Allen Poe (by way of E. C. Comics) met film noir
and pulp science fiction to create a sort of proto-Kubrickian,
nihilistically liberal shout against the smug conformity of the
Eisenhower era. Maybe we'd even pause to wonder at the tragedy this last glimpse of television's era of the "anthology series"

suggested. But by then Serling was dead, his early work and its context long forgotten. It only seemed a faint irony to learn that Serling was the most honored writer in the history of television *before The Twilight Zone*, that when he first announced the series it was seen as a disastrous artistic compromise, a signal of the collapse of his ambition.

It's possible to exalt the *Zone* and still slight the notion of Serling as a writer. We prefer our visionaries to be idiot savants or mediums, to see their wild gifts as outbreaks of zeitgeist or the traumatic subconscious. A Jewish WWII paratrooper from Binghamton N.Y. invented *The Twilight Zone*? That's as likely as a tubercular clerk from Prague writing *The Castle* and *The Metamorphosis*, or a mathematician from Oxford pushing *Through the Looking Glass*. In Gordon Sander's otherwise fine and thorough biography of Serling, that central imaginative leap is never explained, never questioned. But where did *The Twilight Zone* come from? Who was this guy?

Here's who: A kid who grew up listening to Orson Welles's *The Shadow* on the radio and then went to war and then returned, like many thousands of others, to an America as strong as it was strongly in need of reassurance against horror, both past and future. A country trying to find a normative middle between a newly-popularized Id within and a newly-invented Bomb above. Serling wasn't a beatnik, not even a little. He was a striver with a wife and kids in Cincinnati when he began to find his voice, with a clear view from the ground level of the suburban dream—yet Jewish and probably always with that subtle double consciousness of the outsider "passing," ever aware of the possibility of exile and prejudice.

Beginning in radio and quickly moving to television, Serling was from the first a pound-the-words-out storyteller with a passion for controversial social issues and a startling morbid streak. After *Patterns*, a riveting, stripped-down diagnosis of the ruthless new business class, took the country by storm—popular demand resulted in an unprecedented second run-through, a month after the original (and live television could only be re-enacted, since videotape didn't exist!)—Serling overnight joined Paddy Chayevsky and Reginald Rose as emblems of serious television's potential. It was then he became the clench-jawed idol we know as the *Zone*'s host, depicted on paperback collections of his teleplays scowling in front of his typewriter with a cigarette in his knuckles, an intellectual for the age of McLuhan.

Between *Patterns* and *Requiem for a Heavyweight*, the two Emmy-confirmed summits of his career in live teleplays, Serling battled censors and sponsors over the content of innumerable stories of racism, tortured and brainwashed prisoners of war, neo-Nazism, and corruption in government—a struggle which pointed directly to the allegory and indirection of the *Zone*. He struggled as well with his own tendency to purple speechifying, and a weakness for working too quickly, dictating tales good and bad into his tape recorder and seeing them thrown instantly onto the little screen. The best of this work, though, is startlingly good, in a medium Serling helped invent on the spot; live televised noir, with Serling's signature sweaty close-ups written in, and an astonishing compression of means as actors slipped from set to set in the space of what must have seemed like an hour on a tightrope, dodging bullets. Serling was known for his on-set micromanagement of the productions—by his own testimony his diet in those years consisted mainly of "coffee and fingernails."

Don't take my word—find *Patterns* and *Requiem* if you can, not in their inferior, padded-out Hollywood film versions, but in collections of "Golden Age Television," which survive only because the network preserved file copies by pointing a sixteen-millimeter film camera at the screen during the live broadcasts. Especially seek out the lesser-known *The Comedian*, which was perhaps the pre-*Zone* Serling's and the live teleplay's greatest masterpiece. Serling's collaborators on *The Comedian* were Ernest Lehman, who supplied the original story, the young director John Frankenheimer, and Mickey Rooney in a tour-de-force performance in the lead role—a depiction of sadism and ruthlessness as persuasive as James Cagney's in *White Heat*.

Long after declining standards and creeping commercialization had driven his fellow Golden Age writers off to Hollywood, traditional theater and other destinations, Serling persisted—"Television's Last Angry Man" was his biographer's perfect epitaph. Perhaps it was an instinctive match—there was something in Serling's temperament and talent that suited him to the crush of deadlines and the shorter dramatic forms that were typical of television. It would also eventually be his downfall, a medium-turned-marketplace that would tempt his worst instincts and wring him dry. But not before Serling, in one breathless three-year rise and a fatigued two-year decline, created his masterpiece, a definitive statement in 156 nightmarish glimpses.

The Twilight Zone might have seemed a capitulation to series television, but in fact the anthology structure perfectly capitalized on Serling's strengths while sparing him the constant battles for creative control that had come close to driving him away. And in a culture that devalued and marginalized the imaginative and fantastic element everywhere it detected it—save perhaps a Salvador Dali painting or two—the *Zone* certainly struck critics as a retreat from relevant, serious, adult work. The shift into fantasy spared Serling the censorship battles that had scarred his earlier work, simply because literal-minded censors couldn't easily parse the *Zone*'s metaphorical vocabulary. As Serling-esque ironies go, here's a good one: a strong parallel existed in postwar Soviet Russia, where incisive criticisms of the bureaucratic state slipped under state censorship's radar in the form of science fiction stories and short animated films.

The truth was that much of Serling's realist writing was grimly topical, riddled with the sort of lecturing which can make Stanley Kramer's or John Sayles's films run suddenly into a ditch. The *Twilight Zone* episodes wouldn't prove wholly immune to this weakness. But through the medium of fantasy, allegory, and parable Serling found a way to continue to obsess on the great themes of his times—alienation, the Bomb, conformity, McCarthyism, censorship, racism—but in a timeless voice, and one which captured Serling's own fatalistic idealism better than he had all but a very few times before.

He also became a master entertainer, a generator of images and tonalities and phrases that embedded themselves in the culture so completely that their influence can be hard to properly distinguish anymore. What Serling created, above all else, was a homegrown vernacular of alienation, identity slippage and paranoia, and he did it right when it most needed doing, when his audience was starved for a vocabulary to express their uneasiness—and he did it on weekly television. Just the titles of his best episodes read like a found poem of All-American dread: "Where Is Everybody?" "Walking Distance." "People Are Alike All Over." "Time Enough at Last." "The Obsolete Man." "Eye of the Beholder." "Nervous Man in a Four Dollar Room." "The Monsters Are Due on Maple Street." "The After Hours." And so on.

Certainly, Serling incurred debts right and left—Richard Matheson and Charles Beaumont, in particular, scripted some of *The Twilight Zone*'s most memorable shows. And Serling himself was a sponge, absorbing what he needed from science fiction and crime movies and the O. Henry–style short story and pouring it into his vision. What's remarkable is the instinct he demonstrated for distilling the pure communicative essence of his sources and discarding the frills—his science fiction didn't bother with zero-G calculations or any other nerdish jargon, but went straight for space-age estrangement effects. Well before J. G. Ballard's, Serling's astronauts came back to earth weirder and unhappier than when they'd left. Comparisons are rightly made between Serling's nostalgic/horrible You-Can't-Go-Home-Again small town stories and those of Ray Bradbury—and, apparently, Bradbury felt the resemblance was close enough to resent it. Serling holds up better than Bradbury, though—the reason, I think, is that Serling's sometimes overripe and sentimental rhetoric always plays against the scrupulous, cold eye of the televised image, where Bradbury's plays only against itself.

Lawsuits dogged *The Twilight Zone*, but oddly enough intimations of fakery and impersonation seem to have haunted Serling long before—both *Patterns* and *The Comedian* include vivid but non-essential motifs of plagiarism or disputed authorial credit. And of course, the *Zone* itself proved that inauthenticity seemed to Serling a constant danger—one might at any time peel up a strip of skin and discover the android lurking underneath, and any ventriloquist stood in danger of swapping places with his dummy. Serling's confidence as a writer was always fragile, and it had weathered years in the rough and tumble grind of television. Now he retreated to teaching at Antioch, his alma mater, but couldn't put down the tape recorder, couldn't stop dictating scripts in that manual-typewriter voice of his.

Serling never found much success as a Hollywood screenwriter, never really found success in his life after the *Zone* except as a beloved public figure. His script for his old collaborator John Frankenheimer's *Seven Days in May* is solid work. (It was Frankenheimer who came the closest to importing *The Twilight Zone's* vision to feature-length film in *The Manchurian Candidate* and *Seconds*.) He added the famous, and characteristic,

Statue of Liberty twist to *Planet of the Apes*. But Serling had somehow fallen out of touch during the *Zone* years. He spent 1968 researching the new youth culture for a Stanley Kramer film called *Children's Crusade* only to see it discarded in favor of a rewrite by Erich (*Love Story*) Segal. Then came the awkward lapses back to television—*The Loner*, an existential Western series which might have become an American version of *The Prisoner* if Serling had been given half a chance, and *Night Gallery*, which quickly degenerated into the humiliation of hosting other people's third-generation *Twilight Zone* photocopies. When he died from a series of heart attacks at the age of fifty it was a tragedy, but if I rush you past the Jacques Cousteau documentary narrations and heavy drinking of his final years it's only an act of mercy, trust me.

Flip the dial, though, and he lives again. There's a signpost up ahead, and standing beside it in a neat black suit is American alienation's hardboiled auteur, reassuring you that whatever measure of Kafkaesque disjunction you are about to suffer he will be there to guide you back out of it, using nothing more than a few terse phrases out of the side of his wry, enduring smile.

—*Gadfly*, 1999

Mutual Seduction

When you drive Sunset Boulevard, no traffic flow is gradual enough for the sensory occasion. Craning your neck to take in a billboard's extent through the insufficient frame of a windshield, you're seduced into a wild diversity of environments: an idyllic pond in which a band wades fully-dressed (Paul McCartney and Wings), a Sergio Leone western (the Eagles), a soft-edged surrealist fantasyscape (Yes), or the hypnotized front row at a festival show (Neil Young). Or you're enticed onto some other street altogether, say Abbey Road, once the 20-foot-high Beatles have crossed it—but wait, someone stole Paul's head! You might be pulled into a false intimacy with the musicians, as they slouch around a terrace or recording studio, or be swept into Jim Morrison's nostrils, Chaka Khan's cleavage or James Taylor's crotch. Images that originated on album covers or concert posters are transmuted by scale and setting into a vicarious dreamscape by those billboard artists—the genius designers and publicists and painters—whose work is captured in Robert Landau's lavish time-tunnel of a picture book, *Rock 'n' Roll Billboards of the Sunset Strip*.

Sure, the book contains text: extensive, well researched, and full of respectful awe for the largely anonymous creators, especially for the lost guild of those who hand-painted the billboards. Even if it's by definition redundant, and swamped by the pictures themselves, the writing is loaded with any number of amusing specifics as to the genesis or fate of this or that memorable image. Key quote: "For a brief time, it seemed as if everyone was making money." Another, from an interview with the designer Roland Young:

> Those billboards were made to show that the company and the artist agreed, that they shared the same philosophy. At that time it was very important that the record company be perceived as a company aligned with its artist. That's Number 1, and Number 2 is the artists could brag to their friends and family, "Hey Mom, I got a billboard on the Sunset Strip!" Once I understood this, I could solve the design problems, but not many people understood what the problem was.

Philosophy!

It's easy to think we're seeing advertising just now grope into its postmodern phase. On the one hand, Madison Avenue is fetishized for its classical—or modernist?—phase in *Mad Men*. Meanwhile, here in the so-called "present," we enjoy a paranoia-inducing mode in which our products transform us into their own commercials by the subliminal-viral methodology of social networks. Yet even these seemingly straightforward rock billboards document a cargo-cult or allegorical phase in the relationship between advertising's sway over our lives and the notion of commodity. For the idea that these billboards had anything to do with trying to separate a record-store customer from his six bucks seems ludicrous. Landau's book documents a kind of triumphalist tribal ritual, a phase in the heedless monetization of countercultural dreams by a recording industry high on a myth of its own transformational influence. The billboards depict a utopian realm just inches away and yet which refuses your entry utterly. Needless to say, the musicians themselves never attained it.

This mutual seduction, which no consummation could approximate, meets C. S. Lewis's criterion for what he calls Joy: "an unsatisfied desire which is itself more desirable than any other satisfaction." The cynic in me wants to say that the only honest billboard among the many dozens here is that for Pink Floyd's *The Wall*, depicting a bricked-up surface. The cynic in me is in the minority, confronted with the Joy here. Really, what's a lavish coffee-table book but another fetish? This book is reciprocal. It depicts and reenacts the dream of catching with binding and glue and gloss the ephemeral and ineffable; it represents another chance to pay for what can't be bought: a dream. As a happy member of both of the cargo cults in question, I want these billboards on my coffee table. And next time I drive the Strip, I'll rent a convertible.

—*The New York Times*, 2012

VIII

Fan Mail

Carved in Need

I never met Theodore Sturgeon, but I did have a chance to introduce him to my father, in a Sturgeonish fashion. Paul Williams and I were visiting Woodstock, New York, on our way from a convention in Massachusetts, and there we were to meet my father, who had driven to pick me up from and return me to his cabin in the Catskills. In Woodstock Paul and I met Noël Sturgeon, his daughter. We were an hour or so early for the rendezvous with my dad, and, of course, more than a decade late to hope for an encounter in the flesh with Theodore Sturgeon.

This was in 1993, at the start of North Atlantic Books' noble publishing marathon, *The Collected Stories of Theodore Sturgeon*, of which this is the tenth volume. At that time the project was a whisper or a promise. Or perhaps I should say it was a drive in the woods, for that is what it was that day. We went for a drive in the woods and Paul and I contemplated the territory of Sturgeon's life in his Woodstock years, with Noël's eloquent guidance, her narration and her silences. She led us down backroads to contemplate the place where Sturgeon's writing shack had been hidden. We absorbed the presence of his absence, and I absorbed the delicate weight of his daughter's spoken and unspoken memories, and those of her father's friend Paul. I remembered what I knew of Sturgeon, and I remembered the stories and when I'd first read them, when I was a kid. Noël spoke of her childhood with an artist father, and I thought of my own.

Then we went back into Woodstock and met my father in a café. By the time I was able to introduce Noël to my father I felt I was returning a favor, or at least trying to. I felt that I was completing a circle. Leaving Paul and Noël behind, driving off into the Catskills, I spoke to my father of Sturgeon, and I spoke to him differently. That night I slept beside my father in two sleeping bags in a cabin lit only by candles and by the stars, and there I told him more of my life as an adult than I ever had. I was still with Sturgeon, though I was alone with my father, and had never been with Sturgeon at all.

Sturgeon's stories are like that: they speak of human beings connecting with other human beings or attempting to do so at great odds, and at odd angles; of human beings failing at or sabotaging their own best efforts for fear that what they want most doesn't make any sense, or that the odds are too great; of human beings learning again and again that their thin howling selves are part of a chorus which stands shoulder to shoulder in a traffic jam, a mob scene of lonely selves, of members of a great estranged family of beings. Sturgeon wrote miraculous short stories. Some fly, some stumble, but all are miraculous. By that I mean he always wrote of miracles, of deliverance and miracles and of a lust for completion in an incomplete world. He wrote of needs and their denial, with such undisguised longing and anger that his stories are caustic with emotion. His stories are carved in need. Many of the fine examples gathered in Volume 10 are by happy coincidence the first ones Sturgeon wrote in those woods; he moved his family to Woodstock in 1959.

Paul Williams once said, in conversation, that Sturgeon's "only method was the tour de force." That has long seemed to me the only critical remark on Sturgeon's art that needs making. It is impossible to imagine the work arising from anything but the peculiar circumstances of its making. Sturgeon found his urgency directed in becoming, in bursts of stylistic juice, the John Dos Passos, the William Faulkner, the Ring Lardner, the James Thurber, the Virginia Woolf of science fiction. Science fiction gave him the motifs of transcendence and metamorphosis; it gave him, with its lunatic idealism about space exploration, the imperative of optimism. These he needed, to cut against what strikes me as an instinctive morbidity. See how Sturgeon's imagination collapses into the gothic in the non-SF tales; alternately, consider how *The Man Who Lost the Sea*, the finest literary fugue this side of James Salter's *Dusk*, relies on its rocket. Yet Sturgeon's work is the opposite of Pop Art; he never predicted much; his cheerleading's embarrassing. He can seem misplaced in science fiction. I'd argue he'd have been misplaced anywhere. And would he have written his masterpieces without that form to write against? I doubt it.

The results—well, they're as impossible as the foregoing suggests. Theodore Sturgeon's best stories are triumphant Golems. They stride tall while they shake off the entreaties of the clay of the battleground of which they were formed. They have nothing but their voices.

—Foreword to *The Man Who Lost the Sea: Volume X: The Complete Stories of Theodore Sturgeon*, 2005

New Old Friend (A Toast to Kenneth Koch)

I'm subject to an awful temptation here, and that is to lapse into some version of a shameless imitation of one of his own poems in introducing to you my hero, Kenneth Koch. How easy and disastrous it would be to begin *Oh Thank You for giving me the chance of being Kenneth Koch's introducer!* Or *A serious moment for the novelist is when he is asked to draw aside the curtain for his favorite poet!* Or *At a reading, one writer may hide behind another*—And yet I'm going to try to resist this temptation, this seduction, because I know where it leads, or at least I know where it led me once: when I was eighteen my adoration for Kenneth Koch led me to mistake myself for a poet. In 1984 as a college freshman I bluffed my way into a poetry workshop that was meant to be closed to freshman. I did this by appearing in person at the office of the poet who led the workshop, and when he looked at my trembling sheaf and asked me who my favorite poet was I declared proudly Kenneth Kotch! Rhyming it with crotch. I'd never heard the name said aloud. Now I know that that declaration was a very early warm-up for this evening. The teacher-poet corrected my pronunciation and let me into the workshop, and then, in a matter of months, taught me that I was not a poet. Or he allowed me to teach myself. Still, I wasn't done with being seduced by Kenneth Koch, not by a long shot.

A few years later, my then-wife and I began a photocopied zine which we called *Idiot Tooth*, and the motto of the zine, which was printed on the contents page, was "The only thing I could publicize well would be my tooth!" from Kenneth Koch's "Thank You." What is so seductive in those lines I'm compelled to mangle in my parodies, what it is that compels me to read and re-read Kenneth Koch's poems alone and in company, silently and aloud, what it was that once compelled me to read the entirety of "The Boiling Water" to a wedding full of people waiting to dance to a Klezmer band, is the forever-startling freshness and exuberance and generosity of the voice, the mock-effortless way that Kenneth Koch sweeps aside the drab curtain of formality to offer plain talk, wit, rhapsodic inventions, memories, dreams, regrets, fresh air. How odd it is, in a way, to try to introduce poems whose every first line is itself a how-do-you-do, a handclasp, a hot cookie cooling on a tin sheet in a corner of the kitchen when the baker's back is turned.

So often Kenneth Koch has offered us an apparent transparency—the gesture or impulse seemingly recorded naked for the page. Not that we should be fooled for a minute as to the rigor and purposefulness required to deliver such excellence— except, of course, for the endless pleasure in being fooled this way. In an early poem called "The Artist," Koch seems to display his own ambition and restlessness for us to admire:

I often think Play *was my best work.*
It is an open field with a few boards in it.
Children are allowed to come and play in Play
By permission of the Cleveland Museum.
I look up at the white clouds, I wonder what I
shall do, and smile.

Perhaps somebody will grow up having been
influenced by Play.
I think—but what good will that do?
Meanwhile I am interested in steel cigarettes . . .

Well, I'm not a poet, but I am a child who was permitted to play in *Play*. Kenneth Koch, as a writer, showed me the value of paradox and surprise, he showed me the value of intimacy and informality, and when I studied him harder he taught me the value of alertness, and hesitation, and of reading myself as patiently as I read others. He taught me how much of what I love might be allowed into my work—and, beyond that, and writing completely aside, he taught to me consider how much of what I loved might be allowed into my life. I'm terribly grateful to be invited to introduce to you a man who, though we've never met before tonight, is one of my oldest friends, Kenneth Koch.

—Introduction to Kenneth Koch's reading
at the Bowery Poetry Club on March 30, 2002.
Printed that same year in *Crossroads*

Eyes Wide Open

I'm aware of one—*one*—reader who doesn't care for Lorrie Moore, and even that one seems a little apologetic about it. "Too . . . punny," my friend explained to me, resorting to a pun as though hypnotized by the very tendency that had triggered her resistance. For others, Moore may be, exactly, *the* most irresistible contemporary American writer: brainy, humane, unpretentious, and warm; seemingly effortlessly lyrical; Lily-Tomlin-funny. Most of all, Moore is capable of enlisting not just our sympathies but our sorrows. For many readers, the fact that Moore has relieved an eleven-year publishing breach (her last book, the story collection *Birds of America*, concludes with her unforgettable baby-with-cancer story, "People Like That Are the Only People Here," a breathtakingly dark overture to a decade's silence—as if the Beatles had exited on "A Day in the Life") is reason enough to start Google-mapping a route to the nearest surviving bookstore.

If American fiction writers largely find themselves sorted tediously into the category of "natural" at either the short or the long form, regardless of the extent of their commitment to both, then Moore—justly celebrated for her three story collections—has surely been counted as a miniaturist. This book should spell the end of that. *A Gate at the Stairs* is a novel more expansive than either of her two previous novels, the slender,

Nabokovian *Who Will Run the Frog Hospital?* or the structurally dizzy novel-as-set-of-variations *Anagrams*. It's also one that brandishes some "big" material: racism, war, etcetera—albeit in Moore's resolutely insouciant key.

The novel's protagonist and narrator Tassie Keltjin is a student at a midwestern college mecca, daughter of a boutique potato cultivator, who finds work as the nanny-in-waiting for a brainy couple awkwardly on the verge of adoption. This ambiguous assignment takes the foreground in a tale ranging over Tassie's home life and love life—the nest she's just departed and the nest she's hoping to flutter into. Moore's class diagnostics are so exact that she can make us feel the uneasiness not only between town and country in a sole landlocked state, but between different types of farmers on neighboring plots. The book is also set in the autumn of 2001, a fact Moore has the patience to barely deploy for two hundred pages, and then only with a deft sleight-of-hand that will make readers reflect on the ways other treatments of this (unfinished) passage in American life have resembled heart surgery performed with a croquet mallet.

In a 2005 interview, Moore made an allusion to this "post-9/11" aspect of the work that grew into this novel: "I'm . . . interested in the way that the workings of governments and elected officials intrude upon the lives and minds of people who feel generally safe from the immediate effects of such workings." The delicacy of this remark fails to disguise its clarity of purpose, and, as it happens, distant international affairs are by no means the only source of "intrusion" in *A Gate at the Stairs*. Moore's continuing interest in how power imbalances make themselves felt in human encounters fastens here on the Kafka-worthy bureaucracy of adoption agencies and foster homes. Combined with her immaculately tender portrayals of young children, so real you want to pass around their snapshots, this aspect of her novel will do such things to your heart that you may find yourself wishing for the surgeon with the croquet mallet, just for mercy.

Moore's cast is sneaky-large (she's like an athlete you keep wanting to call sneaky-fast, or sneaky-tough). Any of Tassie's relationships—like that with her adoption-seeking employer Sarah Brink, or her vivid goof of a younger brother, or her exotic first love interest, Reynaldo (whom she meets in "Intro to Sufism")—may seem this book's essential one, at least while it assumes center-stage. But the novel's real essence is its sinuous roving spotlight, in which each character and element is embraced in Tassie's wondering and exact sensibility, as when with her brother she revisits a childhood haunt:

> When the gnats weren't bad I had sometimes accompanied him, sat in the waist-high widgeon grass beside him, the place pink with coneflowers, telling him the plot of, say, a Sam Peckinpaugh movie I'd never seen but had read about once in a syndicated article in the *Dellacrosse Sunday Star*. Crickets the size of your thumb would sing their sweet monotony from the brush. Sometimes there was a butterfly so perfect and beautiful, it was like a party barrette you wanted to clip in your hair. Above and around us green leaves would flash wet with sunsetting light. In this verdant cove I recounted the entire plot of *Straw Dogs* . . . Now we stood at the cold stream's edge, tossing a stone in and listening for its *plonk* and plummet. I wanted to say, "Remember the time . . ." But too often when we compared stories from our childhood, they didn't match. I would speak of a trip or a meal or a visit from a cousin and of something that had happened during it, and Robert would look at me as if I were speaking of the adventures of some Albanian rock band.

So I stayed quiet with him. It is something that people who have been children together can effortlessly do. It is sometimes preferable to the talk, which is also effortless.

We found more stones and tossed them. "A stone can't drown," said my brother finally. "It's already drowned."

"You been reading poetry?" I smiled at him.

As for the puns, they seem to me less an eagerness to entertain than a true writerly obsession. Moore's an equal-opportunity japester: heroes and villains both crack wise with Chandler-esque vivacity, so you can't use cleverness as a moral index. The wrinkly recursiveness of her languages seems lodged at the layer of consciousness itself, where Moore demands readers' attention to the innate thingliness of words. This includes not only their plastic capacity as puns, and the oddnesses residing in names for food, foliage and products—for instance, the fact that no bachelor likely ever wore the flowers called "bachelor buttons," or that a fabric's neutral hue can be awarded names as various as pigeon, parmesan, platinum or pebble—but their potential use as deliberate uncommunication: "'Sounds good,' I sang out into the dark of the car. *Sounds good*, that same midwestern girl's slightly frightened reply. It appeared to clinch a deal, and was meant to sound the same as the more soldierly *Good to go*, except it was promiseless—mere affirmative description."

Finally, this book plumbs deep because it is anchored deep, in a system of natural imagery as tightly organized as that in a cycle of poems like Ted Hughes's *Crow*. The motif is birth, gestation, and burial, a seed or fetus uncovering its nature in secrecy, a coffin being offered to the earth. The motif declares itself upfront in Tassie's father's potatoes, which like sleeper cells grow clustered in darkness, and then, unearthed, assume names: Klamath pearls, yellow fingerlings, purple Peruvians and Rose Finns. In *The Gate at the Stairs* it is more than potatoes which adapt themselves for the world behind assumed names, but babies and grownups too.

Great writers usually present us with mysteries, but the mystery Lorrie Moore presents consists of appearing genial, joshing and earnest at once—unmysterious, in other words, yet still great. She's a discomfiting, sometimes even rageful writer, lurking in the disguise of an endearing one. On finishing *A Gate at the Stairs* I turned to the reader nearest to me and made her swear to read it immediately (well, the dog was between us, but doesn't read much, and none of what I recommend). I might even urge it on my dissenting friend.

—*The New York Times*, 2009

Something About a Slice

I shouldn't be writing this with ink or pixels—I should be ladling tomato sauce onto a blank sheet of pizza dough to form the letters, or throwing my laptop up in the air and spinning it around on one finger while you look at me through an open counter window from the street. As a New York City street kid, watching those guys was for me like gazing at a well-appointed beat cop, a three-card monte hustler at his tiny folding table, or the fireman who drove the rear end of a hook-and-ladder—a fundamental exhibition of indigenous authority and style, of blue-collar masculine pizzazz (I hadn't noticed the *pizza* hiding in *pizzazz* until just now). While I never twirled dough myself, I did test myself in the realm of pizza: the day I ate seven slices during a friend's birthday party at a slice house on Livingston Street between Hoyt and Bond in downtown Brooklyn (we were coming back from seeing a Kung Fu movie or a Richard Pryor flick at the Duffield Theater, I'm guessing). That was the day I became a man, my Bar Pitzva. Later, as a punk teen with a fetish for pranks and mail-art, I ate a slice from Queen on Court Street fourteen days in a row, and mailed the cheese-greasy sheet of translucent white paper that had supported each slice—What the hell are those things called? They're a slice's footman, Igor to its Dr. Frankenstein, and no one ever pays them any attention at all, but they're *doing the job*, man, they're *getting it done*—to my friend Eliot, who'd lived in Brooklyn but now lived in upstate New York. This was my way of being a jerk—Hey, I still live in the five boroughs, and you don't—and bragging of my appetites, but also of communing with Eliot on the subject of the sacred everyday things that were underfoot everywhere and needed celebration, the bounteous wrecked worlds of childhood and New York. Just the shakers full of oregano and red pepper flake and garlic salt, oh my: deciding which were your favored toppings, and in what proportion, and then sneering at those choosing otherwise.

Someone once claimed that the New York subways were a great secret neighborhood, running underneath all the others and uniting them—and that person wasn't wrong—but the pizzerias, all so identical and each so snowflake- or finger-print-unique, those are the upper stations of this Pynchonian secret system, the not-at-all innocuous fuel outposts, the crow's nests for scoping out the upper realm—hence the famous syn-chronicity between the price of a slice and the cost of a single fare on the trains. Someday I'd like to pop out once at every sta-tion in the system and gobble a slice from the pizzeria a stone's-throw from the stairwell (you *know* it's there), and someday I will, I swear. To remember pizza is to remember your life, sure, but it's also to dream of days, of slices to come, because the piz-zerias of New York City are like that: stretching out implacably through your past to your untold future. Slow down, smell the dough—maybe grab a slice or two, or even a calzone, hey, you went to the gym yesterday, you deserve it—or hustle past, you type-A freak, they don't care, it's not personal to them. They're not going anywhere, and there's always a next slice.

—Introduction to *The New York Pizza Project*, 2015

Pynchonopolis

Are you ready for Thomas "Screaming Comes Across the Sky" Pynchon on the subject of September 11, 2001? On the one hand, his poetry of paranoia and his grasp of history's surrealist passages, make a perfect fit. Yet his slippery insouciance, his relentless japery, risk being tonally at odds with the subject. Either way, and despite his sensibility's entrenchment in 1960's Californian hippiedom, Pynchon is a New Yorker, with an intimate license to depict the sulfurous gray plumes and tragic tableaus of that irreconcilable moment:

> On the way home she passes the neighborhood fire-house. They're in working on one of the trucks . . . She threads among the daily bunches of flowers on the side-walk, which will be cleared in a while. The list of fire-fighters here who were lost on 11 September is kept back someplace more intimate, out of the public face, anybody wants to see it they can ask, but sometimes it shows more respect not to put such things out on a billboard . . . What makes these guys choose to go in, work 24-hour shifts and then keep working, keep throwing themselves into those shaky ruins, torching through steel, bringing people to safety, recovering parts of others, ending up sick, beat up by nightmares, disrespected, dead?

Thomas Pynchon, meet Pete Hammill? Not so fast. For it is the audacity or recklessness of *Bleeding Edge* also to sound like this:

> Maxine notices this one party out on a remote curve of the bar, drinking you'd say relentlessly what will prove to be Jägermeister and 151, through a Day-Glo straw out of a twenty-ounce convenience-store cup . . . sure enough it's him, Eric Jeffrey Outfield, übergeek, looking, except for the bare upper lip and a newly acquired soul patch, just like his ID photo. He is wearing cargo pants in a camo print whose color scheme is intended for some combat zone very remote, if not off-planet, and a T-shirt announcing, in Helvetica, <p> REAL GEEKS USE COMMAND PROMPTS </p>, accessorized with a Batbelt clanking like a charm bracelet with remotes for TV, stereo, and air condition, plus laser pointer, pager, bottle opener, wire stripper, voltmeter, magnifier, all so tiny that one legitimately wonders how functional they can be.

In fact, the awful day is delayed for three hundred pages, by which time the two airliners crash not only into the twin towers but into an exemplary Pynchon shaggy-dog-novel in full effect. This one, featuring earth notes of Bret Easton Ellis and William Gibson, concerns the diversion of funds, by the shambolic white-collar outlaw Lester Traipse, from a hot Internet start-up called hashslingerz.com to a fiber brokerage called Darklinear Solutions, under the knowing eye of the corrupt dot-com entrepreneur Gabriel Ice. These figures move among dozens, in a conspiracy typically dazzling and ludicrous, as well as impossible (and maybe unimportant) to confidently trace.

We join a good companion in failing to trace it: Maxine Tarnow, fraud investigator and mother of two, who among Pynchon's protagonists is rivaled for tangibility and homely charm only by doper private eye Doc Sportello, from 2009's *Inherent Vice*. Though this book's as long as *V.*, categorists will mark it as Comparatively Stable, with *The Crying of Lot 49* and *Vineland*, as opposed to the Utterly Centrifugal: *Gravity's Rainbow* and *Against the Day*. Maxine pinballs between workplace and family, and among the men in her life: her ex-husband, the commodities-trader Horst Loeffler, her infuriating fake-Zen shrink, Shawn; and the neoliberal death-squad spook Nicholas Windust, Pynchon's latest update of his prototypical cop-heavy. Like Philip Marlowe, Maxine plunges into dive bars armed with nothing but her wits—except Marlowe never stripped for a pole-dance to surveil strip-joint customers from the vantage of the stage. She also visits DeepArcher, a realm of the "deep Web" providing sanctuary for the avatars of fugitive gamers, cyber-anarchists and possibly the 9/11 dead. Pynchon has consistently invoked these sorts of quasi-mystical vales of yearning: spaces outside space, and times outside time. Deep-Archer is his latest bardo.

But wait. I'm acting as if we all know what it is to read Pynchon. In fact none of us do, for figuring out what it is like to read Pynchon is what it is like to read Pynchon. You're never done with it. He'll employ a string of citations to real and imaginary Bette Davis movies, say, or riffs on basketball, much as Pollock uses a color on a panoramic canvas or Coltrane a note in a solo: incessantly, arrestingly, yet seemingly without cumulative purpose. Instead, they're threads for teasing at, or being teased by. Try Bette Davis, who often played good/bad twins or sisters: she resonates—uh, maybe?—with Pynchon's Poe-like attraction to characters split into sinister mirrored doubles. Or try basketball, which in Pynchon's scheme appears to connect disparate persecuted tribes like Mayans, Jews and African-Americans—yet, why, then, does Horst—("a fourth-generation product of the U.S. Midwest, emotional as a grain elevator")—twice hold his head in both hands "as if about to attempt a foul shot with it"?

Well, basketball's Midwestern too. As Hitchcock said, admiring his own *Strangers on a Train*, "Isn't it a fascinating design? One could study it forever." This down-the-rabbit-hole invitation, accepted by generations of fans and scholars, confronts those wishing to join the party with a lost sensation: at which secret mailbox to send away for a decoder ring?

Motifs bleed off the edge of one Pynchon canvas onto the next. Partisans of Pig Bodine, from 1963's *V.*—he of the "remarkably acute nose," who is "never known . . . to guess wrong" about a brand of beer—will thrill at meeting, fifty years later, Conkling Speedwell, "a freelance professional Nose . . . born with a sense of smell far more sensitive than the rest of us normals enjoy." New readers may groan, not least at that reference to "normals"—are Pynchonites merely flashing hipster credentials?

What this misses, though, is the sheer vitality and fascination, the plummets into beauty and horror, the unique flashes of galactic epiphany, in Pynchon's method. Our reward for surrendering expectations that a novel should gather in clarity, rather than disperse into molecules, isn't anomie but delight. Pynchon himself's a good companion, full of real affection for his people and places, even as he lampoons them for suffering the postmodern condition of being only partly real. He spoils us with descriptive flights. Here's uptown in the rain:

> What might only be a simple point on the workday cycle . . . becomes a million pedestrian dramas, each one charged with mystery, more intense than high-barome-

ter daylight can ever allow. Everything changes. There's that clean, rained-on smell. The traffic noise gets liquefied. Reflections from the street into the windows of city buses fill the bus interiors with unreadable 3-D images, as surface unaccountably transforms to volume. Average pushy Manhattan schmucks crowding the sidewalks also pick up some depth, some purpose—they smile, they slow down, even with a cellular phone stuck in their ear they are more apt to be singing to somebody than yakking. Some are observed taking houseplants for walks in the rain. Even the lightest umbrella-to-umbrella contact can be erotic.

This time out, Pynchon may be pursuing a small clarification in his historical pageant of conspiracy. *Bleeding Edge* unnervingly plays footsie with 9/11 trutherism, but I think the discomfort this arouses is intentional. Like DeLillo in *Libra*, Pynchon is interested in the mystery of wide and abiding complicity, not some abruptly punctured innocence: "Somewhere, down at some shameful dark recess of the national soul, we need to feel betrayed, even guilty. As if it was us who created Bush and his gang, Cheney and Rove and Rumsfeld and Feith." Horst, who possesses an idiot-savant gift for profitable investment predictions—Tyrone Slothrop on Wall Street!—observes a dip in certain airline shares the week before 9/11, and wonders: "How could predicting market behavior be the same as predicting a terrible disaster?" Maxine supplies the answer: "If the two were different forms of the same thing."

While paranoia in everyday life believes the worst questions have monstrously simple answers, paranoid art knows the more terrifying (and inevitable) discoveries are further questions. Paranoid art traffics in interpretation, and beckons interpretation from its audience; it distrusts even itself, and so becomes the urgent opposite of complacent art. In Pynchon's view, modernity's systems of liberation and enlightenment—railway and post, the Internet, et al.—perpetually collapse into capitalism's Black Iron Prison of enclosure, monopoly and surveillance; the rolling frontier (or bleeding edge) of this collapse is where we persistently and helplessly live. His characters take sustenance on what scraps of freedom fall from the conveyor belt of this ruthless conversion machine, like the housecat at home in the butcher's shop. In Joyce's formulation, history is a nightmare from which we are trying to awake. For Pynchon, history is a nightmare within which we must become lucid dreamers.

Thomas Pynchon is seventy-six, and this refusal to develop a late style is practically infuriating. The man's wildly consistent: the only reason *Bleeding Edge* couldn't have been published in 1973 is that the internet, Guiliani/Disney Times Square and the war on terror hadn't come along yet. This book, and *Inherent Vice*, make jubilant pendants on his mammoth enterprise, neon signposts to themes he took no trouble to hide in the first place.

Pynchon depicts the world as he sees it, riddled by the depredations of greed, conspiracy and intolerance, of entropies both human-engineered and cosmically imposed. But his novels take the form of the world *as he wishes it*, hence their mighty powers of consolation. The freedoms and duties Pynchon assigns himself are those he desires on our behalf—lasciviousness, punning inanity, attention to the routinely sublime but also to the inevitability of suffering, love for the underdog and a home in our hearts for the dead. Also, license to attempt disappearance into some radical space adjacent to history, and to daily life—what anarchist philosopher Hakim Bey has called "Temporary Autonomous Zones"—even if the costs of such jaunts are, in the end, punishingly high. There's much talk of time travel in *Bleeding Edge*, but getting unmoored is hardly a free ride: "You don't just climb into a machine, you have to do it from inside out, with your mind and body, and navigating Time is an unforgiving discipline. It requires years of pain, hard labor and loss, and there is no redemption—of, or from, anything."

In summary: Despite the lack of personal information supplied about the author, it's plain, from the sweep and chortle of his sentences, from the irascible outbreaks of horniness, from the pinpoint rage at popular hypocrisy and cant, that young Pynchon is a writer of boundless promise, sure to give us a long shelf of entrancing and charismatic novels. I believe he has a masterpiece or three in him. I look forward to seeing what he'll do next.

—*The New York Times*, 2013

To *Cosmicomics*

Now listen, Cosmicomics: *How'd you get so folksy,*
So elegant, so insouciant, when by any paraphrase
You're some sort of staggering cosmic acid journey?
I guess the Grateful Dead pulled off the same trick
But they're nothing like you. Though then again,
If Deadheads ran the public education system
You'd be the high school science class textbook.
(How I'd love to impose you on Texas.)
I'd better explain. In your tales
This unpronounceable character Qfwfq
Appears and reappears in many forms and guises,
And like Marvel's "The Watcher" (another Calvino title, hey!)
Ogles the big bang, evolution, and a whole menu
Of zoological and cosmological happenings.
Each time, he's stuck inside the story, hapless voyager
And yet also an eternal galactic bystander,
One aware he'll jaunt from this exploit to another.
Goofy Qfwfq: he's nobody and everybody,
He has no body, yet he's all of us.
Cosmicomics, *you're silly, and sexy, too; my paperback*
Edition boasts "All at One Point' and 'Games Without End'
Originally appeared in Playboy *magazine"—yowza!*
I guess you could be some kind of angelic stroke book

With pin-ups of the cosmos, which, when unfolded,
Filled all time and space. But then easily folded back, too.
Cosmicomics, *you're like that: bigger on the inside*
Than the outside; as when, while tripping, you
Stare at the housecat and see a sabertooth, or pick
Your nose and find a whole fractal world up in there.

—*Black Clock*, 2015

Anthony Burgess Answers Two Questions

This was 1985—not the Anthony Burgess novel, the year (Anthony Burgess wrote so many books you might have to make that specification about a number of words or phrases—"On going to bed, I read ninety-nine novels—no, I mean I really did go to bed and read ninety-nine novels!"). I was dropping out of college and had begun a novel and returned to New York. A bookstore in Manhattan announced a rare reading and signing by Anthony Burgess, a primary hero of mine at the time, for his autodidact's erudition and braggadocio, and for how he'd gentrified a number of outre genres just by picking them up and mingling them with his erudition and braggadocio. I grabbed a couple of first editions—an unseemly three first editions, actually—and stuffed them in a sack and took the subway uptown. I was hours early, completely certain the event would be standing-room-only. Well, it was eventually, but I was still early. I camped out on a folding chair, front row center. The room filled and eventually the great man was introduced. I don't think he read anything. He pontificated, chain-smoked and wheezed, retailed anecdotes, was charming and spellbinding and ghastly. Soon the chance came for questions from the audience. There I was, front row center, my hand in the air, and as if claiming the privilege of my having arrived three hours early, I was called on first. With great posturing of my own I set up my question, a painfully obvious one: "You recently published a list of the ninety-nine best novels in English in the last century; which of your own would you select to round out the hundred?" It was painfully obvious he'd been asked before and painfully obvious how he'd rehearsed the mock-casual, mock-surprised response. "Well, to be quite honest I hadn't thought I was leaving room for one of my own, humph humph, that wasn't my intention, but I suppose it is reasonable to expect an author to have a favorite among one's own works, hack hack, I'm sure many people will expect me to say *Earthly Powers*, which has been received as a sort of 'chef-d'oeuvre' in many quarters, hem hem, but in truth the book of which I'm fondest, hurr hurr, very likely for private reasons of my own yet it is my vanity to think that among my novels it is the likeliest to endure, heh heh, and certainly no one here will have heard of it, it was given a very negligible treatment either here or in Great Britain, a novel with the odd title '*MF*' . . ."

Burgess may have been about to continue, or not, but in any event he was halted in his progress by the rustling at my feet—at his feet, nearly. For I was seated, just as I've said, front row center, and the riser on which his chair was placed put him only a foot or so above me. Out of my knapsack came the American first edition of *MF*, which I'd brought for him to sign, and now brandished happily for anyone who wished to see it, and to see how I'd punctured his anecdote.

"Ah, yes, hah hah, well, there it is, what are the odds of that?"

He was pissed.

At the signing line, after his talk, I presented the book to him again, along with copies of *The Wanting Seed* and *A Tremor of Intent*, for his signatures. "You're the hic hic young man with the book, very good, very good . . ."

I requested that he sign *A Tremor of Intent* to my friend Eliot, and then asked my second question. *The Wanting Seed*, my favorite of his novels—could it, possibly, by any chance, have been influenced by the writing of Philip K. Dick? (I now know that Burgess's novel was written well before any of Dick's major novels had appeared; the question was foolish.)

"I *don't* read science fiction," Burgess hissed, taking his revenge now.

But he knew who I was talking about.

—*Los Angeles Review of Books*, 2012

A Furtive Exchange

Reading Chester Brown's *Paying for It*, I found myself unexpectedly recalling a trepidatious and exciting visit I once made, in 2000, to an anonymous-looking apartment in downtown Toronto. I went there looking to make a transaction, one in which I would exchange money for something I regard as beyond price, something from a realm *outside* that of transactions and money—but wait, before you leap to any conclusions, let me slow down and explain. Actually, before I explain, let me mention that I regard *Paying for It* as, simply, or not so simply, the most recent in a series of totally characteristic and totally unpredictable masterpieces by one of our greatest—one of our greatest-*ever*—cartoonists, or comic book artists, or graphic novelists, or whatever we're calling them. Note also how I avoided having to say "North American" by saying "our," which I prefer because, *Louis Riel* aside—and that's a big aside—Chester Brown seems to me both more iconoclastic and more universal than "Canadian" or "North American;" he's a citizen of the timeless nation of the dissident soul, as much as Dostoyevsky's underground man. At the same time, he's also a citizen of a nation of one: Chesterbrownton, or Chesterbrownslvania, a desolate but charged region he seems to have no choice but to inhabit, and of which I feel quite privileged to be a regular visitor.

So, what was I seeking at the anonymous-looking apartment

in downtown Toronto in the year 2000?

I was seeking to commission Chester Brown to draw a cover for a small-press book I'd written, a novella, called *This Shape We're In*, that I was designing myself. As it happens. I'd persuaded my publisher-collaborator that Brown was the ideal artist for the project—not difficult to do—and, since, also as it happens, I was intermittently living in Toronto at the time, I made it a fair excuse to impress myself on the man. He was, already then, one of my favorite cartoonists. I wanted to describe the project to him in person, and propose a very particular two-part deal to him, as well: I wanted him to draw the cover image for the book, and I also wanted to own a Chester Brown original, and so I asked if I could arrange to purchase the drawing for the cover in advance.

What happened? Brown welcomed me in, and listened to my wishes, in a kind of attentively distant way, a kind of deadpan but not unfriendly way, one that was of course already somewhat familiar to me from his autobiographical comics and has subsequently become vastly more familiar—and then he agreed. Brown got the gist of what I wanted, and it was okay, he wasn't judgmental of my odd wishes, he could help me with this, yes.

Though this wasn't without its humorous aspects—the fiction I'd written that needed the illustration, nor the situation of my describing it to him (the novella concerned a slumbering army of soldiers living inside a gigantic body, and so the drawing I requested for the cover was of a commander and his lieutenant marching, lost, within an enormous human intestinal tract) the atmosphere between us was oddly furtive and clinical, somewhat clipped and efficient, though, as I said, not in any way unfriendly. The gist of it seemed to be that Brown was able to relieve me of my problem. I think he charged me eight hundred bucks. Or three hundred. Or five hundred. I can't remember.

Now, since I've never paid for sex (thanks to Brown's insinuating rhetorical powers in the footnote sections of *Paying for It*, and because of the pervasive aura of shame that infuses Brown's work this almost feels like an embarrassing confession. Shouldn't I have done so at some point? But no, no, that's not right, I'm over-identifying with my subject right now), what this felt like, to me, was a visit to a drug dealer. I'd found the right address and been welcomed inside and told *sure, I can hook you up*. And, *I'm not going to make you feel like a sick fuck for wanting what you want; some persons just need a drawing of army men lost inside an intestine from time to time. You've come to the right place.*

And I had. Though I ordinarily hate illustrational approaches to my writing, and have fought like a cornered terrier repeatedly to get art directors from major publishers to revert to jacket designs that consist purely of metaphorical or abstract imagery, or of font, there's something about Brown's line that works for me entirely as a representation of what written language does. His lines, his compositions and forms, are both persuasively somatic—grotty, physical, homely, a testimony or confession of the body—and simultaneously a thing of the deep soul-ether; they fuse the actual and the metaphysical as their baseline operation. No matter how hard Brown may work to purge this spiritual, phantasmagorical element from his drawing, and to ground us instead in a flensed and prosaic world (this is a supposition on my part; I have no idea whether he is attempting to do this), it is felt, under the skin. Of course, in describing this tension, I have the benefit of study of his progression of works, from *Ed the Happy Clown*, to the *Gospels*, to the deeply problematic and awesomely hypnotic *Underwater* (a triad of monumental unfinished works, and how unusual is that, for an artist to begin his career with the habit of abandoning gigantic unwieldy canvases?) to the increasing focus on "actuality" in some of the great short works like "Helder" and "Showing Helder" and then of course in *I Never Liked You* (aka *Fuck*) and *Louis Riel* and *The*

Playboy (a triad of finished works, and how odd for the serial abandoner of potential masterworks to become a consummate completer of them!). This progression helps us appreciate the quality of focus and restriction, the sublimely microscopic attentiveness of the style that subsequently evolved—but they also cue us to the atmosphere of the surreal and grotesque and the transcendent, those things which steadily hum just beneath the surface of Brown's contained panels, inside his silent passages, and in his metronomic silences and the dampened body language and facial expressions and blocking of his human figures, all of which are quivering in their containment and with their potential to erupt.

So, what was it like to meet Chester Brown and to make that furtive exchange of cash for sublimity? What was it really like? (I should have probably mentioned up at the top of this piece that I was writing, helplessly, not as a critic but as a total fan.) I'm tempted to joke that *the little man was not little*, or that *the happy clown did not seem particularly happy, but neither did he begin screaming and weeping and snapping his sticklike limbs* but then it is the case that you know these things, because, in the tradition of R. Crumb and Daniel Clowes and Michel de Montaigne, Chester Brown has delivered himself to us, made himself knowable, despite the seeming impossibility of the human desire to be knowable, and Brown's obvious ambivalence at even trying to do so. But what I want to say is this: though I've met many of my heroes, and many of them writers, and many of them writers of great privacy and intensity, and of powerful properties of both empathy and alienation, I think I'll never come as near as I did that day in Toronto in 2000 to being able to imagine what it would have been like to pay a call on Franz Kafka.

—from *Drawn & Quarterly: 25 Years of Contemporary Cartoon, Comics and Graphic Novels*, 2015

Books Are Sandwiches

Books are sandwiches. Between their bready boards lies a filling of information-dense leaves nestled together, an accumulation of layers for cumulative effect. Ratio is everything. Proportion. Too many slices of either meat or cheese can wreck a sandwich's middle passages, the overused fundamental creating a bricky, discursive dry spot in what ought to have been a moist sequence. Too much aoli or chutney or roasted red pepper (always use those soaked in olive oil, never water) can gush, drench bread, run down the hand and destroy a wristwatch. Yet other sandwiches, the tours-de-force, thrive on excess, disunity, a pepperoncini or cherry tomato bursting through the door like a character with a gun in his hand, a rant of watercress or filibuster of brie, an unexpected chapter of flaked oregano inserted like a flashback or dream in italics.

We dislike instinctively those who turn a sandwich and gnaw vertically, against the grain, wrecking the spine and architecture of a sandwich. Their disregard for narrative sequence is as violent as spoiling the plot of a book by gossiping in advance of the outcome. In each sandwich inheres an intrinsic eating speed, shameful to violate. Eating more and understand less? Slow down!

Hors d'oeuvres on tiny crackers are poems, always seeking perfection in elusive gestures, annoying to try to make a meal of. Hot dogs, ice cream sandwiches, and Oreo cookies are like children's picture books, bright and goonish, drawing the eater's eye like a magpie's to something glinting—the clowns of sandwiches. Hamburgers are clowns too, anonymous clowns that pile out of cars, frequently dwarves. Despite the propensity to make hamburgers ever bigger, to boast of ounces, the default hamburger is a White Castle—as Wimpy knows, burgers are eaten in serial, like mystery novels, eye always on the last page, and the burger to follow.

Sandwiches are too often served in public. In fact the reader of sandwiches is essentially engaged in a private act, and becomes steadily irritable at our scrutiny. The Earl of Sandwich may have been a pool player, but the reader of sandwiches has no time for us or the ringing telephone, and only one hand free—for a book.

—*The Book Club Cookbook*, 2004

Acknowledgments

I would like to thank all the individual commissioning editors, and Taylor Kingsbury, Ashley May, Jaime Clarke, Dennis Loy Johnson, Valerie Merians, and most of all Chris Boucher.

Credits

About the Author

JONATHAN LETHEM is the *New York Times* bestselling author of ten novels, including *A Gambler's Anatomy*, *Dissident Gardens*, *Chronic City*, *The Fortress of Solitude*, and *Motherless Brooklyn*, and of the essay collection *The Ecstasy of Influence*, which was a National Book Critics Circle Award finalist. A recipient of the MacArthur Fellowship and winner of the National Book Critics Circle Award for fiction, Lethem has had work appear in *The New Yorker*, *Harper's Magazine*, *Rolling Stone*, *Esquire*, and *The New York Times*, among other publications.

About the Editor

CHRISTOPHER BOUCHER teaches writing and literature at Boston College, and is the managing editor of *Post Road Magazine*. He is the author of the novels *Golden Delicious* and *How to Keep Your Volkswagen Alive*, both from Melville House. He lives with his wife and two children in Watertown, Massachusetts.